W9-CRE-049

Noise and Spirit

Noise and Spirit

The Religious and Spiritual Sensibilities of Rap Music

EDITED BY

Anthony B. Pinn

New York University Press

NEW YORK AND LONDON

NEW YORK UNIVERSITY PRESS
New York and London
www.nyupress.org

Library of Congress Cataloging-in-Publication Data
Noise and spirit : the religious and spiritual sensibilities of rap music /
edited by Anthony B. Pinn.
p. cm.
Includes bibliographical references and index.
ISBN 0–8147–6697–8 (alk. paper) —
ISBN 0–8147–6699–4 (pbk : alk. paper)
1. Rap (Music)—Religious aspects. I. Pinn, Anthony B.
ML3531.N65 2003
782.421649—dc21 2003011888

New York University Press books are printed on acid-free paper, and their
binding materials are chosen for strength and durability.

Manufactured in the United States of America
10 9 8 7 6 5 4 3 2 1

Dedicated
to
the "Spirit" of rap music
and
the Ancestors who nurture it

Contents

Acknowledgments

Jennifer Hammer and I first talked about this project roughly six years ago. I am grateful for her persistence as I moved from reluctance to deep interest in working on this volume. I must also thank Jennifer for her attention to this project and helping me bring the pieces together. In addition, I would like to thank the contributors to the volume for their encouragement and participation in this project. In general terms, the Department of Religious Studies at Macalester College has always encouraged my work (Jim, thanks for supporting my request for time away). In particular, Allen Callahan read early drafts of the introduction and my essay for this volume, and I appreciate his helpful suggestions and challenge to my interpretation of rap music. Our administrative assistant, Toni Schrantz, and our work-study students (particularly Liz Kaziunas, Sarah Chamberlain, and Chrissy Blank) helped me complete this manuscript and handled other tasks for me, thereby allowing time for this project. Thank you. I am particularly grateful for the insights of Kwame Phillips, who worked as my research assistant during the summer of 2002. And, as always, my former student Gregory Colleton helps me think through the nature of hip-hop culture.

As always, I am thankful to my very good friends who provide moments of laughter and much needed "balance." Thank you: Benjamin Valentin, Eli Valentin, Rámon Rentas, Robbie Seals, and a host of others.

Finally, and most importantly, my wife, Cheryl Johnson, has shown me great patience and support. Without her understanding this project would have taken longer to complete and would have been much less enjoyable. (Thanks, "Rev. Ma" and Mother Harris!)

Introduction

Making a World with a Beat: Musical Expression's Relationship to Religious Identity and Experience

Recently, Reverend Paul Scott of Durham, North Carolina, renewed the attack on rap music initiated by Reverend Calvin Butts and C. Delores Tucker.

Butts and Tucker argued that groups such as 2 Live Crew promote a culture of disrespect and immorality that is not in keeping with the best American values and principles of life. Reverend Butts thought some rap music so foul that only a steamroller could adequately deal with the "music." Presenting a mild version of the perspective held by Tucker and Butts, Reverend Scott urged "black people to put black power back into hip-hop . . . to counter the negativity" through giving attention to the positive forms of rap music.[1]

While there is much of questionable social value in rap music as a genre, statements issued by figures such as Reverend Scott, Reverend Butts, and C. Delores Tucker tend to lack any understanding of the complexity of its message, assuming rap can be neatly divided into rigid categories of "good" and "bad" styles. Over the years I've taught my "Religion and Popular Culture" course, some of the students have raised similar questions concerning the content of rap music. For my students, as with Scott and Butts, rap music is most problematic when viewed from the vantage point of religiously charged sensibilities. The two—rap music and religion—are seen as polar opposites. Though there is no doubt that the music is raw, is it not possible that rap artists are modern griots, as Houston Baker and Michael Dyson argue, in keeping with the earlier traditions of the spirituals and the blues? Is it not possible that these artists are continuing a tradition of social critique using an "organic" vocabulary? Hence, at its best, perhaps rap music is a continuation of the creative manner in which meaning is made out of an absurd world by promoting a style of living through which a sense of self and community is forged in a hostile environment.

Noise and Spirit recognizes the deep and messy connections between religious concerns and rap music often expressed in the form of a wrestling between the "sacred" and "secular" that cut across rap style typologies. This introduction, and the larger book behind it, is not intended to provide for religious studies what Houston Baker's analysis of rap music was meant to offer black studies.[2] The field of religious studies needs to get up to speed with respect to rap music and hip-hop culture in more general terms. But, while this volume engages various aspects of a religious-studies approach, its objective is to respond to a basic question: Is there anything of religious significance in rap music?

Before addressing this question, however, a bit of musical context is necessary. The works in this volume suggest that the ultimate questions and concerns of human existence and meaning are played out in many "secular" modes of musical expression, and that paying attention to these strands and what they say about religion and religious experience is important. I begin this process of exploration with the beginning, with the musical expression initiated as slaves first encountered the "New World."

Existential Concerns and "New World" Music

The "middle passage," the path by which enslaved Africans were brought to the Americas, is littered with bodies devoured by the waves and resting on the ocean's floor. Those who survived this journey found themselves in new and strange locations, among a new people. Perhaps the sounds and sights of this experience, this journey, remained alive in the new rhythms of their new world musical expression, first presented through the spirituals.

Stepping off slave ships, weak and shackled, enslaved Africans began to forge a new understanding of life—its pain and possibility—through musical expression. Spirituals recorded in the nineteenth century echo this encounter with an absurd world:

> Sometimes I feel like a motherless child,
> Sometimes I feel like a motherless child,
> Sometimes I feel like a motherless child,
> A long ways from home;
> A long ways from home.[3]

Such songs existed for some time before they were recognized as "rich" in beauty and content, representing the beginning of an African American cultural tradition and experience.

It was through this cultural expression—enslaved Africans' efforts to express a sense of self in a hostile world—that memories of a former home were maintained and were used to make sense of their new existential and ontological space. It was a way of humanizing a dehumanizing environment. The music (and folk tales, decorative arts, and visual arts that make up this new Black culture) represents a style of interpretation, a stylized wrestling with life. It is a way of "moving" through harsh circumstances with dignity and integrity. Through songs developed very early in their "New World" experience, enslaved Africans addressed the harsh and hypocritical practices of white Americans and envisioned the possibility of a better and richer existence. The songs called into question the nastiness of life and provided a vision of fulfillment, expressed with an eye toward the promises of the Christian faith.

> I'm a-rolling, I'm a-rolling
> I'm a-rolling thro' an unfriendly world,
> I'm a-rolling, I'm a-rolling thro' an unfriendly world.[4]

Those who did not find meaning in Christian community and its teachings, as represented in the spirituals, made their presence known through the swaying and sultry sounds of the blues. Just as we cannot accurately date the development of the spirituals as a musical form, we also are uncertain as to when the blues emerged. However, many scholars argue that the blues developed long before they were recorded on "race records" during the early twentieth century. It is likely that the blues emerged during the antebellum period alongside the spirituals, in the fields and during more private moments of slave life.

There are links between the blues and spirituals; for example, country or southern blues, like spirituals, make use of an eight- or sixteen-bar form. In addition, the existential realities encountered in the spirituals—abusive whites and hard work—are also the subject matter of many blues tones. Yet while there are notable similarities between the blues and spirituals in terms of form and thematic structure, there are also major differences. In addition to a shift from communal concerns as expressed in the spirituals, to a radical individualism in the blues, the latter also expresses a rejection of many of the transcendental and supernatural assumptions found in the spirituals. Differing epistemological sensibilities and social codes resulted in friction between these two musical forms—the spirituals and the blues. The shift from a God-based understanding of the world to a human-experience–centered and more pessimistic orientation (including a celebration of sexuality in ways that troubled born-again Christians) resulted in the labeling of the blues as "devil" music by those committed to the spirituals and the black church.[5]

Taken as part of a larger pattern of cultural presence, blues, like spirituals, speak to the creative potential of blacks and to the way in which they made meaning out of a rather meaningless world. What else could they do?

> I worked all the winter
> And I worked all fall
> I got to wait till spring
> To get my ashes hauled
> And now I'm tired
> Tired as I can be
> And I'm going back home
> Where these blues don't worry me.[6]

After the period of slavery, in an attempt by blacks to respond to the existential condition of being free yet oppressed, nascent forms of the blues were spread through popular entertainment venues such as carnivals, medicine shows, gin joints, house parties, and vaudeville shows. With increased mobility, the blues traveled and further developed in northern cities such as Chicago and New York. However, this geographic movement, together with increased exposure, did not translate into a wider acceptance by black Christians, who continued to question its spiritual value. Even blues fans and artists who participated in church activities during the day and swayed to the blues rhythms at night were said to be "flirting with the devil." The blues met with the disapproval of black churches because the lyrical content and seductive nature of the music fell outside the norms, values, and morality advocated by the black church tradition.

Within blues songs, the promises of the spirituals were weighed and tested in light of life's controlling hardships, and utopian ideals were found wanting. Raw or "gutbucket" experiences were poetically presented, critiqued, and synthesized; yet, they were understood as full and unavoidable. No subject was taboo, although most were shrouded and creatively worded. For example, Muddy Waters demonstrates a sexual tone using metaphorical language to mask sexual contact. The symbolism suggested by Muddy Waters was often extended to culinary images such as "jelly-roll" to represent sexual intercourse.[7] Blues men and women such as Robert Johnson, Muddy Waters, Bessie Smith, Ma Rainey, and Koko Taylor preached a politics of pleasure that worked to rethink the beauty and value of black bodies, at least in a limited sense. Using coded language, Ma Rainey had this to say:

> If you don't like my ocean don't fish in my sea,
> Don't like my ocean, don't fish in my sea
> Stay out of my valley, and let my mountain be.[8]

Many may recall the use of gospel music in the Civil Rights movement as a way of creatively expressing outrage with the status quo as well as determination to change oppressive social structures, but of course the social impulse in music predates this iteration. The blues had a humanizing effect, pointing to the tenacity of the human spirit. They were not simply a matter of survival, allowing the musician and listeners to lose themselves in sexual conquest and forget the world around them. Blues also served as a social force by offering a way of creating balance through a recognition of wrongdoing, while suggesting better ways of being in the world.

> Good mornin', blues,
> Blues, how do you do?
> Yes, blues, how do you do?
> I'm doing all right,
> Good mornin', how are you?[9]

The blues played an important role in the formation of consciousness in African American communities. They contain worlds of meaning forged as an early mode of expression born in enslaved Africans as they contemplated the crossing of water in a slave ship named "Jesus."

The blues present an early African American response to the absurdity of the "New World" and an expression of dignity in spite of its dehumanizing tendencies. When things were falling apart, the blues kept body and soul together. The music rejected the dualism (mind versus body) that marked the modern age and served as a humanizing device. In creative ways, this mode of music rejected much of what the "New World" attempted to force upon those of African descent through the creative reworking of cultural expressiveness within the context of a new environment. The formation of healthy consciousness through the use of musical forms such as the blues was deep, so deep that white cultural voyeurs missed much of its meaning and content. While "Uncle Jim" sang his song to white consumers, black listeners received subversive bits of information, such as the miseries of black life based on the hypocrisy of white economic, social, and political dealings. When the blues were played, enjoyment by white folks often entailed a process of signification they failed to "get." Even some black folks could not appreciate the serious nature of play at work in the blues. In fact, just when we think we have dug to the core and really "dig" the music, we discover another layer of complex meaning and vision, another layer of speculation on the meaning of life.

The blues and other musical forms such as the spirituals speak to a style of living, the rhythmic "sway" by which many African Americans have walked through this world. Embedded in the words and the rhythm exists an impulse, a musically defined drive that speaks to the manner in which African Americans have felt the nature of life, measured it, and harnessed it with purpose. It is a meaning that runs counter to the dominant society's efforts to limit the human and cultural worth of black people. As a blues artist notes:

> I wrote these blues, gonna sing 'em as I please,
> I wrote these blues, gonna sing 'em as I please,
> I'm the only one like the way I'm singin' 'em,
> I'll swear to goodness ain't no one else to please.[10]

Through this music one can question, prod, flip, and examine existential circumstances until something useful surfaces. There is in the blues an unflinching confrontation with life, as Ralph Ellison described: "The blues is an impulse to keep the painful details and episodes of a brutal experience alive in one's aching consciousness, to finger its jagged grain, and to transcend it." But this is not a push toward the metaphysical or a type of transhistorical enlightenment. Rather, as Ellison continues, this is a movement of consciousness done by "squeezing from it a near-tragic, near-comic lyricism."[11] The blues, then, is a recognition of the value of African Americans through their ability to shape and control language and thus a world—a world full of sarcasm and tenacious black bodies. This has been a mature depiction of life that recognizes the often absurd nature of encounter in a way that avoids nihilism and calls into question the nature of social crisis. This music teaches that life can be harsh, but these crises are not always "unto death," and in some cases are quite laughable.

> I got the world in a jug,
> The stopper in my hand.[12]

It teaches that life is survivable and more. One need only face it with vision, imagination, and tenacity. Connected to this style of making meaning is a posturing of the body. With the blues, this posture often entailed the sensual movement of bodies across dance floors, while those devoted to spirituals did the "ring shout" across "sacred" space.

For the blues, humanity is fragile, but this is not the problem. The problem is the manner in which fragility is often shown in illusions of superiority and guarded through the aggressive and destructive patterns that whites practice against blacks (and more vulnerable whites), and blacks practice as well. It is an honest depiction in that the music does not paint African Americans in heroic tones. Rather, the blues recognize flaws and point out shortcomings. In this sense, the cruel white landlord is rivaled by the exploiter Stagger Lee (Stackolee or Stack O'Lee). Their crimes are far from the same, but both crimes are rooted in a lack of comfort with fragility and vulnerability. The landlord is exercising a systematically reinforced power. Stagger Lee's exercise of control over his environment does not come with the same systemic backing, but it is vicious:

> I told Stack O'Lee please don't take my life,
> I got two li'l babes and a darling, loving wife.
> [Stack O'Lee remarks] What I care about your two
> babies and your loving, darling wife?
> You done stole my stetson hat and I'm bound to take your life.[13]

Continuation of Religious Orientation in Gospel, Rock, and Jazz

I am not as pessimistic about popular music as, say, Martha Bayles, who writes: "Just as assaultive as the lyrics and images of contemporary popular music are many of the sounds. From the shrieking clamor of thrash metal to the murky din of grunge, from the cheap, synthesized tinsel of pop ballads to the deadly pounding of computerized rhythm tracks, popular music seems terminally hostile to any sound traditionally associated with music."[14] I find a hermeneutic based on a "whatever happened to the *good* music?" sensibility suspect. True, there are lamentable elements in popular music—racism, homophobia, sexism, misogyny, and so on—and these elements must be critiqued. But this critical attention must also appreciate the manner in which some of this music speaks to deeply rooted concerns with hard and pressing questions of life, questions of ultimate value and ultimate meaning. No particular genre can be disregarded for the sake of some type of musical "purity."

Music is a "fluid" art, a mode of cultural production marked by perpetual movement. The general aesthetic and musical quality of the blues, along with the spirituals, flows in a variety of directions—gospel, rhythm and blues, rock 'n' roll, rock, and so on—because, as Ralph Ellison notes in response to Amiri Baraka's *Blues People,* "the master artisans of the South were slaves, and white Americans have been walking Negro walks, talking Negro-flavored talk (and prizing it when spoken by Southern belles), dancing Negro dances and singing Negro melodies far too long to talk of a 'mainstream' of American culture to which they're alien."[15] That is to say, the "American" musical idiom of the United States is indebted to and drawn heavily from the creativity and ingenuity of African Americans, and from this community of sun-kissed skin it moved outward.

Gospel, rock, and so forth owe something to earlier musical forms such as the blues and maintain their commitment on some level to exploring the ultimate questions of life, speaking about religious, or what some might refer to as a spiritual, orientation. There is a confirmed wrestling between sacred and secular in musical production, and the resulting friction represents an attempt to address the deeper issues of life. (How else could the creator of the blues hit "It's Tight Like That" also be the creator of the gospel song "Take My Hand Precious Lord"?) This wrestling is presented in the friction between the spirituals and the blues, and it continues in the often uneasy tension between the "sacred" and the "secular" within contemporary forms of music such as gospel, rock, and jazz that marks the presence of religious sensibilities and commitments in popular music.

Many of those who sang the blues were also religious in a traditional, church-derived way. Twentieth-century "born-again" blues folks, most notably Thomas Andrew Dorsey, were responsible for the development of a blues-influenced form of religious music called "Gospel Blues" or "Gospel Music" that got underway in 1921 with Dorsey's first song, "Someday, Somewhere." Gospel music became a part of black church worship because Dorsey and gospel singer Sallie Martin traveled across the nation singing and helping congregations develop gospel choirs. The music would change, influenced by new technology and social circumstances such as the Civil Rights movement.[16] The gospel sound changed the aesthetics of black church worship as choirs imitated the music on Sundays and the choir's attire became more dramatic to compliment the more explosive sound.

Sensitive to the theological claims of traditional gospel music, contemporary gospel music during the 1970s attempted to reach the unchurched, to draw them in by avoiding a message of repentance and salvation that was too confrontational. Contemporary gospel, as written by figures such as Andre Crouch, contained a subtle message of Jesus Christ and the merits of salvation that addressed the ethos created by the Black Power movement, Black Arts movement, and other movements developed with respect to growing black consciousness.[17] Contemporary gospel has offered the "traditional" message in a new package, with a more subdued approach to evangelization. It was because of this more subtle message, combined with the funk and rock of contemporary music, that one could hear gospel singer Tramaine Hawkins's proclamation of the Holy Spirit's presence being pumped into nightclubs during the early eighties, and on gospel-format radio stations during the same period.

Soulful singers such as Al Green have moved between gospel and more "secular" modes of music, while Little Richard expressed a call to ministry.[18] Sam Cooke was the son of a minister and sang with the Soul Stirrers, and some suggest that "to compare his gospel recordings with his better secular recordings is to be struck by the resemblance, and in some cases, the identity between the two."[19] Cooke's "A Change Is Gonna Come" influenced other musicians such as Curtis Mayfield to address the deeper questions of life in important yet subtle ways, not with explicit utilization of Christian theological categories but with a wrestling over issues of self-consciousness.[20] And who can forget the musical importance of Marvin Gaye? His "What's Going On" incorporates a grappling with existential and ontological concerns plaguing humanity, and concludes with a prayer that undoubtedly connected Gaye with his childhood religious encounters and framed them in terms of his musical successes.

Are these and other examples really odd when one considers that R & B is a child of gospel, swing, and the blues? So many musicians have roots in various religious communities, and the questions and concerns generated within these communities continue to maintain a hold on the epistemological rings of these artists. According to a recent article in *Vibe* magazine:

> Historically, most R & B singers have grown up singing in church; still today, artists from Snoop to Lil' Kim have sung in the choir as kids. And the two genres have met in the middle any number of times, from the Teddy Riley–produced Retrun by the Winans, in 1990, to L. L. Cool J's 1991 track "The Power of God." . . . The Edwin Hawkins Singers' "Oh, Happy Day" was a chart smash in 1972, and the Clark Sisters' "You Brought the Sunshine" lit up discos in 1982. And who could forget M. C. Hammer's 1990 "Pray"?[21]

From gospel to the Christianity-influenced lyrics of R & B, to its "kissing cousin" rock, religious sensibilities and visions bleed through the lyrics and lives of blues-indebted musicians.[22]

Emerging in the 1950s, with figures such as Chuck Berry and Elvis Presley, rock defines a hybrid musical form and cultural sensibility drawn from a variety of sources, including the blues and gospel music that was popular in churches. Over the years, rock artists have used technological advances such as multitrack recording and drum machines to give expression to questions of ultimate meaning and place in the world. This discussion often took place through the language of religiosity. Who can forget, for example, the religious sensitivities put on public display by Elvis Presley on numerous occasions? Or the magic Jimi Hendrix performed with his electric guitar, though he did not live long enough to develop the "Electric Sky Church" he talked about:

> We're trying to save the kids . . . to help them realize a little more what their goals should be. We want them to realize that our music is just as spiritual as going to church. The soul must rule, not money or drugs. You should rule yourself and give God a chance.[23]

In response to some of the excesses of rock culture, including the type of drug use that took Jimi Hendrix's life, new movements within rock emerged as alternatives to the dominant ethos. Rather than advocating a radical individualism and hedonism as the language of this musical form, groups emerging in the 1980s such as U2 sought to present a more complex and socially conscious message often expressed in the language of religious commitment. While the religious orientation or commitments of some artists has been questioned by music critics and fans, U2's allegiance to the Christian faith has been for the most part simply a given, shaping its music and message. Even those within formal religious institutions speak to this; in fact, as one minister deeply familiar with the group notes:

"Whether on records, on stage, on video or in interviews—they have never denied their faith, even if at times they have questioned how that faith fits with the events of their generation. They have constantly kept spiritual issues at the heart of all they have done, whether looking at the light or the darkness around them."[24] There is an ethical accountability, a musical articulation of liberation theology, tied to the Christianity of this group that is not as developed in the religious wrestling of most. According to Bono, "Faith in Jesus Christ that is not aligned to social justice—that is not aligned with the poor—it's nothing."[25] CDs such as the 1987 *Joshua Tree* point to the importance of religious questions and concerns for U2, tied as they are to a perpetual search for more meaning, and so Bono sings, "but I still haven't found what I'm looking for."[26]

Questions of a religious nature continue to find expression in musical production. What Michael Dyson says concerning Michael Jackson is true for a larger range of artists, including U2, insofar as much of their music has clear links "to the spiritual roots that have nourished its beginning and that continue to sustain its expanding identity."[27] The words and images associated with these songs are pregnant with religiously based wonderings.

Jazz also has been involved in this struggle with religiosity and with the ultimate meaning of life. First articulated in the 1830s and 1840s through plantation brass bands and minstrel troupes and through the later development of ragtime in the 1890s, jazz marks a blending of African American musical sensibilities from the blues, for example, and European harmonic structures. Finding a home in places such as New Orleans and Chicago, jazz greats like the New Orleans Rhythm Kings, Jelly Roll Morton, and Louis Armstrong refined this musical art form. With time, the improvisation that marked Jelly Roll Morton's work among others was further developed into the swing style exemplified by figures such as Duke Ellington. Religious themes and issues were not lost on jazz musicians. For example, in Duke Ellington's "Sacred Concerts" as well as Billie Holiday's "God Bless the Child" and Nina Simone's "Sinner Man" religious questions are at play.

The music continued to evolve from swing through incarnations such as bebop and cool jazz, each bringing a creative take on the relationship between music and existential realities. But perhaps one of the best-known examples of jazz's religious sensibilities is John Coltrane's album *A Love Supreme*, recorded in 1964. As Coltrane writes to listeners, the religious preoccupation that guides this musical project is clear: "This album is a humble offering to Him. An attempt to say 'thank you God' through our work, even as we do in our hearts and with our tongues." This struggle with the presence of divinity was inspired, Coltrane notes, during his "spiritual awakening" in 1957. As a result of this conversion experience, Coltrane "asked to be given the means and privilege to make others happy through music. I feel this has been granted through His grace."[28] The importance of this particular jazz recording for those seeking religious (or, as some put it, "spiritual") fulfillment has taken numerous forms, but none is more attention grabbing than the Church of Saint John Coltrane African Orthodox Church in San Francisco.

In 1971, Bishop F. W. King organized a chapel called the One Mind Temple Evolutionary Transitional Body of Christ as a religious community dedicated to "live cleanly, do right . . . offering praise to God and service to man." This development was inspired by "the dedicated triumph of John Coltrane's life over many obstacles, his music, and his testimony."[29] This church, dedicated to the example of John Coltrane, became an affiliate of the African Orthodox Church in 1982, and the name was changed to Church of St. John Coltrane African Orthodox Church. Over the course of the past two decades, numerous programs and projects such as the Human Outreach Program have developed as a way of extending the call for righteousness and proper living outlined in *A Love Supreme.*[30]

Rap Music's Religious Sensibilities and Concerns

What happened to musical movement and intent during the late twentieth century, in urban areas? Where does one turn for a raw and "natural" presentation, for an extension of the nitty-gritty expressivity found during earlier periods? The answer is easily located. It manifested itself anew in rap music, the mode of musical expression developed first in New York City during the late 1970s.[31]

Through the spirit of the spirituals and the blues came a variety of musical forms with creative alterations of existing styles and with sensitivity to the existential circumstances of their creators. There should be no wondering, then, about the birth of rap music as a vital—and often troubled and troubling—mode of musical expression. "Rapper's Delight," the 1979 hit by the Sugar Hill Gang, brought what had been the skills of the streets, parks, basements, and clubs to the attention of a much larger audience—including Canada and Europe, where the single reached the top five and top ten, respectively. Eventually it became the "black single of the year" in

1980, with earnings of more than $3 million on sales of over 2 million records.[32] "In retrospect," cultural critic George Nelson notes, "rap or something like it should have been predicted. Each decade since World War II has seen the emergence of some new approach to black dance music [and more, I suspect]. The 1940s brought forth rhythm & blues, the 1950s rock & roll, the 1960s soul, the 1970s funk and disco. Something was due in the 1980s."[33] This "something due" expressed in clear terms the hybridization of music through a bold and creative manipulation of established genres. It brought together without apology jazz, disco, rhythm & blues, and so on; and in the process, through high-tech conjuration, presented musical ancestors within a new context. These conjurers looked at what they had produced and could not help but say, "Damn, it's dope!"

While the music is important, Houston Baker is correct to note that the voice finalizes the process. Language and the spoken word have their own materiality that moves the music because "the voice, some commentators have suggested, echoes African griots, black preachers, Apollo DJs, Birdland MCs, Muhammed Ali, black street corner males' signifying, oratory of the Nation of Islam, and get-down ghetto vernacular. The voice becomes the thing in which, finally, rap technology catches the consciousness of the young."[34]

Indebted to U.S. and Jamaican aesthetics and oral traditions, rap artists, as "new-style troubadours,"[35] expressed the concerns and preoccupations of young people living in urban centers of late-capitalism's America using linguistic manipulations and alterations fed through a system of creative technological arrangements. As Mark Costello and David Foster Wallace have noted: "Rap, like the avant-garde, deploys digital multi-tracked sampling to blow open the musical and political boundaries of the soul and funk that are the rapper's Bach and Beethoven."[36] The lyrical wing of a larger movement, referred to as hip-hop culture (which includes dance, the visual arts, and an aesthetic displayed through creative clothing choices), rap would grow and multiply into a variety of styles, with a complex typology—progressive, gangsta, and so on. Many assumed it was a fad, a stylistic virus easily contained and ended; but instead, rap artists have grown in stature, created production companies and record labels, and have moved into other areas of popular culture. These artists have used technological advances to signify the American vision of life and labor, and in so doing captured the imagination and dollars of an eager public.

As pop artists such as Andy Warhol produced work that raised philosophical questions concerning the nature of the visual arts, rap music raised a host of questions concerning the form and content of musical expression. Some, like the abstract expressionists who despised the innovations of pop art, lamented the substitution of "noise" for "music," while more insightful listeners recognized the musical creativity and compelling (though often troubling) presentation of sociohistorical and psychological realities and fantasies of life in the post–civil rights years. At its best, rap music provides listeners with critical insights "as energetically productive as those manned by our most celebrated black critics and award winning writers."[37] But we must also acknowledge that when not at its best, rap music provides a celebration of radical individualism and nihilism over against community and hope.

In the early years, "back in tha day," this stylized depiction of life's meaning was rapped in the grab and poetry of Grand Master Flash and the Furious Five, KRS-One, Public Enemy, and others who looked at the world and critiqued it in "black." Rap music has changed since those days. Like many others, I lament some of its current lyrical and visual twists, such as the more objectifying videos. But I see glimmers of the quest for meaning, a stylized defense of subjectivity, an aesthetic that serves to harness and interpret human interaction and the world in which it takes place.

Continuation and experimentation with black orality is the hallmark of rap, taking the themes and sensibilities housed in musical expression for centuries and giving them a postindustrial twist. Rap music explores "grammatical creativity, verbal wizardry, and linguistic innovation in refining the art of oral communication."[38] Yet, what is most significant about rap for the purposes of this book is expressed not simply in terms of the process of fusion—grammatical, verbal, and linguistic manipulations—but through the morphing of content. The importance of rap music rests on this morphing process because "the rap artist appeals to the rhetorical practices eloquently honed in *African-American religious experiences* and the cultural potency of *black singing/musical traditions* to produce an engaging hybrid."[39] Michael Dyson points to an interesting interaction, a stylization of self and community, addressing ultimate meaning within the context of a musically significant "process of repetition and recontextualization,"[40] deserving greater attention.

As the contributors to this volume argue in various ways, the implicit claim here must be made explicit: one of the major and documented functions of musical production such as rap has been the articulation of responses to the "ultimate" questions of life. In this sense, it has engaged religious traditions and religious issues in both overt and covert ways. There are explicit examples in efforts to foreground Nation of Islam and Nation of Earths and Gods theologies within the music of Queen Mother Rage, Eric B. & Rakim, Isis, Paris, Public Enemy, and Poor Righteous Teachers, among others. While one may question the consistency, sophistication, and "thickness" of the presentation, references to Islam abound within rap music. The educational process such rap music seeks has had benefit. According to Sister Souljah, "hip-hop is a blessing because the [Poor] Righteous Teachers, Brand Nubian and KRS-One have actually been the educational system for Black kids, in place of the so-called educational system that is entirely financed by the American government. And in the absence of the voice of young people in hip-hop, we would have even more chaos than we have today."[41]

From the nebulous celebrations of Malcolm X to the more explicit and focused attention to the teachings of the Honorable Elijah Muhammad and Minister Louis Farrakhan, rappers highlight the commonly recognizable elements of the Nation of Islam's faith, such as the importance of self-knowledge as the key to all other developments. Others, moving from the early days of Africa Bambata to more recent figures, point to the teachings of the Nation of Earths and Gods (also known as the Five Percent Nation), highlighting the cosmic value and importance of blacks. Yet, "orthodox" Islam represents one of the fasting-growing religious groups in the United States among African Americans, and it too is represented in rap music. As rap artist Mos Def, a Sunni Muslim, notes in projects such as *Black on Both Sides* (1999), individual fulfillment and communal development are dependent upon spiritual awareness, a recognition of God, a devotion to prayer. In his words:

> I really believe that none of our efforts are gonna work until we turn our attention to the Creator . . . and really start to have a spiritual program, as opposed to a political program. To even have a spiritual program, first, you have to be attentive to what's in us, before we can say, "Okay , this is how we can affect public policy." We gotta be going inside first, and then come out. . . . There's a Creator of all this and for me, and this is true for everyone, that when you focus your attention on trying to be as close, or as cognizant or as mindful of that presence, then all those other things fall into place.[42]

Not every artist presents religious sensitivities and theological vocabulary in such a straightforward manner. Rap artist Nuwine, for example, argues that his music is not necessarily religious (in the strict sense). Rather, it is his attempt to discuss the events of his life that eventually lead him to the church. During various interviews, Nuwine, who records on boxer Evander Holyfield's label, talks about his early childhood. As a preteen he dropped out of school and became involved in gang activity. In 1990 this activity resulted in gunfire: "I was shaking hands with a guy when a rival gang saw us, and started shooting. They got me with the first shot." This experience did not stop the activities that eventually took him before a judge. At that point, while awaiting his court appearance, "I noticed a white guy across the room staring at me. After a while, he boldly interrupted me. 'You don't know me,' he said, 'but God loves you, man. God forgives you and has a purpose for you.' Suddenly my whole macho attitude caved in. I fell on my knees and cried."[43]

After this conversion experience, Nuwine began using his rap abilities to spread the story of his transformed life. Beginning with CDs sold from his trunk, to a record deal, Nuwine is concerned with music that moves beyond the mere nihilism present in some rap to a modest optimism based on the Christian faith. Nuwine argues that his music may be a little "hard," but this is appropriate because it speaks to people who are in need. In his words: "That's what ministry is about. Reachin' out to those who don't know God. Reachin' out to the sick, the rebellious, the angry, the hurting. That's what it's for. Jesus did it. He spent very little time in the synagogue. Why do the well people need a physician? It's the sick people that need a physician."[44] In another interview he elaborates on this point by clarifying the meaning behind the title of his 2001 CD, *Ghetto Mission.* He says: "The meaning speaks for itself. Look at the world—the world is a ghetto. You have problems in suburbs and the cities, and that problem is people are hurting, man. People want answers, they want to know why they're here, why they're broke, why people are killing each other. So [*Ghetto*] *Mission* is like a mission statement. I'm reaching out to the ghettos, you know, and saying that God loves you."[45]

A few, such as Reverend Run (Joey Simmons of Run-DMC) have taken this concern with spreading a Christian message even further by entering a formal Christian ministry. Reflecting on his life prior to his conversion, Reverend Run critiques the materialism and radical attitude of consumption that marks so much rap music, the effort to uncover meaning through goods: "I thought I had all the riches, but I was really poor. It was then the Lord came into my life and raised me up, and I started to feel better and all those worldly things didn't mean anything to me anymore."[46]

Educator and part-time rapper from the 1990s, Sister Souljah, made a similar message clear by presenting a centered life marked by respect for self and community and a relationship with God as the hallmark of existence. The title track from her album, *360 Degrees of Power,* and other tracks such as "My God Is a Powerful God" speak to this reevaluation of life purpose and meaning.[47] Regarding the connections between her conviction and lyrics, Sister Souljah says:

> Having grown up on hip hop, I always considered the drum and beats and bass to be strong and moving. It captured the feeling of the energy of our experience in white America and reestablished Black masculinity, rebellion, self-instruction and information distribution. I believe that Chuck D and Hank Schocklee asked me to be a member of Public Enemy because my life represented what they were rhyming about. Not only had I lived it, I challenged it, rebelled against it, organized and created solutions, and stayed rooted and humble in my blackness.[48]

For some, there is a paradox at work, a form of existential slippage between stated commitments to a particular religious vision and the system of ethics expressed in the music. Take, for example, Snoop Dogg, whose lyrics often portray an image not necessarily in keeping with the religious sensibilities claimed for his personal life: "I've got a responsibility to God. He put me here. He'll take me down in a heartbeat the minute I start tripping on myself and how great I must be because of all the people telling me all the time. . . . I tried to keep it real, never to sell the truth, but always to tell the truth. And if there's one reason why you know the name Snoop Dogg and I don't know yours, it's because telling the truth has given me the props I need to carry out God's purpose and plan."[49] One might wonder about the nature and meaning of central terms here: Truth? Providence? What is the doctrine of God represented here? And, what are the ramifications with respect to ethics, even if we dismiss, as we should, warped puritanical ethics? Yet, regardless of one's take on such matters, as vital as they are, there remains here an important tension, a battle between existential realities and religious sensibilities. We may not find the resolution offered by certain artists appealing, when such sensibilities do not raise a critique concerning oppressive attitudes and behaviors. Nonetheless, this should not mean a lack of attention paid to the nature of confrontation with the "religious" that is expressed in their work. Snoop Dogg and others provide rudimentary elements of a theological system, a theology of rap, complete with an epistemology of encounter:

> Thinking back on it now, I understand that God was reaching out to me, even then. It wasn't like I saw His face in a cloud or heard His voice thundering in my ear, like fucking Charlton Heston in a Bible movie or something. In my experience, God doesn't work that way. He lets His will and His plan be known to His children by the people and situations He brings across their paths. At the right time, and the right place, there was always someone there to guide me, to point me in the right direction. And even when I chose to go my own way, I still had the clear choice laid out in front of me. It takes time to learn to do the right thing, but God is patient and He'll bring you along, if you let Him.[50]

The line between religious belief and life practice is often blurred. The lyrical content with its expressed religious vision often creates a paradox. But this is not a problem that wipes out the value or vitality of the religious imagination within rap music. Rather, it might point to the linguistic "playfulness" within the music, drawn from vernacular practices within black oral and aesthetic traditions. In other words, it is quite likely that much of what is expressed in rap music is not meant to be taken literally, in the same manner in which numerous biblical stories are quite troubling if taken literally.[51] The sexism expressed by Saint Paul and other biblical figures and the homophobia that marks both testaments have not resulted in a huge theological backlash requiring the destruction of the Bible as a viable and sacred text. The same hermeneutic of multiple meanings may extend to rap lyrics and their creators. This is not to say these artists should not be held accountable, or should not be critiqued with regard to behavior and opinions. It simply means that we should recognize the often problematic relationship between theological pronouncements and arguments, and practice that plagues the history of religion in *and outside* hip-hop culture. Recognizing the great difficulty with which humans exercise and explain the religious, explicit theological or religious pronouncements in rap music are worth one's time and attention not because of perfection of practice but because of what they say about the musically expressed encounter with questions of meaning, those with great existential and ontological weight. Such consideration fosters, for the benefit of those in religious studies, cultural studies, and so forth an opportunity to follow the *flow* of the religious within cultural production, and in this way to better recognize and analyze both religiosity (themes, practices, etc.) and an important cultural ethos marking our new century.

In addition to explicit moments that reflect a type of hip-hop evangelicalism, there are also more "shadowed" engagements with religious themes and religious traditions in rap music, often lyrically fused in metaphor, signs, and symbols. Perhaps this approach is what rapper Big Boi of OutKast has in mind when discussing the need to address pressing issues and themes within the music: "We feel that—just like KRS-One said—when you get on this microphone, you have to educate as well as entertain. We feel that responsibility, but not in a preachy way. We're gonna party with y'all and slip something in there every now and then—maybe a word or a phrase or a question. And you might be like, 'Damn, I wonder why they said that?'"[52] The rapper known as Common addresses a similar sensibility, one that moves from self-consciousness outward. When speaking about the motivation and intent behind his CD *Resurrection,* Common says:

> At that point I was just tryin' to become a better artist. At the same time I started becoming a better person. Just the things I exposed myself to. Or the things I got exposed to. . . . I started getting more in tune with myself spiritually and not just following the Christian upbringing that I had. Not just sayin' Jesus is God for this reason. I'll put it this way: Resurrection was more of an understanding. I started understanding things more and actually started to apply 'em more too. But it was an understanding. And the focus on that album was just to be creative and put a mark on this Hip Hop Game. And make people notice what myself and No ID was doin'.[53]

Rap music often fails in its effort to transform thought and action because artists forget their work must begin with self-consciousness. Otherwise, what is the lesson being taught to others? For the student of rap music and hip-hop culture, wondering "why" often points to religious sensibilities and themes within rap music that are not limited to Christianity and Islam. One must also be mindful of the meaning of Buddhism and humanism, for example, within the lives of particular artists. This is certainly the case with the Beastie Boys' Adam Yauch's conversion from Judaism to Tibetan Buddhism, and underground artist Sage Francis's apparent embrace of free thought (or humanism). It is worth noting that the influence of religiosity on rap music and hip-hop culture in more general terms is not limited to those at the microphone. Pioneers such as Russell

Simmons recognize the importance of spiritual practice. (He uses the term "spiritual" as opposed to "religion" to connote the noninstitutional basis of his practice.) In his autobiography, *Life and Def: Sex, Drugs, Money, + God,* he speaks to the importance of yoga for a sense of centeredness. In his words:

> The practice of yoga changed my life. Over the past six years I've been practicing yoga, and in that time found a spiritual center to my life. My spiritual sense is stronger than ever, so the teachings of all the great religions sound good to me. The yoga practice of quieting the mind through asana practice, as well as meditation, is about clearing the mind of fluctuation so that you can one day know your true self. . . . My experiences with yoga have taught me the practice of finding God everywhere—especially within myself."[54]

The impact of this quest for greater meaning holds consequences for Simmons's perspective on hip-hop culture:

> Over the last few years I have begun to walk toward God or service to God, whether it is through promoting political initiatives that I believe could help the masses—from reforming the prison industrial complex to increased involvement in electoral politics—or by focusing more on the numerous charities I am involved with. I am in a unique position to organize some hip-hop for the better of the masses.[55]

Locating the Discussion

What is the significance of religious or spiritual considerations in the world of rap music? How should such considerations affect the manner in which we understand, explore, and discuss rap music and religion?

A good deal of academic work has been done on rap music, particularly using the methodological tools of literary theory, musicology, history, sociology, and so on. Work by scholars such as Tricia Rose, William Perkins, and Brian Cross and more "popular" treatments by Nelson George, James Spady, and David Toop discuss rap along these lines. Within these studies, which represent only a small sampling of the available literature, primary attention is given to the historical development of this musical genre as a creative, cultural response to certain social, political, and economic forces. The emphasis is most often on rap music as a secular response to pressing issues. However, as Jon Michael Spencer and others argue, there is no clear distinction between the sacred and the secular; they flow together, merging in unexpected places. Hence, "Locations within the secular world must also be examined for disclosures of the religious if we are ever to be able to understand what people are really thinking religiously and how those thoughts influence their behavior in the real world."[56]

Some, such as Ernest Allen, have explored rap music with respect to issues of black nationalism, noting connections with the Nation of Islam and the Five Percent Nation. Although this work has been extremely important and insightful, there is something religious/theological in much of this music that is not fully captured with this approach. Like the spirituals, the blues, and gospel, rap music has profound connections to the various religious traditions found within African American communities. It grapples with the questions of meaning that are intimately connected to religious organizations and their thoughts and practices. Those in religious studies are in a unique position to isolate and explore connections between rap music and religious faith. In addition, those with primary expertise in other areas enhance their discussion of rap music by employing the questions, concerns, and frameworks associated with religious studies.

This volume does not seek to provide yet another history of rap. Rather, it uses religious studies (including theological exploration) as a means of providing additional depth to our understanding of rap music by surfacing its more religious dimensions. There are a few treatments that address the need for a religious-studies (e.g., theological) analysis of rap music. Two prominent examples are several issues of Jon Michael Spencer's now defunct journal *Black Sacred Music* and Michael Eric Dyson's *Between God and Gangsta Rap*. Work by Dyson and Spencer is invaluable because it creates dialogue between popular culture and religious studies. However, these treatments of religion and rap are limited to a discussion of religious themes related to the Christian tradition and, in some cases, the Nation of Islam. If this exploration is to grow, we must also consider rap's relationship to a variety of other religious traditions and sensibilities—both institutional and noninstitutional.

Noise and Spirit seeks to fill this void by offering essays exploring rap music's exploration of Christianity as well as traditions such as humanism, Rastafarianism, and Islam (Nation of Islam as well as the Five Percent Nation). However, the religious sensibilities of rap artists are not limited to dialogue with established religious traditions. Some artists, without adherence to any particular tradition, explore basic religious/theological questions. Several essays within this volume thus break away from the religious-institution model and give attention to a more general religiosity or spirituality that informs the development and production of certain forms of rap.

With this in mind, the volume is divided into several sections. The first explores rap's association with more easily recognizable religious traditions and communities. The next presents discussions on important considerations such as death and "naming" (e.g., the "Queen") as spiritual practice. The final unit in the volume discusses ways to theologize the relationship between the sacred and the profane in rap.

There is a thickness and complexity to this study that results both from the various angles from which rap is explored as well as from the manner in which contributors often address the same artists but with differing outcomes. This offering of varying perspectives allows for an acknowledgment of the necessary nature of the struggle for life-meaning found within cultural production in general and within the depth of rap music in particular. In addition, this project as a whole recognizes the value of context, sound, and lyrics for the discussion of raps' relationship to religion.

Although not all the contributors to this volume have primary expertise in religious studies, all in some way make use of the questions, categories, and concerns associated with various religious-studies approaches. Their approach to the subject, along with the concern with a variety of religious orientations, distinguishes this project from existing treatments of rap music. It seeks to explore the variety of religious sensibilities present in the genre. Using various dimensions of religious studies as a method of study, it expands common perceptions of religious themes in rap to expose its true complexity and diversity. Furthermore, the essays are not only descriptive in terms of presenting rap music's "borrowing" from various religious traditions; they are also constructive and critical in that they provide a discussion of rap's critique of these traditions, and the depth of rap's engagement with doctrine from these traditions in descriptive and theoretical ways.

We have attempted to dig into the religious sensibilities and themes present within rap music as a way of extending and expanding the conversation concerning this musical form. Only readers, however, can measure the success of this effort. There are shortcomings, to be certain, yet it is my belief that even these blind spots and oversights might serve to inspire more work on this important topic as a way of taking scholarship "to another level."

NOTES

1. *African Americans for Humanism Examiner* 12, no. 1 (Spring 2002): 8.

2. These questions are based on a statement made by Houston A. Baker, Jr., in *Rap, Black Studies, and the Academy* (Chicago: University of Chicago Press, 1993), 83.

3. James Weldon Johnson and J. Rosamond Johnson, eds., *The Books of American Negro Spirituals* (New York: Da Capo Press, 1969), ii, 30–31.

4. R. Nathaniel Dett, ed., *Religious Folk-Songs of the Negro as Sung at Hampton Institute* (Hampton, VA: Hampton Institute Press, 1927), 186.

5. For additional information on the spirituals and blues, see Paul Oliver, *The Meaning of the Blues* (New York: Collier Books, 1960, 1963); Charles Keil, *Urban Blues* (Chicago: University of Chicago Press, 1966); Eileen Southern, *The Music of Black Americans: A History* (New York: W. W. Norton, 1971; 2d ed., 1983); William Barlow, *"Looking Up at Down": The Emergence of Blues Culture* (Philadelphia: Temple University Press, 1989); Christa K. Dixon, *Negro Spirituals: From Bible to Folk Song* (Philadelphia: Fortress Press, 1976); Dena J. Epstein, *Sinful Tunes and Spirituals: Black Folk Music to the Civil War* (Urbana: University of Illinois Press, 1977); John Lovell, Jr., *Black Song: The Forge and the Flame; The Story of How the Afro-American Spiritual Was Hammered Out* (New York: Macmillan, 1972); Robert Palmer, *Deep Blues* (New York: Viking Press, 1981); Jon Michael Spencer, *Blues in Evil* (Knoxville: University of Tennessee Press, 1993); Howard Thurman, *The Negro Spirituals Speak of Life and Death* (Richmond, VA: Friends United Press, 1975).

6. Eric Sackheim, compiler, *The Blues Line: A Collection of Blues Lyrics* (Hopewell, NJ: Ecco Press, 1993), 45.

7. Paul Oliver, *The Blues Fell This Morning: The Meaning of the Blues* (New York: Cambridge University Press, 1979, 1990), 109–114.

8. Ma Rainey's "Don't Fish in My Sea," in Eric Sackheim, ed., *The Blues Line: A Collection of Blues Lyrics from Leadbelly to Muddy Waters* (New York: Ecco Press, 1993), 47.

9. James H. Cones, *The Spirituals and the Blues* (Maryknoll, NY: Orbis Books, 1972, 1991), 110.

10. Ibid., 97–98.

11. Ralph Ellison, "Richard Wright's Blues," in Robert G. O'Meally, ed., *Living with Music: Ralph Ellison's Jazz Writings* (New York: Modern Library Edition/Random House, 2001), 103.

12. Ibid., 114.

13. Mississippi John Hurt, "Stack O'Lee Blues," in *The Blues, vol. 2* (Washington, DC: Smithsonian Collection of Recordings, 1993).

14. Martha Bayles, *Hole in the Soul: The Loss of Beauty and Meaning in American Popular Music* (Chicago: University of Chicago Press, 1996), 4.

15. Ralph Ellison, "Blues People," in Robert G. O'Meally, ed., *Living with Music:*

Ralph Ellison's Jazz Writings (New York: Modern Library Edition/Random House, 2001), 130.

16. Melva Wilson Costen, *African American Christian Worship* (Nashville: Abingdon Press, 1993), 103–104.

17. Issues related to the mass appeal of contemporary gospel fostered questions related to white appreciation of this art form. The interplay between black musical production and whites has always been an issue. Beginning with the debate over the origin of black spirituals and the origin of gospel music, African Americans have fought off claims to their musical production. Add to this the movement of white musicians into various areas of jazz and hip-hop. In recent years, a new challenge has arisen. It is the presence of white artists in gospel music, and it has resulted in a question probed in numerous publications and in more private conversations: Are whites co-opting gospel music? Evidence of this "crossover" has been apparent. For example, Angelo Petrucci and Veronica Torres won the Dove Award for the best contemporary *black* gospel recorded song in 1995!

Resentment over this development is heightened by what some artists understand as the industry's racism. White executives over black gospel divisions of labels have caused tension that is matched by the episodes of racism at major gospel festivals. Black artists eventually formed a new organization to address their interests, named the United Gospel Industry Council. Although white artists have made inroads into gospel music, it remains clear that African Americans dominate the market and in their recordings and concerts offer a somewhat "personalized" connection to a particular history of suffering based on race and celebration of triumph over racialized suffering.

18. "R. Kelly: From Raunch to Religion," *Ebony* magazine, June 1997, 106.

19. Bayles, *Hole in the Soul,* 156.

20. Ibid., 228–229.

21. Alan Light, "Say Amen, Somebody!" *Vibe* magazine, October 1997, 92.

22. One cannot forget the religious imagery and symbolism present in countless music videos such as R.E.M.'s "Losing My Religion," Tupac Shakur's "I Ain't Mad at Cha," Madonna's "Like a Prayer," or Joan Osborne's "One of Us." One could certainly add Moby to the list of artists for whom religious themes and ideals are fair musical "game." His recent recordings play off the religious aesthetics of the spirituals (and blues) as a way of exploring his sense of "spiritual" awareness. His present stance may be a matter of evolution—a movement from youthful years in the Presbyterian Church, to time spent as a rather conservative Christian, to a philosophical preoccupation with Marxism, to a more recent incarnation as one who is spiritually aware and appreciative of the teachings of Christ. Much of this comes across, for example, in a recent project titled *Play* that is heavily indebted to the African American spirituals tradition. Many of Moby's fans claim his music promotes a type of "spiritual" reaction. Yet for some there is an ambiguity or opaque quality to Moby's spiritual self-description that makes categorizing him

rather difficult and the intended epistemological focus of his work hard to capture with any certainty.

23. Quoted in Bayles, *Hole in the Soul,* 236.

24. Steve Stockman, *Walk On: The Spiritual Journey of* U2 (Lake Mary, FL: Relevant Books, 2001), 5.

25. Quoted in ibid., 53.

26. U2, "I Still Haven't Found What I'm Looking For," on *The Joshua Tree,* Polygram Records; ASIN: B000001FS3.

27. Michael Eric Dyson, *Reflecting Black: African-American Cultural Criticism* (Minneapolis: University of Minnesota Press, 1993), 40.

28. John Coltrane, liner notes to *A Love Supreme,* AS-77, MCA Records, 1964/ MCA Records 1995/GRO Records, Inc., 1995.

29. Church of St. John Coltrane African Orthodox Church, "Saint John Will-I-Am Coltrane." Found at: <http://www.saintjohncoltrane.org>.

30. Finally, one might turn to Sun Ra and the "cosmic" as well as "New Age" sensibilities informing what makes up "Cosmic Tones for Mental Therapy/Art Form for Dimensions Tomorrow." Sun Ra's spirituality, a stretch for most people, I would imagine, involved claims to birth on Saturn and elements of the Egyptian mystery systems and cosmological structures.

31. A presentation of rap music's social and intellectual history is beyond the scope of this essay. For an excellent presentation of rap music's origins and development, see Tricia Rose, *Black Noise: Rap Music and Black Culture in Contemporary America* (Hanover, NH: University Press of New England, 1994). Also see Mark Costello and David Foster Wallace, *Signifying Rappers: rap and race in the urban present* (New York: Ecco Press, 1990); Brian Cross, *It's Not about a Salary . . . Rap, Race and Resistance in Los Angeles* (New York: Verso, 1993); Adam Krims, *Rap Music and the Poetics of Identity* (New York: Cambridge University Press, 2000); Jon Michael Spencer, ed., *The Emergency of Black and the Emergence of Rap,* a special issue of *Black Sacred Music: A Journal of Theomusicology* 5/1 (Spring 1991); William Eric Perkins, ed., *Droppin' Science: Critical Essays on Rap Music and Hip Hop Culture* (Philadelphia: Temple University Press, 1996).

32. Nelson George, *The Death of Rhythm & Blues* (New York: Pantheon Books, 1988), 169, 191.

33. Ibid., 188.

34. Houston A. Baker, Jr., *Rap, Black Studies, and the Academy* (Chicago: University of Chicago Press, 1993), 91.

35. Sherley Anne Williams, "Two Words on Music: Black Community," in Gina Dent, ed., *Black Popular Culture* (Seattle: Bay Press, 1992), 167.

36. Costello and Wallace, *Signifying Rappers,* 58.

37. Baker, *Rap, Black Studies, and the Academy,* 59–60.

38. Dyson, *Reflecting Black,* 12.

39. Ibid.

40. Rose, *Black Noise,* 73.

41. Quoted in Ernest Allen, Jr., "Making the Strong Survive: The Contours and Contradictions of Message Rap," in William Eric Perkins, ed., *Droppin' Science: Critical Essays on Rap Music and Hip Hop Culture* (Philadelphia: Temple University Press, 1996), 182.

42. Interview of Mos Def. Found on <http://www.poundmag.com/magazine/features/articles/mighty/mosdef.html>

43. http://search.netscape.com/google.tmpl?search=nuwine.

44. Manhunt.com. Manhunt features: Interview by s2.

45. Nuwine Chat, February 1, 2000. Twec.com.

46. Quoted in Russell Simmons, with Nelson George, *Life and Def: Sex, Drugs, Money, + God* (New York: Crown, 2001), 217.

47. Sister Souljah, *360 Degrees of Power* (New York: Epic ET48713).

48. Quoted in William Eric Perkins, "The Rap Attack: An Introduction," in Perkins, ed., *Droppin' Science: Critical Essays on Rap Music and Hip Hop Culture* (Philadelphia: Temple University Press, 1996), 35.

49. Snoop Dogg, with Davin Seay, *The Doggfather: The Times, Trials, and Hardcore Truths of Snoop Dogg* (New York: William Morrow, 1999), 2–3.

50. Ibid., 106.

51. Robin D. G. Kelley, *Yo' Mama's Disfunktional! Fighting the Culture Wars in Urban America* (Boston: Beacon Press, 1997), 38–39.

52. Sacha Jenkins, "The End of the Ice Age?" *SPIN* magazine, March 2001, 85.

53. Meshack Blaq, interview with Common. Posted on *Kronick Magazine Online*: <http://www.kronick.com/2.0/issue30/common.shtml>.

54. Simmons, *Life and Def,* 217–218.

55. Ibid., 219.

56. Jon Michael Spencer, "Overview of American Popular Music in Theological Perspective," in *Theomusicology,* a special issue of *Black Sacred Music: A Journal of Theomusicology* 8, no. 1 (Spring 1994): 216. The intertwining of the "sacred" and "secular" that I suggest throughout this introduction is embraced to varying degrees by the contributors to this volume.

Part I

Rap and Religious Traditions

1

African American Christian Rap

Facing "Truth" and Resisting It

Garth Kasimu Baker-Fletcher

African American Christian rap has not received much critical analysis. One may find many descriptions of the artists—Lil' Raskull, L. G. Wise, Tru to Society, B. B. Jay, Knowdaverbs, E-Roc, and Tonex (pronounced "Toe-nay"), and so forth—with not so much as a mention of to what religious depth the rappers have plunged. Perhaps this is because music journalists feel that they must simply "report" what they have "seen" and "heard." The task of the scholar of religion is more telling, and more difficult, because she or he must call upon the resources available to make the best kinds of analytical judgments regarding how African American Christians utilize Christian rap's structure, message, and musicality within the continuum of contemporary music—in particular, hip-hop culture and African American culture.

Format and Methodology

In this chapter, which is based on the powerful work of historian of religion Charles Long, I examine rap music from two broad angles: first opacity, and then oppugnancy. *Opacity is the experience of oppressed persons to live with their contradictory negativity and at the same time transform and create an-other reality.*[1] Opacity for African Americans, according to Charles Long, meant that Black people faced the fact of their blackness in a white society that promoted itself as being the most free society in the world. In the facing of such "truth" came an amazing capacity to transform the contradiction of freedom in dominant society into life-affirming spiritual health. *Oppugnancy,* or *creative forms of resistance to the embedded forms of oppression in society,* occurred in slave society, according to Long, along several levels. These included the conversion experience itself, through which the power of an Almighty God intervened into the very historical modality of individual religious consciousness itself.[2] Although they are beyond the scope of this study, many excellent analyses of slave narratives and slave conversion experiences are readily available.[3] It must also be historically underlined that two of the most significant slave uprisings, or to use Long's rhetoric, *events of oppugnancy,* occurred under the leadership of men who had a religious following—Nat Turner and Denmark Vesey.

I use the two scales of judgment above, oppugnancy and opacity, to delineate the parameters of this chapter's analyses concerning Christian rap music. Other parameters could have been how "evangelical" or "evangelizing" Christian rap's lyrics might be (an earlier temptation that crossed my mind, to be sure!); or, another parameter might be to ignore the "evangelical" aspects of Christian rap's message, searching instead for its sociopolitical or sociocultural critiques. Further, in this chapter I reject looking at Black Christian rap as another manifestation of what is taken to be a tendency of religiously oppressed peoples to use religion as a psychological "opiate" (the view most forcefully articulated by Karl Marx). I reject this "explanation" of or *reductionist view* of religion in general because such "explanations" ultimately lead to a denigration of any religious experiences, a priori or a fortiori. Rather, I shall look at the ways in which the Christian message is expressed in rap music through the polarities of oppugnancy and/or opacity using religious symbolism and language. This is a difficult task but a necessary one. So doing, we tease out symbolic meanings (of Christian religious meaning) that lie directly in the hearer's grasp, rather than possible inferences that might miss the mark entirely.

"Homies," "Da World," and "Da Streetz" for Christian Rappers

The three categories of "homies," "da world," and "da streetz" encompass a critical space of spiritual critique for African American Christian rappers. Broadly speaking, Christian rap sets about its task of proclaiming the saving message (or "Gospel") of Jesus Christ within the space inhabited by "homies" who live in "da world" on "da streetz." In this sense, all of these are categories of both opacity and oppugnancy.

"Homies" are people, usually but not exclusively male, with whom one has grown into maturity, lived in the same "'hood" (neighborhood), and had an affinity of interests on da streetz. Several of the most successful Christian rappers such as L. G. Wise and Lil' Raskull base their lyrics on testimonials which proclaim their former lives *before* they had a living and personal relationship with Jesus Christ. What is interesting is that they still see themselves as homies, but as homies transformed by the Gospel of Jesus Christ. As transformed homies their current mission is to "save" the souls of other homies so that they might also join the new family of "homey Christians" who are moving toward a glorious future in heaven. Lil' Raskull's "Wonder Years"[4] provides an excellent window into how a Christian rapper exposes the world of homies and how they are trying to live successfully on da streetz without Jesus guiding them. In one section he cries out that there are too many "homies" loving material things and the "money they've got," while the women in their lives are selling their bodies for the same. The "world" Lil' Raskull describes is not the racist one of Jim Crow segregation, but one of the post–civil rights era. It is a "world" of poor, urban youth whose search for respect and love draws them out into the streets—"da streetz"—of the ghetto. The predators, evildoers, and torturers of "da streetz" are not described as "the Man" (white men or white people) but other Black men from other 'hoods, interested in "busting a cap" (shooting) into your body.

For Christian rapper E-Roc, "da world" is a place filled with the spirit of Hannibal Lecter, as he notes in his song "Modern Day Cannibals."[5] Lecter, made known through two blockbuster Hollywood movie hits, is perhaps one of the most noxious human beings to have ever hit the screen. A notorious cannibal, Hannibal was known to keep the carved-out body parts of his victims and save them in his refrigerator for months, drawing a strange sense of "comfort" and "warmth" from their presence. Hannibal was known to have sautéd the organs in butter, particularly the liver, his favorite organ. E-Roc's lyrics decry the world as being filled with "modern-day cannibals," *eating us* like Hannibal. The sense of overwhelming, uncontrollable lust for eating the very flesh and body of women and men in the 'hood is realized by the scourges of drug trade and its concurrent usage of heavy gunfire, and prostitution of women with its corrosive deleterious pimping by men. The "modern-day cannibal" E-Roc warns against is not just someone or something outside of himself or a "them," but the possibility of *corrupting hypocrisy within himself and other Christian rappers* (read other Christian ministers/Christians). This corrupting hypocrisy "eats" one's heart and soul, according to E-Roc, and the result is that one's behavior embarrasses "your crew" or the group of people who depend upon the upright steadiness and righteousness of your walk with God. Further, "modern day cannibals" are those afflicted with a soul-sickness that leaves them prone to mocking Jesus. In another reference to a Hollywood blockbuster film—the *Star Wars* hero Anakin Skywalker who eventually becomes corrupted into the infamous intergalactic villain Darth Vader—E-Roc warns that the "cannibal" tendency can turn a good person into one representing evil.[6]

E-Roc has a tremendously imaginative way of using even traditional biblical imagery in new ways. In another song he uses the image of the "Devourer"—borrowed from the Angel of Death found in Exodus 12—as the spirit of death plaguing the African American community. He notes in his song that the Devourer seeks to "eat" and "destroy" all those who fail to come to "hear" and "decide" to "follow Christ, for He is the only way to come out of the world." He compares this capacity of the Devourer to "Megaton Bombs," whose destructive capacity is unmatched in human imagination.[7] This profession of Christian faith, however narrow and prejudicial it might sound to the ears of those who practice other beliefs, seems to satisfy E-Roc's sense of theodicy and divine fairness. We shall return to questions of theodicy later.

B. B. Jay refers to "da world" as a place of emotional pain. Earlier in his life, as he testifies at the very beginning of his CD *Universal Concussion,* he was the "punch line" to everybody else's jokes, the butt of their teasing remarks.[8] He has nothing good to say about what da world had to offer him, or anyone else, for that matter. Furthermore, B. B. Jay insists that his Christian rap is his way of expressing how he was slapped around, put down, and how eventually he learned to survive with the hope that someday he might "blow up" ("become a success"). Lil' Raskull, E-Roc, and L. G. Wise[9] all agree that da streetz and da world are the loci of pain, seduction, and misplaced desires for their homies. They all testify that da streetz serve as places where quick money could be obtained through drug trafficking, the traffic of bodies (usually female), and the so-called defense of these transactions with automatic guns. Such behavior, note the Christian rappers, leads to the pain of a life in and out (and in again) of prison. Both Lil' Raskull and L. G. Wise pepper most of their songs with references to, and supportive commentary for, the homies who are locked up behind the bars in prison.

Sometimes young male Christian rappers, like their secular rap counterparts, use the term "hoochies" as a term of derision for a woman who sells her body for money, or a prostitute. Lil' Raskull uses this term in

"Wonder Years" as a counterterm to his derision of the materialism of homies on da streetz. He decries women selling sexual favors, saying that it is "treating yo' body like scotch."[10] A problem occurs as we analyze whether or not one can speak of prostitutes as being "materialistic" in the same way as homies who rely on their vast treasures of money. Those who utilize even a gentle feminist/womanist critique do not find enough intellectual "space" placed by Lil' Raskull between the two phrases.

Fortunately, Christian rappers *never* refer to female "homies" as "hoes." African American Christian rappers also never refer to women using other extremely derogatory words frequently used by secular rappers. There is, in fact, quite a large difference between the care L. G. Wise's "Ain't Gotta Be Like Dat" shows toward young women caught up in the sexual industry and the fixated, stunted, and truncated name calling that secular rappers regularly refer to when addressing women. "Ain't Gotta Be Like Dat" is a story-rap L. G. Wise "spits" (the slang word for "really *telling* a story with emphasis"). He picks up a young teenage female friend to drive her to wherever she would like to go. Wise is shocked to find out that the young lady is going to "work" as a stripper in the local erotic dance joint. He tells her "ain't gotta be like dat" over and over again, reminding her that the true love that she seems to be seeking can only be found in a living relationship with Jesus Christ.[11] The musical background Wise uses reinforces his message of potent rebuke because its bass line, keyboards, and drumming all overlay each other as one. This overlaying of musical, rhythmic, and harmonic levels reinforces for the listener the importance of the message.

Male Christian rappers like B. B. Jay go beyond rebuking "worldly" and sinful acts by women, finding ways to uplift the plight of female "homies" caught up in the ways of da world without insulting them. B. B. Jay's song, "For the Ladies," extols every woman as a "diamond" whose strength is greater than any male's, even though she is considered as the "weaker vessel" biblically.[12] B. B. Jay goes on to note that a "lady" is one who stands by her homey as the police wagon hauls him away, coming through with the bail, even if it is "four in the morning." As such, this woman, this "lady," is "unique." Every woman, according to B. B. Jay, is unique in the world, however abused. The overwhelming sentiment presented in the song is that men need to start treating women as the queens they are. Furthermore, B. B. Jay makes sure that all the generations are mentioned—grandmothers, sisters, aunts, mothers, and so forth. Finally, he exhorts the women of the 'hood to meditate on Jesus to alleviate the ills of their lives and overcome hardships, transforming them into blessings.

Is such commentary noteworthy for its resistance (oppugnancy) or its transformative facing of otherness (opacity)? If we are careful to note what is going on in the lyrics as well as in the forcefulness of the rhythmic presentations and music, I believe that we can come up with answers. For example, B. B. Jay's "For the Ladies" presents a message of hope and uplift to the female homies of poor African communities (in particular). His musical backbeat is not "male" in the sense that it rocks with a machismo heaviness that overwhelms the lyrics, but has a kind of (dare I say) "soft" and rolling "pop" sound more in character with popular female groups like Destiny's Child or Trin-i-tee 5:7. Such a presentation *itself* transforms and transgresses expected boundaries and moves the listener toward an openness that would not occur had B. B. Jay used another musical presentation.

The message of "For the Ladies" is a mixture of both Black Power ideology (treat Black women like Queens) and biblical knowledge (women are the weaker vessel that serves and cares for family and community). This combination is unstable and tricky, to say the least, but B. B. Jay, like many African American males in the church, believes that it is a necessary combination. The strength of the combination is that a Queen is undoubtedly a leader, a force to be reckoned with, and a visionary in the community. Unfortunately, queens in Western culture can also simply be put on pedestals and silenced. African Americans have had so little actual sociopolitical and economic power that it is difficult to say which valence of the term "queen" would actualize itself. Likewise, Black women have revealed themselves to be quite able to lead as servants in the various circles, societies, sororities, and clubs they created within churches and throughout various African American communities. Historically, it was these groups that took a strong leadership role in denouncing lynching in particular, right alongside male-dominated groups like the NAACP. This strength, seeing oneself as giving service to the community, ought not to be denigrated but incorporated into a fuller understanding of what African American oppugnancy means. Thus, resistance did not always involve open rebellion, or flaming rhetorical flourish, but could be accomplished just as thoroughly by the means of women gathering together, resisting in their own way the violence of their own lives—daily threats of rape, the threat of lynching for their men, the atmosphere of constant tension, and so forth.

Have I answered the pertinent questions about the Christian rappers? Yes, and no! True, I have given more of a history lesson. Yet, it is out of that historical background that we can appreciate how and why Christian rappers articulate a particular vision of life. Insofar as issues about opacity and oppugnancy concern and relate to women, perhaps they are better served by Elle R.O.C. (Her name means "Woman Representative Of Christ," or as she says, a "Femcee for Christ.") Of note, Elle R.O.C.'s entire CD, *I Die Daily*, never devotes an entire song to the "worldly situation" of women over and against men, nor does it choose to honor women any more or less than men. Rather, Elle's piece "Circular Motion" speaks of the ways in which da world has young women (in particular, but not exclusively) in a "circular motion of sin." This "circular motion" turns young females into confused human beings who believe that having a baby as an unwed teenager is the only way to have love. Even after realizing that this is not the "way," Elle points out that most of these "sistazz" find themselves "doing the same thing over and over again." There seems no way out of their dilemma, even though they recognize a need for a change.

Elle R.O.C. paints with strongly poetic words the opaque situation in which young women in the 'hood find themselves. At the same time, she does not leave her sistazz or brothers with only a *recognition* of the problem, and no call for *transformation* (the other side of genuine opacity). Elle uses the story of a fifteen-year-old with two babies whose life choices seem caught up in a "circular motion" of sin. Elle pleads with this sistah, who is on the way to more babies, heartache, and complications, to "make a change" and "rearrange" her life. At the same time, she makes the poignant comment that while we may realize our need for a change (male or female), we cannot do so without divine help.[13]

Lil' Raskull's "Ghetto Dreams" is an exceptionally good example of opacity. It confronts the lifestyle of homies living with no self-respect and with so much grief, violence, and death. Raskull prays for the soul of fallen homies who have died while pursuing "ghetto dreams" of material wealth won by cocaine profits, hoping that their "souls have found God" before they passed. The singers continue to repeat the refrain, making a plea for strength in hard times. Lil' Raskull thanks God that he has learned how to lead a family now, whereas before he used to simply lie around and waste time, living a life of self-disrespect. He goes on to note that most fathers in his 'hood are forced to leave their homes fatherless because of their self-destructive lifestyles, and that this has created a crisis in the 'hood that cannot be ignored. Raskull refuses to overlook the crisis in "Ghetto Dreams," but has a strong message that any crisis can be overcome by the spirit of Christ.[14]

How is such rap an example of opacity? It reveals a way of spreading the Gospel of Jesus Christ that varies radically from most standard church-speak. First, it speaks with a beat that arises from da streetz. Second, it directly addresses the dilemma of living, dying, and attempting to survive on those streetz as it critiques the basis of error upon which the streetz ethos seduces homies to strive for a self-destructive form of success. Naming this form of suicidal success a "ghetto dream," Raskull denies that such a dream has anything to do with really positive dreaming. Without saying so, he disconnects the "ghetto dream" from the "dream" of Martin Luther King, Jr., whose dream was a vision that called for far more than mere survival. King's dream, as an unspoken yet inferred ghost to Raskull's ghetto dream, sought to heal old wounds between races, dispel hatred across boundaries, and seek ways to live out the Kingdom of God here on this earth. Raskull's prayer calls for Christ to strengthen our minds to "survive in these times." Opacity is the ability to call to account one's situation, face to face, and then create an-other anyway, despite all the odds. Lil' Raskull does this with skill and power.

The "Devil" as the Personal Force of Evil

The devil is not an objective, impersonal "it" for African American Christian rappers. Christian rappers, or as they call themselves, "Gospel Rappers,"[15] follow a strictly evangelical reading of the Bible, a reading that sees the devil as a personal entity—the Father of Demons. This reading emphasizes that the devil has set himself up as a false counterpart to God as the father of demonic entities—"principalities, rulers in high places"—that attempt to manipulate, control, and corrupt the behavior of humanity. For most Gospel rappers, the devil is the root cause of "drama" in the lives of homies, be they Christian or otherwise. Drama is chaos, confusion in one's life. Drama is the incarnation of all that is bad and evil. L. G. Wise, E-Roc, Lil' Raskull, and Tru to Society all note that "drama" causes Christians to lose their focus on praising God and loving one another.

The devil is the cause of the radiating forces of spiritual "ill-ness." Rappers call this "ill-ing," and E-Roc sees his lyrics as illuminating that spiritual "ill" with what he calls "ill-Radiation."[16] This "ill" philosophically defined is a term of ontological evil—the opposing (b)eing to Being, or to use Augustinian language, the "diminishing of the good" or "privation of being."[17] This privation of being is evil because it leads to hatred, envy, malice, concupiscence, adultery, murder, stealing, war, and all other forms of violence. Gospel rappers use the medium of rap lyrics to deal with the late twentieth century, early twenty-first century manifestations of the privation of being. The Bible simply called this activity "sin," a "falling short of the mark" (Romans 3:23).

The devil, for Lil' Raskull, is a "hater."[18] His activity continually stirs up malice toward one another in the hearts of homies, leading to the competitive acts of self-disrespect that ultimately lead to violence. The hate-mongering activity of the devil is intolerable for Christian rappers like Lil' Raskull and E-Roc because their mission is so focused on saving those whose lives have been devastated by what they perceive to be the personal intervening power of the devil.

Another rapper, Easop, elaborates a demonology beyond most others in scope and character on his CD *The Time Has Come.* In the songs "How It Used to Be," "Life or Death Til I Die," and particularly "Images," Easop describes not only the ways in which there is a leading evil personal entity called the "devil," but he rhymes about ways in which the entire host of demons under the devil's reign of influence wind up turning human individuals into devils. He warns about the ways in which devils can seduce one to do things here on da streetz because they are so filled with the evil power of the devil that flows through them.[19] Human devils are an evil to which Easop is particularly attuned, and his songs mention them alongside of demonic forces described so vividly in Ephesians 6:12

> For our struggle is not against enemies of blood and flesh, but against rulers, against the authorities, against the cosmic powers of this present darkness, against spiritual forces of evil in the heavenly places.

Easop and other Christian rappers seem determined to remind, exhort, encourage, and uplift both the faithful and those not yet within the fold of Christian belief to see that their experiences on da streetz have given them a particular ministry of identifying E(e)vil in all of its forms. As such, there is an attitude of determined condemnation of anyone and anything that would water down the corrosive and corrupting seduction of the devil to both the believer and nonbeliever.

For Gospel rappers, the devil is the personification of all the negative cosmic forces that come to "steal, kill, and destroy" life (to paraphrase John 10:10). He is that entity that one must recognize as the genuine enemy of life and living. Thus, Gospel rappers do not single out European

Americans or the white man as the problem facing young Black males living in the 'hood. According to Gospel rappers, the opacity of the Gospel of Jesus Christ enables the ability to get beyond looking outside of the 'hood for the root of the 'hood's evils, and placing the blame squarely at the spiritual feet of the entity causing the problems. Since whites are not called out for blame, the devil appears as the real thief that steals "lost souls" for Lil' Raskull, requiring a "necessary murder" of that aspect of the human nature that can be easily controlled by satanic forces—"the flesh." "The flesh" is the "old humanity" of 2 Corinthians 5 that can be renewed by the "new humanity" we receive in Christ. Lil' Raskull sharpens the conflict of an "old" nature needing to be replaced by a "new" human nature. He goes beyond the imagery of life and death that Elle R.O.C., Easop, and other Gospel rappers use. Raskull believes that the devil must be "murdered" in our "flesh" in order for the "new man" to live. He prays for a "187" (police code for murder) on the devil.[20] Raskull sharpens oppugnancy toward the devil into an actual frontal confrontation through which he is certain Christians can emerge victorious.

The devil not only personifies negative cosmic forces, he also represents all those aspects of negativity destroying homies. A Los Angeles Gospel rap group called Priesthood speaks of "loving thugs," even though their lives are caught up in all of the negative things of da streetz. The devil controls, manipulates, tempts, and seduces thugs, according to Priesthood, into negative lifestyles. Priesthood calls on the homies to resist the evil of the devil. As a personification of all the evils facing homies, the devil is the one toward whom oppugnancy is directed. Gospel rappers make it abundantly clear that resistance is the only proper relationship with the devil. They clarify their opposition to all things evil, including the "devils in the recording industry."[21]

Setting things in a very Johannine sense of "darkness" and "light," the devil is the King of Darkness. Gospel rapper Knowdaverbs portrays a nightmare vision of persons who are living under the influence of this "darkness." Calling nonbelievers "Zombies," Knowdaverbs notes that da world is filled with "dead people yet still walking," caught up in the satanic dimension of necrophilia. Loving "death" and "darkness" so intensely, these people are perceived by Knowdaverbs to be writing their own names on their tombstones because their life energies are caught up in ghastly patterns of evil pleasure. Knowdaverbs, for all of his condemnation of the Zombies, still has confidence that such "creatures of the night" can be positively turned by spiritual "exposure to the Light."[22]

New Gospel rapper King Cyz identifies an even more insidious spiritual poisoning that needs to be resisted by homies—suicide. "Should I Go On" is a Gospel rap anthem in which King Cyz utilizes the ancient musical form of call-and-response to answer the vexing query of a suicidal soul: "Tell me why should I go on?" With encouraging phrases, King Cyz keeps on lifting the downcast spirit, responding to the mournful query with a positive exhortation to "keep on looking to the Sonshine." The entire address from King Cyz arises from a paraphrase of Psalm 139's paean to the comforting omnipresence of God, often in the midst of evil circumstances.[23] The piece is important to this chapter because it reveals another dimension of the spiritual oppugnancy (resistance, rebellion, and move toward freedom) that Gospel rap believes it represents.

Jesus Christ as Saving Force

Jesus Christ is the "only way" of salvation for Christian rappers. Uniformly one finds a straightforward evangelical interpretation[24] of John 14:6, "Jesus said to him [Thomas] I am the way, and the truth, and the life. No one comes to the Father except through me." Jesus is the personification of God on earth, come to "save sinners before they loved God," a very important religious/theological point that Christian rappers of all stripes repeat in many creative ways. For thugs, homies, and all those whose lives have been affected by the powerful negativity of da streetz, this offer of salvation has a particular significance. For Elle R.O.C., Easop, and King Cyz, the lyrics on their CDs emphasize the daily giving up of one's will to the will of Jesus Christ that lives within one's spirit. Elle R.O.C.'s theme song is entitled "I Die Daily," throughout which she reiterates the theme of "dying to self" to "live in Christ."[25] King Cyz places responsibility for life and death on the choices made by individuals. For him, as for most who adhere to a strict reading of John 14:6, one *chooses* to live or die—and those choices have eternal consequences.[26] Furthermore, after one makes a choice, Jesus Christ enables one to become a "Man of God" whose choices are decisive because his or her will is strong like the "Man of Steel." With repeated blasts of a French horn imitating those of a Jewish *shofar* (an ancient ram-horn that makes a hornlike sound), King Cyz happily repeats the chorus, "Cats don't want to bang with us" because the Christian lives a life "victorious." While "streetz" gangs go around "banging," hanging out, selling drugs, and doing various activities both righteous and unrighteous, King Cyz translates the

Gospel work of Jesus Christ (what is called in theological circles "soteriology" or "saving work") to be the creation of a righteous gang. Cyz's "Man of God" not only has the support of a "righteous" gang, but each individual within that group has the strength of a Superman—the popular TV character, not F. W. Nietzsche's amoral and cruel *Übermensch*.

Other Gospel rap groups like Unity Klan envision the saving work of Jesus Christ as enabling the truly global, multicultural Body of Christ. Unity Klan takes Jesus to be God, not just the personification of God, but God God's-Self. As Jesus Christ works in the hearts, minds, and lives of believers, Unity Klan sees that "the blood that washes us clean" also unites people across ethnic, cultural, and racial boundaries. In "Whatever Happened," Unity Klan calls for the "anointing" of Jesus—or infilling of the Holy Spirit sent by Jesus—not merely to be "holy" in an abstract sense, but to "break the power of principalities." These principalities stop Christians from living out the riches and fullness of life that is promised them.[27]

Can a reading of the Gospel rap message such as that of Unity Klan be both opaque and oppugnant? A careful hearing of Unity Klan's work, especially "Rida," in which they reach out to homies that are "rida's" on the streetz, reveals their awareness of the connection between the style of musical presentation they have chosen and its material source. Their self-understanding is different than that of a B. B. Jay (from Brooklyn, New York), or Easop (from Oakland, California), whose roots and ministry are more pointed toward da streetz. Unity Klan, alongside of many Christian rappers—many of whom are not African American—see rap as a medium to translate the Gospel for a generation acculturated to hip-hop and rap musical styles. Their view of what must be recognized and transformed is not the same as that of former "gangstah homies." They believe that what must be overcome is more broadly conceived, less concretely tied to African American communities—or poor Black urban communities specifically. Rather, their view of what Jesus Christ has come to "save" is directed toward bringing together different peoples, formerly filled with enmity toward one another. They resist easy categorization as "Black" Christian rappers because they hail from the United Kingdom, so their material situation is different than that of American-born Africans. Their oppugnancy, as a male and female duo, is toward the kinds of manifestations of racism, sexism, and so forth that occur in the United Kingdom. Such a different focus of opacity and oppugnancy is important for anyone interested in understanding the diversity of Gospel rappers currently proclaiming their messages.

Another example of difference in opacity and oppugnancy is Knowdaverbs. He emphasizes living a life in Christ that is "phullon empty." Christians seek to be "empty" of their former "selves" in order to leave room for the infilling guidance of the Holy Spirit. We speak of the Holy Spirit here under the aegis of the saving force of Jesus because Jesus is the One who indwells the believer through the medium of the Holy Spirit for Gospel rappers like Knowdaverbs. So the categories of Holy Spirit and Jesus Christ cannot be separated artificially for Knowdaverbs, but must be examined as a single salvific piece. Knowdaverbs proclaims the surrender of personal will as key to living a properly "Christian" life. "Advancing" in life is predicated on the deflation of self-will, a paradox Knowdaverbs interprets as genuine knowing and living in Christ.[28]

Focusing on Knowdaverbs a bit longer, one notes that his message is not politically or socially quietist. He calls on Christians to be like an "action figure" in which the "Word" (another term for Jesus Christ as well as the Bible) is "put into motion" in life actions. Like the television and movie character of *Mission: Impossible,* Christians, for Knowdaverbs, are "called" by Christ to do what is "impossible" unless they move forward with the proper "information" from the Bible, and have the courage to speak in language "prophetic."[29] The Word spoken by Knowdaverb's action figure penetrates into the "heart" of nonbelievers, "killing" the "flesh" in order for others to join the ranks and become action figures in their own right. Here we see the rhetoric of murder turned toward that aspect of human nature that is not in synch with Jesus Christ, but is directed toward the devil. One might ask at this point whether this rhetoric is less effective than that of Lil' Raskull, or whether its effect is the same. Both appear as a linguistically violent form of oppugnancy toward evil—Raskull locating resistance in working against the evil entity (the devil), and Knowdaverbs redirecting these energies toward human nature itself. We shall return to these differences later.

Los Angeles Gospel rapper Priesthood speaks of Jesus as "Lover of My Soul" in "Take Me Away." Asking for "the Lord" to ease the pain of corrupt living and heartlessness, Jesus' love is presented as a potent counterbalance to the uncaring selfishness of "da world." Over an extremely smooth ballad-kind of musical groove, Priesthood presents Jesus as the one whose love provides the kind of "hope" persons need to survive with dignity. In fact, throughout Priesthood's CD *Keepin' It Real,* the overwhelming presentation of Jesus is that of lover of one's soul and spirit. While maintaining strong and occasionally danceable rhythms and beats, the deepest "reality" of Jesus, as "All about You" reiterates, is Christ's transforming operation in the lives of Christians. Priesthood offers the insight that such divine love can transform terrible and evil individuals and situations into beautiful, livable ones.[30] The saving force of Jesus is central to the specifically Christian aspect of Gospel rap.

Inasmuch as all of the Gospel rappers I studied seem to understand Jesus in a uniformly evangelical fashion, the metaphors and images of Jesus arose from the Bible rather than from the artistic imagination referred to elsewhere in this chapter. Evangelical theologian Carl F. H. Henry explains this move away from imaginative forays most succinctly by stating that Protestant reformers "strenuously resisted" allegories that encouraged "looking beyond the *sensus litteralis* to some obscure meaning." Further, Henry quoted John Calvin as discerning "satanic influence at play in the notion that the 'fertility' of a text determines its true meaning and nurtures a hidden import."[31] So, while Gospel rappers experience and encourage a certain figurative and metaphorical freedom in "translating" the Gospel for hip-hop generation listeners, they find it much more difficult (as a group) to look for such "freedom" in relationship to matters concerning Jesus.

Mission and Theodicy

L. G. Wise, B. B. Jay, Lil' Raskull, King Cyz, E-Roc, and Easop all were homies from da streetz. The feeling, tone, and attitude of their rap music is similar to that of secular rappers like Eminem, Dr. Dre, Snoop Dogg, Notorious B.I.G., Tupac Shakur, Bone-Thugs-N-Harmony, and Ja Rule. Their overall sound "reaches homies" because they still sound like homies—just "sanctified!" Gospel rappers believe that they have been saved from the violence, mayhem, and self-destruction of da streetz in order to go back and "reach a generation for Christ," as Elle R.O.C. has put it.[32]

B. B. Jay is particularly concerned with explicating a Gospel rap message for those caught in the impoverishment of the ghetto. In "Po' No Mo'" Jay articulates a message of rejecting both spiritual and material poverty. What is unusual about this message is that not many Gospel rappers pay attention to the material conditions of ruthlessness on da streetz, but seem more focused on spiritual issues. In "Po' No Mo'" Jay remarks that he knows "joy cometh in the morning," but he wonders how much longer it will be before that morning arrives![33] Most Gospel rappers speak in such an unconditionally positive manner about all things pertaining to both this life and the next that B. B. Jay's message might seem to be spreading more doubt than faith. Rather, B. B. Jay is speaking to a hardened group of homies, addressing the kinds of material worries, fears, and motivations that drive their lives. By saying that he does not want to be "po' no mo'," Jay both identifies with these homies, and presents his Christian desires as being in touch with their material needs. His interpretation of Gospel rap is not divorced from basic material wants or needs. B. B. Jay even speaks prophetically, reminding "America" that it needs to "open the door" for the poor. Further, he sees the United States, not just da streetz, as being a "troubled land." He prays that God will give him the "wisdom and power" to take the Gospel message to the land, a message that he is certain is potent enough to "break the yokes and shackles" that enslave people in evil ruthlessness, "drama," and all those aspects of a "sabre-tooth society" that inflict pain. But in the end B. B. Jay is confident that God does, in fact, have the "whole world in his hand." By not separating the spiritual Gospel from the material, B. B. Jay represents both an opacity of recognizing how things are, and a fierce desire to resist the status quo—oppugnancy. The end of Jay's appeal is for a genuine "peace on earth" that reaches all humanity and "keeps the 'Hood' alive!"[34]

B. B. Jay also addresses poverty and hard times in "His Love." Calling himself a "Chocolate Child" that looks at "da world mad critical," because it is so cold-hearted, with "no reconciliation, no healing," Jay calls for "self-respect," in whatever language, tongue, or ethnicity. Again, striking a prophetic tone, Jay does not see any way out except through "the Word of God," expressed in the love of Jesus Christ.[35] What B. B. Jay sees in "His Love" is Jesus as the "Holy Revolutionary" calling Christians into a revolutionary kind of lifestyle.[36]

This view of Christ, as well as the role of Gospel rap as the medium for conveying this "revolution," is also reflected in Tonex's interpretation. In his "Nureaupean Anthem" Tonex demands that the old presentations of the Gospel represented by most churches be silenced. He calls for a "revolution" that is "not asking for permission" but is simply *taking over things as they stand.* Obviously tired of waiting for traditionalists to "get used" to new presentations, Tonex and others like him call for something like a "hostile takeover" of Gospel.[37] Such boldness is repeated by Unity Klan as well as local Dallas favorite, Dooney, whose message is a bit less confrontational. Placing his view of Gospel rap on the front lines with other Gospel rappers, Dooney calls his interpretation part of the "trendsettaz" who are moving from a small minority in the Gospel music industry to a majority position.[38]

Other Gospel rappers present Christianity as not caring for issues of poverty, violence, and oppression. DJ Maj, for example, is an excellent "DJ," or mixer of various musical samples into one musical presentation, but he never raps about issues like L. G. Wise, Lil' Raskull, B. B. Jay, or other former "streetz" persons. DJ Maj's CD *Full Plates* celebrates presenting the message of the Gospel without specifically naming the kinds of situations facing oppressed persons. While the song "Full Plates" purports wanting to transform the "culture" of hip-hop and rap into "His image," the rest of the CD pays no attention to the details of that "culture," except insofar as it relates to specific record deals, music industry types, and occasionally the materialism of rap artists in general.[39] Curiously, there is a rap on the CD entitled "The Revolutionary," but the revolution it points to is the very *fact* of Christian rap (and its values) in the midst of the secular medium of rap music in general. B. B. Jay, and others like him, seem much more pointedly concerned about the homies on da streetz than DJ Maj.[40] While one might say that the concerns of the streetz ought not be the sole focus of Gospel rappers, it is also clear that Gospel rappers like B. B. Jay find ways to present the Christian message in an opaque and oppugnant fashion in relationship to the evils of oppressed urban culture.

For Gospel rappers from da streetz like B. B. Jay and Lil' Raskull, finding and being found by Jesus Christ meant being saved from almost certain self-destruction. B. B. Jay thanks God throughout his CD for saving him from almost certain jail time, drug addiction, or death. Lil' Raskull raps about the many brothers who are no longer alive with whom he had grown up. For such Gospel rappers, the medium of rap enables expression of their conversion testimonials. It also gives them a way of interpreting and presenting to the homies, thugs, and other streetz folk the Gospel message of Jesus Christ. There is not only a sense of joy that exudes from such testimonials, but a profound sense of gratitude that God has given their lives an opportunity to serve in this fashion.

Shifting "Truths": Presenting the "Truth" of the Gospel

To conclude, there are three different kinds and types of Christian presentations of the Gospel message in Gospel rap. These three types, while adhering to the traditional evangelical interpretation of Jesus Christ as being the "only Way" to find salvation, are not uniform in how the Gospel message can transform the lives of believers. In the first type, for those like

B. B. Jay, Elle R.O.C., King Cyz, and Lil' Raskull, for example, the Gospel message purges individual souls of the "devil" *and* provides a meaningful alternative to the cultural "drama" of "da streetz." Applicable both to specific evils plaguing women and African Americans, these Gospel rappers interpret the Christian message as one that is both individual and social. For these kinds of Gospel rappers there is a clear-cut relationship between recognizing the work of the devil and its evil (their understanding of "opacity"), and moving toward strategies of living that transform groups and social situations (oppugnancy).

The second type is represented by groups like Unity Klan, which see the Gospel message as salvific for individuals by opening the barriers that separate various warring ethnicities and cultures. Their understanding of individual salvation is directly related to a vision of the "Body of Christ," be it the Church or believers in general. The "Body of Christ" cannot claim Christian salvation unless and until attempts are made to move beyond the singular focus of "da streetz" and on the specific woes of poor, urban African Americans. Their rap reveals an interpretation that recognizes the nonbelieving "world" as divided in irreconcilable ways—opacity. They celebrate the power of the saving force of Jesus Christ as having the ability both to transform such divisions and to create new structures of a loving community—opacity and oppugnancy.

The third type of Gospel rappers, such as Knowdaverbs and DJ Maj, present the individual salvation of Christ as enough of a focus for the message of Gospel rap. Recognizing one's own sinfulness and need for Christ is enough—their understanding of what we call opacity in this chapter. Resisting the devil, temptations, and the material seductions of the world is their version of oppugnancy.

These different levels of interpreting and presenting the Christian Gospel form differing, shifting levels of "truth" in relationship to what all would agree is the truth of the Gospel message. They are *shifting* types because no particular Gospel rapper is *only* concerned with being one type or the other. There is a shifting, malleable relationship among the types.

Finally, further research and analysis need to be done on the kinds of rhetoric Christian rappers utilize. Earlier I noted that there was a linguistic violence present in both Lil' Raskull and Knowdaverbs. Lil' Raskull directs the violence toward "the devil," while Knowdaverbs directed such energies toward the preredeemed/unredeemed aspects of human nature itself. Is such violence a part of all rap in general? If this is so, then in what ways is Gospel rap truly different from other kinds of rap music? Is such violence a necessary aspect of credibility for Gospel rappers, without which they could not reach the homies they are trying to address? Such concerns go beyond the purview of this chapter, but point to fertile ground for further scholarly inquiry.

NOTES

1. "Perspectives for a Study of African-American Religion in the United States," in Timothy E. Fulop and Albert Raboteau, eds., *African-American Religion: Interpretative Essays in History and Culture* (New York: Routledge, 1997), 27.

2. Ibid., 30.

3. "Slave Songs and Slave Consciousness: An Exploration in Neglected Sources," in Fulop and Raboteau, *African-American Religion,* 55–87; John W. Blassingame, *The Slave Community* (New York: Oxford University Press, 1972); Eugene Genovese, *Roll, Jordan, Roll: The World the Slaves Made* (New York: Vintage, 1972). Of course one of the classic treatments of slave conversion experiences is Albert Raboteau's *Slave Religion: The "Invisible Institution" in the Antebellum South* (New York: Oxford University Press, 1978). More recent interdisciplinary studies include Gayraud S. Wilmore, ed., *African American Religious Studies: An Interdisciplinary Anthology* (Durham, NC: Duke University Press, 1989); and Milton C. Sernett, ed., *Afro-American Religious History: A Documentary Witness* (Durham, NC: Duke University Press, 1985).

4. "Wonder Years," on Lil' Raskull, *Certified Southern Hits,* Grapetree Records, 1999, distributed by Chordant.

5. "Modern Day Cannibals," on E-Roc, *Avalanche,* Grapetree Records, 1999, distributed by Chordant.

6. Ibid.

7. "Megaton Bombs," on E-Roc, *Avalanche.*

8. "Intro" of B. B. Jay, *Universal Concussion,* Jive Records, 2000, distributed by Zomba Recording Corporation.

9. L. G. Wise refers to the hardships and pain of "da streetz" with particular eloquence in his piece "Hard Times" on *GT Compilation Volume II: Muzik Ta Ride 2,* Grapetree Records, 1997, and in "Ghetto Fables," a testimony partially taken from his own extended family of cousins as well as "homies," on L. G. Wise, *Ghetto Fables*: Da Ain't Told, Grapetree Records, 2000, distributed by Chordant.

10. Cf. note 4, "Wonder Years."

11. "Ain't Gotta Be Like Dat," on L. G. Wise, *Ghetto Fables.*

12. "For the Ladies," on B. B. Jay, *Universal Concussion.*

13. "Circular Motion," on Elle R.O.C., *I Die Daily,* Bettie Rocket Record, distributed by Diamante Records.

14. "Ghetto Dreams," on Lil' Raskull, *Certified Southern Hits.*

15. Elle R.O.C. is particular about this point. She speaks of "rhyming Gospel" at an early age. See "Holy Hip-Hop Awards," on Elle R.O.C.'s Internet connection: http://www.elleroc.com/news2.htm, pp. 1–4. Another term she uses that is also used by other rappers is "Christian Emcee."

16. "Ill-Radiation," on E-Roc *Avalanche.*

17. Augustine's first reflections on this occur in *The Confessions,* Book 7, part 12 (Hammondsworth, UK: Penguin, 1984), 148. He returns to the theme later in a more systematic fashion in Book 19 of *City of God.*

18. "One Fo the Sick," on Lil' Raskull, *Certified Southern Hits.*

19. See other songs on Easop, *The Time Has Come,* Life or Death Records, 1999, Distributed by Grapetree.

20. See "Lost Souls" and "Necessary Murder," on Lil' Raskull's *Certified Southern Hits.* Also look up his treatment of "killing the Devil" in "Satan Wants Yo Mind," on *Gory to Glory,* Grapetree Records, 1997, GTC0163.

21. Easop calls out what he sees as a satanic system running the recording industry on "How It Used to Be," and "Here We Come" on his *Time Has Come* CD.

22. "Zombies" on *Knowadverbs: The Action Figure,* Gotee Records, distributed by Chordant.

23. "Should I Go On" on *King Cyz: Life or Death,* Nu Wyne Records, distributed by Grapetree.

24. By an "evangelical interpretation" of the Bible, I refer to Carl F. H. Henry's definition of what evangelicals mean by a "literal" interpretation: "Evangelical consensus today would generally agree with Harold Lindsell who says, 'All that is meant by saying that one takes the Bible literally is that one believes what it purports to say. This means that figures of speech are regarded as figures of speech. No evangelical supposes that when Jesus said 'I am the door,' he meant He was a literal door." See Harold Lindsell, *The Battle for the Bible* (Grand Rapids, MI: Zondervan, 1976), 37. As Bernard Ramm writes: "The 'liberal' meaning of a word is the basic, customary, social designation of the word . . . To interpret literally (in this sense) is nothing less than to interpret in terms of normal, usual designation." See Bernard Ramm, *Protestant Biblical Interpretation* (Grand Rapids, MI: Baker Book House, 1982), 90–91. See also Carl F. H. Henry, *God, Revelation, and Authority: God Who Speaks and Shows,* vol. 4 (Waco, TX: Word Books, 1979), 104.

25. "I Die Daily," on Elle R.O.C., *I Die Daily;* three songs by Easop—"Life or Death till I Die," on *Dead but Alive* (Party Mix), and "Dead but Alive" (Street Mix), found on *The Time Has Come;* and "Life or Death (Intro)," on King Cyz, *Life or Death.*

26. "Life or Death (Intro)," on King Cyz, *Life or Death.*

27. "Whatever Happen" on Unity Klan, *As It Is Written,* Eternal Funk Records, distributed by Diamante.

28. "Phullon Empty," on Knowdaverbs, *The Action Figure.*

29. "Action Figure," on Knowdaverbs, *The Action Figure.*

30. See "Keep It Real," "All Right," "I'm Free," and "Luv or War," as well as "Luv for My Thugs," on Priesthood, *Keepin' It Real,* Metro One Music, distributed by Word Distributing.

31. Henry, *God, Revelation,* 105.

32. Elle Roc stated it this way during the "Hip-Hop Awards"; see n. 15.

33. "Po' No Mo'," on B. B. Jay, *Universal Concussion.*

34. Ibid.

35. "His Love," on B. B. Jay, *Universal Concussion.*

36. Ibid.

37. "The Nureaupean Anthem," on *Tonex Presents Ms. Dynasty: The Hostile Takeover,* Tommy Boy Records, 2001, Tommy Boy distributors, TRC 1488.

38. "Trendsettaz," on Dooney, *Peculiar Records Compilation, Volume 1,* Peculiar Records, 2000, distributed by Midwest Records.

39. See "Full Plates," "Reception," and "Champion Sound" in particular on DJ Maj, *Full Plates,* Gotee Records, distributed by Chordant.

40. "The Revolutionary" on DJ Maj, *Full Plates.*

2

A Jihad of Words

The Evolution of African American Islam and Contemporary Hip-Hop

Juan M. Floyd-Thomas

A Jihad of Words

Malcolm X gained international prominence through his role as the controversial spokesperson for the Nation of Islam (NOI). Malcolm's notoriety was largely driven by his relentless attack on the causes and consequences of racism as the nation's civil rights struggle gradually reached its apex. Coupled with his fiery invectives against the cruel injustices of Jim Crow in America, Malcolm's ascendancy in public life was also fueled by his representation of a growing Islamic presence in the United States. In a postwar America struggling to come to terms with its racial and religious transformations, Malcolm emerged as an enigmatic celebrity for the American public. In order to satisfy the public's growing interest in his life and career, in addition to chronicling his own personal quest for social justice and spiritual wholeness, Malcolm X agreed to compile his personal recollections into a book-length project.

In the wake of Malcolm X's untimely death, *The Autobiography of Malcolm X* stood as a testament to the formation of Black racial identity. Malcolm X's collaboration with author Alex Haley during the last years of Malcolm's life has served as the definitive articulation of the rage, struggle, and hope of African Americans in the late twentieth century as illustrated through personal tales of pain, loss, and rebirth.[1] Furthermore, for countless readers, Malcolm's memoirs provided unprecedented insights into African American Islam "as a religion as well as a weapon of protest and a means of self-definition."[2] Within the narrative of Malcolm's life, readers found a wellspring of frank, honest, and scathing indictments of American society from a person who had seen the worst side of life.

Malcolm's social critique and political vision, couched within a religious commitment, attacked the destructive tendencies of American culture. In fact, it has been suggested that Malcolm was engaged in a verbal jihad marked by a "talking back at white America—which translated as offering blacks a psychological alternative, a perhaps nonpacifist plan for fighting back."[3] Theologian Richard Brent Turner asserts that Malcolm X's "jihad of words" was advanced by his "extensive and thoughtful reading, debating, and serious contemplation" of the racial inequality and social injustice which eventually "raised his religious and political consciousness about the situation of black people in America and the world."[4]

Even as Malcolm used his mastery of logical exposition, reasoned disputation, and moral persuasion to attack white supremacy, capitalist exploitation, neocolonialism, and a multitude of comparable societal ills in an outward manner, such an enterprise had an indelible inward effect. This is also in keeping within the greater Islamic tradition of a dual essence to jihad: the first—*jihad bil nafs*—addresses "striving within the self"; the second—*jihad fi sabil Allah*—emphasizes "striving in the path of Allah."[5] Turner indicates that Malcolm's realization of and response to such negative aspects of the human condition eventually instilled him with the virtues, discipline, and wisdom needed to submit himself more fully to the will of Allah. Therefore, even as he sought to end oppression both here and abroad, Malcolm's jihad of words gradually made him a better, more devout Muslim. In many regards, the events and circumstances that defined the last few years of Malcolm's life demonstrated how political and moral concerns were contingent on one another. In his history of the Black Power movement and its relationship to American culture, William Van Deburg notes: "Following his death, Malcolm's influence expanded in dramatic, almost logarithmic fashion. He came to be far more than a martyr for the militant, separatist faith. He became a Black Power paradigm—the archetype, reference point, and spiritual adviser in absentia for a generation of Afro-American activists."[6]

What is of primary importance for this chapter is the manner in which Malcolm X's jihad of words provides the framework by which many rappers address both their religious sensibilities and social outrage. It must also be noted that this jihad of words, although initiated through the rhetoric of Malcolm X, is continued in the religious rhetoric and social critique offered by his most noteworthy successors such as the Honorable Minister Louis Farrakhan of the Nation of Islam, Father Allah of the Five Percent Nation, and Imam Warith Deen Muhammad of the American Muslim Mission. This essay argues that there has been a synergy of African American Islam and hip-hop over the past few decades which has forged a profound and complicated relationship between these two phenomenological forces that must be studied more closely by students of religion and popular culture in the contemporary world. I make an effort to develop this argument through attention to *both* the historical development of various modalities of Islam in black communities and the articulation of these developments in the lyrical content of rap music.

Application of the Jihad of Words, I: Nation of Islam

Although many scholars have written about the rap group Public Enemy (PE), little attention has been given to PE's overt references to NOI doctrine, icons, and rhetoric. The lyrics, for example, from "Party for Your Right to Fight," on PE's 1988 album *It Takes a Nation of Millions to Hold Us Back* reflect an open adoption of Malcolm X's "jihad of words." Many of the lyrical insights in this song are patent examples of NOI ideology within a hip-hop idiom: "It was your so called government / That made this occur / Like the grafted devils they were. . . . Word from the honorable Elijah Muhammad."[7] A few years later, Public Enemy's song "White Man's Heaven Is a Black Man's Hell," from their 1994 album, *Muse-Sick-N-Hour-Message,* served as a tribute both in title and spirit to a classic calypso tune of the same name recorded by Louis Farrakhan.

The rapper KRS-One offers another manifestation of Malcolm's jihad of words. When KRS-One and DJ/producer Scott La Rock, as the seminal group Boogie Down Productions (BDP), released their debut album, *Criminal Minded,* in 1987, they were among the vanguard of East Coast rappers who anticipated the advent of gangsta rap through rhymes filled with murderous violence, sexual braggadocio, and youthful frustration. On the brink of commercial success and critical acclaim within gangsta rap, the group underwent a profound transformation largely marked by the murder of Scott La Rock, in 1987, as he attempted to break up an altercation in the Bronx. With the release of *By All Means Necessary,* BDP's sophomore album, in 1989, it was evident that the group had drastically altered its sense of purpose. Both the cover art and title of the album reflected KRS-One's desire to appropriate much of Malcolm's symbolic and rhetorical arsenal. The album's title mimics one of Malcolm's most recognizable slogans, "By any means necessary." Moreover, the album's cover art consists of KRS-One standing with an automatic weapon next to a window in a state of constant readiness, serving as a direct visual allusion to a classic photo of an armed Malcolm X that was popularized during the 1960s. With these two gestures, KRS-One initiates a process wherein he infuses his aspirations to serve as hip-hop's reigning "teacher" with the essence of Malcolm X, the organic intellectual and cultural revolutionary. This is most evident in BDP's overt decision to compose and perform music that was more politically conscious and empowering in nature following the tragic loss of Scott La Rock. From 1989 onward, KRS-One and BDP penned songs that attempted to advance the general level of discourse within rap music beyond thoughts about cars, clothes, jewelry, dance moves, and other trendy topics that had dominated rap music during its early years.

By the start of the 1990s, this expression of black nationalist/Afrocentric rap was on the verge of becoming a nationwide force. This is best represented by the solo work of the rapper Ice Cube during this period. Through *Death Certificate,* Ice Cube infused his social commentary about racial and class inequality during the Reagan-Bush era with the imagery and ideological tenets of Louis Farrakhan. Designed as a concept album, Ice Cube divided the songs equally between "Death" and "Life." The "Death" side is intended to expose the internalized pathology and nihilism that fomented the self-destructive tendencies that surfaced in poor/working-class African American youth culture during the 1980s and 1990s. Conversely, the "Life" side focused on generating a rebirth of consciousness by using incisive social critique to target problems, generate intracommunal dialogue, and ultimately work toward a concrete agenda for racial uplift. In many regards, Ice Cube's *Death Certificate* represented the musical transliteration of Farrakhan and the NOI's ideological platform. From the outset, the album marked a considerable departure from standard hip-hop fare, serving more as political polemic than party record.

By embracing Farrakhan's teachings within his musical purview, Ice Cube merged the moral authority of the NOI with his street credibility as a pioneering gangsta rapper in order to scrutinize black people's complicity in their own devastation. It was only after his adoption of NOI beliefs, no matter how cursory, that Ice Cube assumed the quasi-religious/quasi-political position of a "prophet of rage." I do not want to give the impression that such a gesture was intellectual posturing or some sort of career move. Instead, this move was a serious confrontation with spiritual malaise and social injustice by a young Black man, in the rhetoric of the NOI, "no longer deaf, dumb, and blind." At a moment when gangsta rap was making steady and lucrative inroads into mainstream America, Ice Cube complicated his image as hip-hop's "Nigga You Love to Hate" by asking (and in some instances forcing) his listeners to do something they had never done before—take a deep breath, muster courage, and dive into the most confused, dissonant recesses of the black psyche.

The jihad of words once promised by NOI-influenced rap music of the late 1980s and early 1990s met its untimely end through the renaissance of Malcolm X as pop culture icon. In 1992, director Spike Lee mounted a dizzying publicity campaign to advertise the long-awaited film adaptation of *The Autobiography of Malcolm X*. The hype surrounding the motion picture soon spawned a proliferation of posters, baseball caps, clothing, and various other forms of merchandising bearing an "X" logo which began surfacing across the United States and overseas. This gross reduction of Malcolm X and his jihad to a letter "X" emblazoned on all kinds of cheaply manufactured goods sold by countless bootleggers helped dilute and ultimately diminish the intellectual and moral gravitas that Malcolm had personified at the zenith of his public notoriety. Even as artists like Public Enemy, KRS-One, and Ice Cube tried to imbue rap with the fiery spirit of the "jihad of words," the commercial and media feeding frenzy inspired by Lee's cinematic homage to the fallen black Muslim leader ironically led to the evisceration of Malcolm's life and beliefs. As the late Joe Woods states:

> To understand the reemergence of Malcolm we begin by considering his iconic power. In these hostile times, many African Americans are hungry for an honorable sanctuary, and Black spirit fits the bill. . . . But are the buyers, African American or not, angry or not, Black believers? Not necessarily, because Black spirit has never meant one thing . . . which is its great power *and* failure. Spirit has no spine; it bends easily to the will of the buyer.[8]

Journalist Greg Tate elaborates on this problem by stating that the murder of Malcolm X left African Americans with "their first revolutionary pop icon. . . . We celebrate the death of Malcolm X for what it is—the birth of a new black god. . . . He's like the Elvis of black pop politics—a real piece of Afro-Americana. That's why Spike's X logo is branded with an

American flag. Malcolm couldn't have happened anywhere else."[9] One need not share Tate's satiric outlook to appreciate the implicit crisis of transforming one of postwar America's most profound political voices into a fashion accessory. Furthermore, the commodification of black America's "shining prince," to borrow from Ossie Davis's eulogy, left many African Americans with cognitive dissonance about the revolutionary potential of black nationalism and Afrocentrism.

Jihad of Words, II: The Five Percent Nation and Rap Music

African American Islam and rap music underwent major transitions during the early nineties. From the early heyday of Ice T and NWA (Niggaz With Attitude) to the crossover appeal of Dr. Dre and Snoop Dogg, the preponderance of West Coast rap emphasized musical postulations of "life in the ghetto" that were deeply apolitical, predatory, and nihilistic in nature. Though the artists were neither the first nor only purveyors of this more ruthless edge of African American popular culture, this trend hit its apex during the early 1990s largely due to the fact that white middle-class teenagers in suburbia were buying gangsta rap music at a phenomenal rate. Also, whereas the urban black communities along the eastern seaboard of the United States certainly had their own indigenous gang subcultures, those gangs never achieved the same essential function or cultural relevance for urban black youth on the East Coast during the 1980s as gang culture had out West.

This geographic displacement also marked the diminution of the strong black nationalist/Afrocentric fervor that once dominated rap. In the matter of a few years, the politicized school of East Coast rap soon gave way to the increasingly shallow and virulent gangsta consciousness that served as West Coast rap's stock-in-trade. Through a process of signification—the process of naming and subsequent identity formation as a means of self-definition—Dr. Dre's renunciation of "medallions, dreadlocks, and black fists" in "Dre Day" marked those symbols of the hip-hop generation's pro-black militancy as archaic and useless relics.[10] As Todd Boyd notes, "The emergence of gangsta rap has seen an open rejection of politics by those involved."[11]

The East Coast hard-core scene responded to the prevalence of West Coast gangsta rap by emphasizing its most esoteric and exclusive collective, namely the Five Percent Nation of Islam (also known alternatively as the Five Percenters and the Nation of the Gods and Earths).[12] The Five Percent Nation was founded by Clarence 13X. After joining the NOI, Clarence 13X was assigned to Temple No. 7 in Harlem in the early 1950s and subsequently became a lieutenant in the Fruit of Islam (the NOI security force) and a youth minister. During this period, Clarence 13X worked closely with Malcolm X and found much inspiration in his de facto mentor's direct challenges to the NOI's hierarchy and dogma. There were several concepts that were central to the NOI that Clarence 13X later canonized within the teachings of the Five Percent Nation: black people were the "original" people in the world and emanated from Asia; Christianity was an integral tool used by white slave masters to control the minds of black people; white people were a devilish and grossly inferior race created by a mad scientist named Dr. Yacub some six thousand years ago as the living embodiment of evil on earth; and the only hope for black people in America is total separation from whites and self-reliance.

In the early 1960s, Clarence 13X began to question the NOI doctrine that God had appeared in Detroit in 1930 in the person of Master Fard Muhammad. He reportedly began to question whether or not Fard was actually God, since the NOI taught that the Original Man qua Asiatic Black man was Allah. This seemed contradictory to Clarence 13X since Fard Muhammad looked white. Clarence 13X began to teach that every black man was the physical manifestation of God. He was reprimanded in 1963, left the NOI along with a few followers, changed his name to Allah, and began preaching to the youth on the streets of Harlem. In emulation of the Middle Eastern sites made legendary within historic Islam, Clarence 13X and his growing cadre of followers changed the names of Harlem, the Bronx, and New Jersey to "Mecca," "Medina," and "New Jerusalem," respectively.

Father Allah, as his followers came to call him, taught that the Five Percenters are black men who have acquired "knowledge of self" and use this knowledge to release the hidden resources of the black man. Once a man has tapped his hidden talents, he is a God. In fact, most members refer to themselves as Gods rather than Five Percenters, reserving the latter term for those who have only begun studying the knowledge. The general premise is that 85 percent of the black population is manipulated and otherwise victimized by the 10 percent who are the "bloodsuckers of the poor." According to the teaching of Fard Muhammad, as later disseminated by Father Allah, the 10 percent includes the grafted, blue-eyed white devil and those, such as those in the Nation of Islam, who have knowledge and power but who use it to mystify and abuse the 85 percent. The Five

Percenters are the poor righteous teachers who preach the divinity of the (black) man—the god who is "manifest" in living flesh (not a spook, not a mystery god). They also believe they, through their teachings, will save the 85 percent from destruction.

In its orientation, the belief system of the Five Percenters represents a form of African American gnosticism. Generally speaking, gnosticism refers to the mystical perception of transcendent spiritual knowledge that is disseminated and interpreted only by spiritually mature adherents and initiates.[13] For example, within the Judeo-Christian experience, the gnostics of the ancient world viewed Jesus as a great teacher rather than as divine messiah and believed that the ultimate essence of Jesus' real teaching was that the kingdom of Heaven was a present, corporeal reality to be experienced through personal comprehension of sacred truth.[14] Therefore, inasmuch as the Five Percenters developed an integrated system of mythology and metaphysical teachings intended to explain the creation of the world, the genesis of humankind, and the perfectibility of the human soul, the Five Percent Nation operates in a fashion similar to classic gnosticism. In keeping with gnosticism as an esoteric school of thought, the Five Percent Nation philosophy revolves around fundamental principles such as the divine origins of the cosmos; the presence of evil that corrupted humanity; and recovery of humanity by nurturing the inner life of true believers.

Father Allah willfully spread Fard Muhammad's secret teachings, known as the "Lost-Found Muslim Lessons" to black youth who were outsiders to the NOI.[15] (During the 1960s, NOI members were not allowed to discuss the tradition with outsiders, maintaining a great deal of secrecy about their core beliefs, rituals, and practices.) Father Allah also developed his own system of teachings, known as the Supreme Mathematics and the Supreme Alphabet. The "divine sciences" of Supreme Mathematics and Alphabet are sets of principles and an evolving system of analysis, attached to numerals as well as the letters of the alphabet, which serve as the keys to divine knowledge. For Five Percenters, the "science of Supreme Mathematics is the key to understanding man's relationship to the universe." Islam, for them, is a mathematics-based science, a way of life and not a traditional religion. For Five Percenters, "the science of Supreme Mathematics is the key to understanding man's relationship to the universe."

The Supreme Alphabet of the Five Percenters has been instrumental in making members extremely adept at the "breaking down" of words, in order to arrive at their true, esoteric meaning, in accordance with the lessons provided by Master Fard and Father Allah. "Knowledge is the Foundation of all in Existence," according to Father Allah's Supreme Alphabet, "It is the Original [Asiatic Black] Man, who 'knows the ledge' or the boundaries of himself and knows that there is 'no ledge' or no ending to his circumference. . . . Wisdom is your Wise Words, Ways and Actions. . . . Wisdom is developed from the knowledge of Self, which allow[s] One to be Wise or Speak Intelligently from the Dome or the Mind." For instance, rap artists Pete Rock and CL Smooth's "Anger in the Nation" illustrates this theme: "Libraries, broken down as lies buried/Television tell a lie vision."[16] In addition, the hip-hop group Brand Nubian's song "All for One" asserts "You got to know the ledge of wise and dome/And understand your culture of freedom."[17]

When using the Supreme Alphabet to ascertain the true meaning of Allah, the Five Percenter visualizes each letter of the Arabic term for "God" to be part of the following acronym: "Arm, Leg, Leg, Arm, and Head." By depicting God in this very anthropomorphic fashion, the Five Percenter equates this use of word play with the fundamental belief that black men are the living embodiment of divinity in the world. Likewise, using the Supreme Alphabet to decode the meaning of Islam, the Five Percenters transform the term, which means "submission" in Arabic, into the following statement: "I Self Lord and Master." In doing so, this alternative definition of Islam by the Five Percenters directly contradicts the historic interpretation of the word from its Arabic origins. But the Five Percenters do so in order to advance a more personal and empowering theology that places black people as well as their desire for human dignity and self-governance squarely at its center.

There is also a noteworthy material culture that coincides with the ideology of the Five Percent Nation. For example, the Book of Life, also known as the "Power Papers" by the Five Percenters, is circulated in the form of photocopied pamphlets that are passed hand-to-hand from initiated members of the group to new recruits. The Book of Life represents the amassed teachings of Father Allah and serves as the main source for the Five Percenters' "lessons." In addition, the Book of Life was central to the bitter feud between the NOI and the Five Percent Nation. As a former youth minister for the Nation of Islam's fabled Mosque No. 7 in Harlem, Father Allah was privy to numerous doctrines that were handed down by Fard Muhammad himself and were closely guarded secrets of the NOI's leadership. With Father Allah's departure from the NOI, he incorporated these secrets into the Five Percenters' Book of Life.[18] In addition, the

"Power Flags" used by the Five Percenters have an eight-pointed star with an encircled number 7 in the center of it with the motto "In the Name of Allah" imprinted above it.[19]

Of great significance to the gods is the number 7. It stands for the seventh letter of the alphabet, G, and, by extension, for God.[20] According to Fard Muhammad's *Lost-Found Muslim Lesson* no. 2, the Original Man has 7-1/2 ounces of brain when compared to the white devil, whose brains weighs only 6 ounces. This symbolism is extended further: the flag of the Five Percenters, also known as the Universal Flag of Islam, contains a 7 (symbol of God) surrounded by a crescent moon (signifying the black woman) and a star (signifying the child). Rappers who embrace the teachings of the Five Percent Nation note the significance of this number. Famed rapper Rakim, for example, has produced lyrics such as those in the song "No Competition" which declare "I'm God/G is the seventh letter made," reflecting the centrality of seven as the number of divine perfection.[21]

Anyone who is remotely aware of Five Percent jargon is cognizant of the racial essentialism that fuels believers' assault on white supremacy. As for the subject of the white people, Five Percent lyrics often refer to them variously as "snakes," "serpents," "the Yacub crew," "skunks," "cave dwellers," and so on. Poor Righteous Teachers and Gang Starr, for example, represent the most adamant position. In the song "Word from the Wise," Wise Intelligent of Poor Righteous Teachers asserts, "Most definitely Poor Righteous Teachers never be down/We're with the kings and crowns not clowns/No blue eyes and blonde hair is over here."[22] Guru, the rapper from Gang Starr, expounds, "And yo, the devil's got assassination squads/Want to kill niggaz cuz they're scared of God" in the song "Tonz O' Gunz."[23] In both instances, the lyrics illustrate the level of racial antagonism and mistrust that emanate from the belief that any contact with whites will result in the downfall and subsequent demise of blacks.

It must be noted that the Five Percent rappers grapple with this issue of race in a very complex and varied manner. Taken at face value, Rakim's classic lyric from the song "In the Ghetto"—"It ain't where you're from, it's where you're at"—appears to summarize a postmodern or antiessentialist argument that political identity and geographic location are what really matter more than biological origin and cultural heritage.[24] Yet most observers generally pay no attention to other lines within the same song that arguably denote the racial essentialism and ethnic absolutism at the core of Five Percenter thought. For instance, in keeping with the classic iteration of NOI/Five Percenter racial theory, Rakim mentions those who "lived in the caves" (the white men) and "they couldn't cave me in/cause I'm the Asian" (the Original Asiatic Black man). Furthermore, while repeatedly emphasizing the power of his "third eye," a direct reference to the mind used in Five Percent terminology, Rakim states, "From knowledge to born back to knowledge precise." This serves as another Five Percenter allusion indicating the constant personal and spiritual evolution that came from the acquisition of self-knowledge.

Central to the mission of the Five Percent Nation has been an attempt to move beyond a critique of nihilism into a mode of empowerment for poor and working-class African Americans who are otherwise disenfranchised, disaffected, and desperate. When considered in light of Cornel West's definition of nihilism as an all-encompassing specter of "psychological depression, personal worthlessness, and social despair,"[25] the song "Life's a Bitch" by rappers Nas and AZ vividly illustrates the manner in which the beliefs of the Five Percent Nation can be perverted. The duo provides a fascinating insight into this fundamental crisis by re-creating the ghetto mentality of New York City's underside through the pensive, albeit frustrated, voices of those who have to contend with the harsh realities of the "mean streets." The song begins with the two rappers discussing how to split money that the listener assumes they have gotten through nefarious means. After they expound on the relative merits of fifty, twenty, and one dollar bills, respectively, Nas says, "That's what this is all about right . . . /Clothes, bankrolls, and hoes—ya know what I'm sayin?!" From that starting point, AZ's initial verse sets the stage for an exploration of how this materialistic zeal is embraced in spite of their best intentions: "Visualizin' the realism of life in actuality/Fuck who's the baddest/A person's status depends on salary/And my mentality is money orientated/ I'm destined to live the dream for all my peeps who never made it/Cause yeah, we were beginners in the hood as five percenters." Furthermore, AZ insists that "Even though we know somehow we all gotta go/But as long as we leavin' thievin' we'll be leavin' with some kind of dough/And so, to that day we expire and turn to vapors/Me and my capers will be somewhere stackin' plenty papers/Keepin' it real, packin' steel, gettin' high/Cause life's a bitch and then you die!"[26]

Nas and AZ's exchange declares their intent to satisfy a desire for goods, wealth, and sensual pleasure as the definitive interests that give life meaning and substance. Their song reflects Cornel West's warning that the nihilistic tendencies for urban black youth can be summarized as "fortuitous and fleeting moments preoccupied with getting over—with acquiring pleasure, property, and power by any means necessary."[27] Rap music inherited the fearless audacity and racial empowerment that was central to the examples of Malcolm X and Louis Farrakhan as noteworthy Black Muslims in recent memory, but the Five Percenters were largely bereft of the NOI's political sensibility as well as its moral compass.

Young black men have been drawn to the Five Percent Nation because, for example, of the movement's emphasis on male leadership. Much like the NOI had done previously, the Five Percenter teachings were able to criticize black men for abdicating their "rightful" place as leaders both in the public and private spheres while affirming their role. Thus Five Percenters' beliefs challenged African American men to assume control over their destinies, and they responded in kind. Black women within the Nation of the Gods and Earths—referred to as Earths or Queens—are taught to respect themselves, to submit to the will and authority of men, and to manage the affairs of family and home. Ironically, a growing number of young black women are attracted to the Five Percenter movement because they appreciate the strength of the men and the protective posture toward them in a society that either denigrates or ignores black femininity. Moreover, according to Five Percent beliefs, only a man can achieve the level of perfection symbolized by a 7, whereas a woman can only reach a 6. In the song "Can I Start This," the Poor Righteous Teachers illustrate this gender dynamic by proclaiming, "Peace to all the Queens/Submitting to the sevens."[28] Women are to subordinate themselves to men just as the Earth revolves around the Sun. Furthermore each woman, or "Earth," must cover three-quarters of her body by wearing head coverings and long, loose-fitting garments, just as three-quarters of the Earth is covered by water. While this is often dismissed as symbolic gesture or ritualistic code of dress, one must note that this practice is deeply imbued with concerns over male concepts about and control over the black female body.

As becomes clear, much of what is taught within the Five Percent Nation has served to reify modes of patriarchy that are insidious and regressive. For instance, it is important to note that there are only a handful of female Five Percenters in the entertainment industry.[29] Also, unlike her male counterpart, a female Five Percenter is known as a "Muslim," because she bears witness to the fact that her man is Allah and willingly submits herself to the black man.[30] In the song "Love Me or Leave Me Alone," the members of Brand Nubian declare, "I ain't down for a honey who don't wanna submit/See I'm not the kind to let a woman run it."[31] To a generation of urban black youth who are unaccustomed to the security of a strong nuclear family with traditional gender roles, the Five Percent Nation provides a welcome social structure. The underlying message of the Five Percenters is that the disorder they had experienced up until then had been caused by outside forces beyond their control, evil influences they were now able to overcome through self-mastery. Although the Five Percenter movement proclaims empowerment for the entire black community and tends to treat black women with respect, their sexist orientation provides little space for female Five Percent rappers or the unrestricted articulation of women's issues.

Jihad of Words, III: Sunni Islam and Rap Music

The NOI underwent several dramatic changes following the death of the Honorable Elijah Muhammad in 1975.[32] Under the brief leadership of Warith Deen Muhammad, one of the Honorable Elijah Muhammad's sons, the original Nation of Islam was transformed. The name of the organization was changed to the Bililian Community, and later to the World Community Al-Islam in the West (WCIW). To this day, members continue to be known as Bililians, in tribute to Bilal ibn Rabah, an Ethiopian Muslim who was born and lived during the seventh century A.D. and served as the first muezzin, the one who calls Muslims to prayer.

Although Warith made membership and participation in the WCIW open to people of all races, its membership remained predominantly black. Nonetheless, expansion of the organization marked a profound move from a black separatist movement with quasi-Islamic traditions to a black Sunni Muslim collective that aligned itself with global Islamic orthodoxy. Warith Muhammad restructured the NOI, not only to give the organization an orthodox Islamic sensibility but also to integrate black Muslims more fully into mainstream America. Over the past three decades, Imam Warith D. Muhammad made greater attempts to foster better relations with the United States government and foreign Islamic governments. More than that, the changes made by Warith Deen Muhammad were important because they brought the WCIW in line with other Islamic nationalist movements around the world.

Warith D. Muhammad sought to align the doctrine of the organization with the Qur'an. He boldly did away with Elijah Muhammad's doctrine of racial separation. He struggled to dismantle the overly secretive and hierarchical structure of the former NOI. After nearly a decade of his vilification by top-ranking NOI ministers, Warith made a deliberate effort to restore Malcolm X to a position of honor within the WCIW, most notably by renaming Mosque No. 7 in Harlem after his fallen friend. Also in direct contradiction to his father's teachings on racial separatism, Warith began honoring the U.S. Constitution and encouraging his members to participate in the political process. In another drastic move, Warith made certain that most of the organization's real estate holdings were quickly sold off. He also redefined W. D. Fard as a "wise man" and began to teach the five pillars of orthodox Islam.

Meanwhile, due to intense differences with Warith Deen Muhammad concerning the political and economic perspectives of the parent organization, Louis Farrakhan separated from the WCIW in 1977 yet retained the organizational name "Nation of Islam." As Edward Curtis notes, Farrakhan's attacks deemed Warith Deen Muhammad's efforts to reform the NOI into a Sunni Islamic entity as "a misguided departure from Elijah Muhammad's teachings" and subsequently charged Warith with establishing new policies that "ignored the issue of racism."[33] This newly formed NOI was clearly intended to be a political, as opposed to religious, enterprise. It is crucial to note how, under Louis Farrakhan's leadership, the NOI has actually constricted rather than expanded discourses on race, religion, and politics in the minds of the American public.

There has been resurgence in scholarly and popular interest about the NOI in general and its chief spokesperson, Minister Louis Farrakhan, in particular, largely based on the media attention generated by the Million Man March. On October 16, 1995, the NOI brought about one million African American men together to the National Mall in Washington, D.C., in support of what Louis Farrakhan called a "Day of Atonement," an event that garnered Farrakhan a great deal of publicity and influence within American politics. Despite this media visibility and overtures to the American mainstream, the future of the NOI is a matter of great debate. Like Elijah Muhammad and Malcolm X before him, Farrakhan is radical in his racial outlook, yet quite conservative in his political and economic views. Yet, unlike his predecessors, the inflammatory rhetoric of Louis Farrakhan has brought the NOI into the American sociopolitical mainstream. Mattias Gardell notes that "it is difficult to determine where on a political scale Farrakhan and the NOI should be placed. As a religio-political ideologist, Farrakhan moves in a different universe than secular politicians, making the left-right scale an inadequate tool of classification."[34] Even though the NOI has held a fairly prominent position within American society, the organization is losing ground because of its long-standing unwillingness to either embrace Sunni Islam or assimilate itself into American life by denouncing its race-based theology. In either case, the ideological tensions that once ensured the significance of Farrakhan and the NOI—racial separatism, black cultural pride, economic self-help, and political neutrality—now cause the man and the organization to become increasingly questionable to blacks and whites alike.

At the turn of the century, Minister Louis Farrakhan proclaimed a new direction for his organization. On February 26, 2000, a day the NOI designated as "Savior's Day," the NOI leader declared that he and his followers would accept orthodox Islam as the basis of their faith. After decades of eschewing any attempts to enter the larger Islamic community worldwide, this was an implicit shift away from the racialized mythology that epitomized the NOI's theology and religious practice under the Honorable Elijah Muhammad's leadership. In turn, this act greatly assuaged the prolonged ill-will that existed between Farrakhan and Warith Deen Muhammad.

This public acceptance of orthodox Islam by the NOI also represented a transition from the race-based theology and black nationalist ideology it embodied toward a worldview that still awaits true definition. Nevertheless, it is evident that the future of the NOI seeks to embrace the multiracial, multiethnic dimensions of the Muslim world yet retain its own core doctrines and definitive organizational structure. With the broad scope and great diversity of Islamic traditions and communities within the United States, the NOI led by Louis Farrakhan has actually been overshadowed and now stands as one of the smallest expressions of African American Islam in the nation. There are nearly twenty subgroups of Black Muslims within the United States today, ranging from Imam Warith Deen Muhammad's American Muslim Mission, to the Anser Auset (Nubian Islamic Hebrews of Brooklyn), to the Tijaniyah Sufis from Africa, to the Dar al-Islam Tabligh movement of Sunni Muslims.

The influence of African American Sunni Islam within rap music is neither a coincidence nor a marginal cultural phenomenon. Mos Def, Talib Kweli, Common, A Tribe Called Quest, Everlast, the Intelligent Hoodlum, Encore, Divine Styler, and the Roots are among a select constellation of hip-hop artists who have emerged as the musical vanguard of rap artists who are either Muslims or who have pro-Islamic tendencies. Two members of the critically respected hip-hop group A Tribe Called Quest, Q-Tip (who has since changed his name to Fareed Kamal) and Ali Shaheed Muhammad, whose last two albums are *Beats, Rhymes and Life* and *The Love*

Movement, are Sunni (orthodox) Muslims. The Roots, a hip-hop group whose renowned use of live instrumentation and lengthy improvisational jams have garnered favorable praise by fans and critics alike, is a unique collaboration among members who are both Sunnis and Five Percenters.[35]

While they still constitute a minority presence in hip-hop, Sunni Muslim rappers have gained much respect in media and industry circles for their stylized depiction as "conscious rappers." This recent manifestation of the black Muslim presence in hip-hop has been positioned and marketed as a bulwark against the more facile, materialistic, and thuggish elements that tend to mark the current state of mainstream rap music. In the song "Fear Not of Man," the rapper Mos Def provides a stark contrast to the prevalent trend in hip-hop during the late 1990s. The song begins with Mos Def uttering the *Basmala,* a solemn Arabic invocation, *Bismallah ir Rahman ir Raheem,* which means "In the Name of God the Most Merciful, the Most Compassionate." The *Basmala* is traditionally done without musical accompaniment in a tone akin to a reverent whisper. By offering the Basmala as the first words on his album/CD, Mos Def performs *dhikr,* a brief yet poignant prayer intended to assert one's full awareness of the union between God and the faithful believer and to purify the Muslim of all that is bad. Thus, Mos Def expresses an intention to commit himself and his musical work to divine will by repeating the name and attributes of God in the hopes of drawing himself closer to God. This deceptively modest gesture can be seen as a profound shift in the articulation of African American Islam in contemporary rap music.

In many ways, the rapper Common has emerged to represent a conscious effort to raise moral and artistic reflection within black youth culture in general and rap music in particular. Common raps in the song "The Sixth Sense," "Some say I'm too deep, I'm in too deep to sleep/Through me, Muhammad will forever speak."[36] In the song "G.O.D. (Gaining One's Definition)," Common explores the possibility of a truly ecumenical expression of black religiosity by stating: "Who am I or they to say to whom you pray ain't right/That's who got you doing right and got you this far/Whether you say 'in Jesus's name' or 'Al um du'Allah'/Long as you know it's a being that's supreme to you/You let that show towards others in the things you do."[37] In his lyric, Common indicates that religion, for him, transcended concerns about its functional (what it does) and substantive (what it is) dimensions and must focus on its definitive (what it means) aspects.

Aside from his strictly religious overtures, the greatest controversy in Common's musical career arose from his first ode to rap music entitled "I Used to Love H.E.R." As the rapper has stated, the H.E.R. in the song's title stood for "Hip Hop, in its essence, and real." In the song, Common provides an allegorical history of hip-hop's evolutionary migration from an underground East Coast subculture to a mainstream West Coast phenomenon in terms of his romance that had gone awry with a female lover. For Common, the disintegration of his love affair with rap music was keenly reflected in his fiery comments in the song. By way of illustration, he comments: "Talkin' about poppin' glocks, servin' rocks, and hittin' switches/Now she's a gangsta, rollin' with gangsta bitches/Always smokin' blunts and getting' drunk/Tellin' me sad stories, now she only fucks with the funk/Stressin' how hard core and real she is/She was really the realest, before she got into showbiz."[38]

In 1996, prominent West Coast rapper Ice Cube verbally attacked Common in a guest verse on "Westside Slaughterhouse" for Common's negative depiction of gangsta rap as a flawed expression of hip-hop culture. In turn, Common responded by producing an independent underground record called "The Bitch in You" in which he levels a contentious musical reproach of Ice Cube. In that song Common criticizes Ice Cube for going after quick cash in his Hollywood and later recording career, which glamorized everything that violated his staunch beliefs as a Muslim. Common delivered clever albeit scathing lines to highlight Ice Cube's many transgressions, such as: "Hypocrite, I'm filling out your death certificate/Slanging bean pies and St. Ide's in the same sentence/Shoulda repented on [the] 16th of October/Get some beats besides George Clinton to rock over."[39] In this one rhyme, Common brought to public attention how Ice Cube's present activities diverged greatly from *Death Certificate,* the musical testament to the rapper's conversion to the NOI. Moreover, Common argues that Ice Cube's decision to participate in the NOI's brand of self-help capitalism (the reference to "bean pies") while also serving as an advertising spokesman for a leading alcoholic beverage that was ravaging urban black America (the mention of "St. Ide's") is incongruous as well as contemptible. By arguing that Ice Cube "shoulda repented" during the Million Man March, Common is calling into question Ice Cube's moral commitment to the collective welfare of black people in the United States. This point is finally leveled as an indictment of Ice Cube's banal choice of recycling musical samples from George Clinton and other 1970s funk musicians, a move that simply followed the dominant trend within gangsta rap rather than making musical or aesthetic choices that might either challenge listeners or bring forth innovations within rap music in general.

With the intense schism between the East Coast and West Coast leading to the violence that might have contributed to the murders of Tupac Shakur and the Notorious B.I.G. during that period, there was much concern that a battle between Common and Ice Cube, whether lyrical or otherwise, might result in unwanted bloodshed and further public disgrace for the hip-hop community. As a result, Minister Farrakhan called a summit in which both parties were called to NOI headquarters in Chicago to parlay and work out their grievances amicably. As much as the Million Man March promoted a sense of personal responsibility and moral atonement for black men of all ages across the nation, Farrakhan's direct mediation of this potential feud helped establish a paradigm for crisis management and peaceful negotiations for the hip-hop generation.

Final Thoughts

To summarize, this chapter has analyzed how the evolution of African American Islam in the postwar era coincided with the growth and development of hip-hop. Rather than simply illustrating a unilateral imposition of Islamic influences upon this African American art form, I have argued that a heightened concern about black consciousness, adherence to complex rhetorical/ideological codes, and establishing a diverse system of aural/lyrical/visual aesthetics affected African American Islam and hip-hop to equal degrees from the 1960s to the present.

By using the "jihad of words" as an analytical rubric, it is vital to reconsider the ways in which African American Islam and rap music revise dominant notions of the relationship between religiosity and artistic creativity. As historic analogues, both African American Islam and hip-hop exposed codified as well as unwritten myths, ideologies, and stereotypes. They rejected the normative logic and realities of dominant society, creating alternative formulations that were far more relevant to the lives and experiences of black people. While black Muslims have provided the vision for new levels of social critique and spiritual renewal, the creative work of rap artists provided the means and rationale for the transformation of daily reality. By the coevolution of Islam and rap music within the African American experience, it is possible to contemplate how religion and popular culture operate in tandem to provoke many people to consider evil and strive toward social justice.

It is interesting to note that the development of a more "orthodox" turn in rap's Islamic sensibilities mirrors the general shift in the Islamic orientation within the larger black community. As demonstrated herein, the various manifestations of the black Muslim presence in hip-hop has been positioned and marketed as a bulwark against the more facile, materialistic, and thuggish elements that tend to mark the current state of mainstream rap music. While we have a sense of what this turn in hip-hop and the larger community means in terms of the diversity of both cultural production and religious sensibilities in black America, it remains to be seen how this complexity will ultimately manifest itself in years to come.

NOTES

1. Malcolm X, *The Autobiography of Malcolm X* (New York: Ballantine, 1973).

2. Steven Barboza, "Allah's Will in America," in Steven Barboza, ed., *American Jihad: Islam after Malcolm X* (New York: Doubleday, 1993), 14.

3. Ibid., 18.

4. Richard Brent Turner, *Islam in the African American Experience* (Bloomington and Indianapolis: Indiana University Press, 1997), 185.

5. Barboza, "Allah's Will in America," 17.

6. William L. Van Deburg, *New Day in Babylon: The Black Power Movement and American Culture, 1965–1975* (Chicago and London: University of Chicago Press, 1992), 2.

7. Public Enemy, "Party for Your Right to Fight," on *It Takes a Nation of Millions to Hold Us Back,* Def Jam, 1988.

8. Joe Wood, "Malcolm X and the New Blackness," in Joe Wood, ed., *Malcolm X: In Our Own Image* (New York: St. Martin's Press, 1992), 6–7.

9. Greg Tate, "Can This Be the End of Cyclops and Professor X?" in Joe Wood, ed., *Malcolm X: In Our Own Image* (New York: St. Martin's Press, 1992), 185.

10. Dr. Dre, "Dre Day," on *The Chronic,* Death Row/Interscope/Priority Records, 1992.

11. Todd Boyd, *Am I Black Enough for You? Popular Culture from the 'Hood and Beyond* (Bloomington and Indianapolis: Indiana University Press, 1997), 39.

12. Among the commercially successful and critically hailed rappers who belong to the Nation of Gods and Earths are Rakim Allah of Eric B and Rakim, MC Ren, Shorty from Da Lench Mob, K-Solo, Daddy O from Stetsasonic, Big Daddy

Kane, Poor Righteous Teachers, Busta Rhymes, Guru of the group Gang Starr, Pete Rock and CL Smooth, Brand Nubian, Digable Planets, and Mobb Deep. All members of the hip-hop collective Wu Tang Clan such as the RZA, Method Man, Ol' Dirty Bastard, the GZA, Raekwon, and Ghost Face Killah belong to the Five Percent Nation.

13. The author is aware that gnosticism has been viewed historically as the designation given to certain heretical sects among the early Christians who claimed to have superior knowledge of things spiritual, and interpreted the sacred writings by a mystic philosophy. It is my attempt herein to utilize a broader, more contemporary connotation of this term.

14. Mary Pat Fisher, *Religion Today: An Introduction* (London: Routledge, 2002), 187.

15. There has been speculation that the format of the NOI lessons, which are arranged in question-and-answer format, might have been modeled after the Freemasons' catechism.

16. Pete Rock and CL Smooth, "Anger in the Nation," on *Mecca and the Soul Brother,* Elektra/Asylum, 1992.

17. Brand Nubian, "All For One," on *One for All,* Elektra/Asylum, 1990.

18. There are allegations that Father Allah's disclosure of the NOI secrets motivated the organization to have him condemned to death. Father Allah was found murdered in 1969 under mysterious circumstances.

19. The Five Percent Nation has been condemned by various state and federal law enforcement agencies as nothing more than a criminal "gang," citing the group's involvement with the burgeoning underground drug economy and other illicit activities. In addition, critics from across the American political and social spectrum have denounced the Five Percenters as an assembly of criminals and thugs who use Arabic sayings and Islamic aesthetics as a means of justifying their unlawful activities and self-indulgent practices. There has been an increasing number of complaints from incarcerated Five Percenters in recent years against the Departments of Corrections in New Jersey, South Carolina, and other states about the violation of their civil liberties. Many of the members of the Five Percent Nation have had their constitutional right to religious freedom curtailed by prison authorities because of their unwillingness to view the Nation of the Gods and Earths as a legitimate community of faith. I want to suggest, however, that this treatment of the Five Percenters is both unbalanced and oversimplified. It disregards the significance of the group's beliefs, practices, and value system for individual members. Additionally, such pejorative views of the Five Percent Nation deny the exigent circumstances that gave rise to the Five Percenter phenomena.

20. Five Percenters originated the salutatory expression, "What's up, G?" whereby "G" originally stood for "God," not "gangsta," as has been stated recently.

21. Eric B. and Rakim, "No Competition," on *Follow the Leader,* Universal, 1988.

22. Poor Righteous Teachers, "Words from the Wise," on *Holy Intellect,* Profile Records, 1990.

23. Gang Starr, "Tonz O' Gunz," on *Hard to Earn,* Capitol, 1994.

24. Eric B. and Rakim, "In the Ghetto," on *Let the Rhythm Hit 'Em,* MCA, 1990.

25. Cornel West, *Race Matters* (Boston: Beacon Press, 1993), 13.

26. Nas, "Life's a Bitch," on *Illmatic,* Sony Music, 1994.

27. West, *Race Matters,* 5.

28. Poor Righteous Teachers, "Can I Start This," on *Holy Intellect,* Profile Records, 1990.

29. Female adherents of the Five Percent Nation who have gained recognition in the past few years are Erykah Badu, Lady Mecca of the Digable Planets, and Blue Raspberry, a female member of the Wu Tang roster.

30. Yusuf Nuruddin, "The Five Percenters: A Teenage Nation of Gods and Earths," in Yvonne Y. Haddad and Jane I. Smith, eds., *Muslim Communities in North America* (Albany: State University of New York Press, 1994), 128.

31. Brand Nubian, "Love Me or Leave Me Alone," on *In God We Trust,* Elektra/Asylum, 1993.

32. Due to his advanced Qur'anic education and extensive travels through the Middle East and North Africa, Wallace Muhammad (later renamed Warith Deen Muhammad) had a profound effect on Malcolm X's theological views during the late 1950s and early 1960s. Prior to Malcolm's controversial rift with the Honorable Elijah Muhammad and the NOI hierarchy in 1963, it was Warith who initially distanced himself from the organization for what he deemed to be false Islamic teachings. By most accounts, it was evident that the more Warith read the writings of W. D. Fard, the more he questioned his father's claim to be the "messenger of Allah." Although they were going through their own respective crises of faith regarding their affiliations with the NOI, both Warith and Malcolm eventually concluded that it was unreasonable to believe that Fard was Allah himself. In spite of being separated by considerable amounts of time and space, both men came to similar conclusions and hence began to lean more toward orthodox Islam.

33. Edward E. Curtis IV, *Islam in Black America: Identity, Liberation, and Difference in African-American Islamic Thought* (Albany: State University of New York Press, 2002), 130.

34. Mattias Gardell, *In the Name of Elijah Muhammad: Louis Farrakhan and the Nation of Islam* (Durham, NC: Duke University Press, 1996), 283.

35. Furthermore, in addition to Islamic doctrine in rap music, the resurgence of Middle Eastern musical textures within today's rap music has been noteworthy. Most recently, songs such as Missy Elliott and Timbaland's "Get Ur Freak On," Norega's "Nothing," Erick Sermon and Redman's "React," and Truth Hurts's "So Addictive" have been major R & B/hip-hop hits that use Middle Eastern rhythms and melodic structures to give their recordings some exotic flourishes. The latter song was further accentuated in this regard not only by the stellar

production by West Coast rap legends Dr. Dre and DJ Quik, but also with the lyrical assault by the penultimate hip-hop lyricist and Five Percenter, Rakim Allah. If we think that some of these doctrines are problematic or heretical, we need to try to understand them, to engage them, and to try to work to change conditions that produce them.

36. Common, "The Sixth Sense," on *Like Water for Chocolate,* MCA Records, 2000.

37. Common featuring Cee-Lo, "G.O.D. (Gaining One's Definition)," on *One Day It'll All Make Sense,* Relativity, 1997.

38. Common, "I Used to Love H.E.R.," on *Resurrection,* Relativity, 1994.

39. Common, "The Bitch in You," on *Relativity Urban Assault,* Loud Records, 1996.

3

Rap, Reggae, and Religion

Sounds of Cultural Dissonance

Noel Leo Erskine

In both the United States of America and Jamaica, rap and reggae create a conduit for African-American and Afro-Caribbean culture. Addressing issues of identity and location that are relevant for both rap and reggae, Tricia Rose explains: "Rappers' emphasis on posses and neighborhoods has brought the ghetto back into the public consciousness. It satisfies poor young black people's profound need to have their territories acknowledged, recognized and celebrated. These are the street corners and neighborhoods that usually serve as lurid backdrops for street crimes on the nightly news."[1] Addressing a similar social context, in which Bob Marley and the Wailers hammered out reggae music, Don Taylor states:

> Trench Town and the rest of West Kingston were beginning to show a flare up of the ghetto problem which had started to become noticeable in the early fifties: there were larger tracts of wasteland crammed with the makeshift houses of the itinerant rural squatters who captured every square inch of living space, as they moved from country to town. The shacks were built cheek-by-jowl and somehow the politicians thought the way to solve the problem was to bulldoze them all down and build large and concrete structures. . . . This was where Bob ended up, in the area the country would later call "Concrete Jungle."[2]

Don Taylor points out that although the roots of reggae preceded rap by a couple of decades, the social context out of which both emerged was quite similar. In Jamaica, the association with Marley, Peter Tosh, and Bunny Livingston begins in the "Concrete Jungle" where they lived, in the reality of being an integral part of the ghetto world in which there were no regular paying jobs.

> Many idle days were spent by the majority of young ghetto dwellers in a world without regular work and opportunities. A world where the only escape seemed to be in the learning of a trade for the boys and the cleaning of white people's house for the girls, or in migration to "foreign" by first the mother and finally the family.[3]

And rap music emerges from a similar world of economic struggle, political deception, and social absurdity.

In this chapter I examine the historical development of rap and reggae, noting the lines of convergence and divergence. I call attention to a similar social context that triggers the ethos that produced rap and reggae, looking specifically at the history of these two musical forms, their religious sensibilities, and the dilemma of sexism as a challenge to religious vision.

Historical Considerations: Rap and Reggae

Tricia Rose has helped to make the connection between the early beginnings of rap in the South Bronx and reggae in Trench Town, Jamaica, through her study of hip-hop culture. In both cases, the ghetto serves as a black popular narrative. Through music, the poor and marginalized find voice and are able to acknowledge and celebrate their identities and neighborhoods. In a context in which "few local people are given opportunity to speak, and their points of view are always contained by expert testimonies, . . . young mostly male residents speak for themselves and for the community, they speak when and how they wish about subjects of their choosing. These local turf scenes are not isolated voices; they are voices from a variety of social margins that are in dialogue with one another."[4]

Because of the advent of the transistor radio in the 1950s, in Jamaica the poor and marginalized youth in Trench Town could listen to and move to the rhythmic beats of Fats Domino, Louis Jordan, and the Timpani Five. Reggae, like rap, emerged from Afro-Caribbeans and African Americans giving voice to their social reflections on poverty, the fear of adulthood, their views about absent fathers, frustrations about black male sexism, female sexual desires, racism, homophobia, daily rituals of life as an unemployed teen hustler, safe sex, raw anger, violence, and childhood memories.

Rap and reggae are also the home for the creative use of language, the freedom to name one's world, and the freedom to retain the power of definition in relation to one's world and self. It is a powerful medium for storytelling and spiritual and cultural messages.[5]

Rap and reggae have been linked since rap's inception. Kool Herc, a Jamaican immigrant to New York City, is credited with playing an instrumental role in the development of rap as a segment of hip-hop culture. Drawing from the musical genius of Lightening Rod and James Brown, Kool Herc provided rhythmic patterns that would define the genre of rap as he created a new art form infused with energy of reggae.

> Herc was deft at the early art of mixing and fading one record into the next without missing a beat in the interchange. He did this mostly by ear. His vast repertoire of music, including some reggae beats that though loved in the streets were very hard to find, and his thundering speaker system known as 'The Herculords' made his music highly danceable, rhythmical and unavoidable.[6]

Having lived in New York City during the early 1970s, I can attest to the vibrant Afro-Caribbean—particularly Puerto Rican and Jamaican—culture that shaped the youth during this period. In this ethos, rap music emerged as a cultural art form giving expressive power to voices that emerged from the margins. Rap arrogates to itself the power of definition, which comes to the fore through storytelling, "accompanied by highly rhythmic, electronically based music. It began in the mid-1970s in the South Bronx in New York City as part of hip-hop, an African American and Afro-Caribbean youth culture composed of graffiti, breakdancing and rap music."[7]

Hip-hop culture serves as an alternative resource for identity formation and social status in a setting in which the older local support institutions have become irrelevant for many youth. In an earlier time, the African American church provided a means of identity formation and the setting in which local identities were formed. For many young people today, the church does not provide this basis for identity formation and social standing in the community. Hip-hop has provided an alternative culture in which a new language, new names, and new communities (posses, neighborhood crews) have emerged. What is decisive in this context is that many hip-hop fans, artists, musicians, and dancers have maintained the power of self-definition and belong to an elaborate system of crew or posses.

The pressure to belong, to have a support system, to have a group identity, provides a basis for posses or neighborhood crews to become an alternative family. Coupled with this search for identity and family is the void experienced in the job market. Many of the artists and musicians turn to hip-hop because the jobs for which they are trained are socially irrelevant and economically limiting. Tricia Rose encapsulates the issue for us:

> Early Puerto Rican, Afro-Caribbean, and black American hip hop artists transformed obsolete vocational skills from marginal occupations into the raw materials for creativity and resistance. Many of them were "trained" for jobs in fields that were shrinking or that no longer exist. Puerto Rican graffiti writer Futura graduated from a trade school specializing in the printing industry. However, as most of the jobs for which he was being trained had already been computerized, he found himself working at McDonald's after graduation. Similarly, African-American DJ Red Alert (who also has family from the Caribbean) reviewed blueprints from a drafting company until computer automation rendered his job obsolete. Jamaican DJ Kool Herc attended Alfred E. Smith auto mechanic trade school. Salt and Pepa (both with family roots in the West Indies) worked as phone telemarketing representatives at Sears.[8]

Although most scholars speak of three foci of hip-hop—graffiti, break dancing, and rap music, I highlight rap because it emerges as the most prominent facet. The DJs were the central figures in the emergence of rap. They would connect their turntables and amplifiers to any available electrical source, including streetlights, turning public parks and streets into venues for community socializing.[9] The performative style of the DJs attracted large crowds. At some point, the crowds began to dance less and spend more time observing the DJs. "It was at this point that rappers were added to the DJs' shows to redirect the crowd's attention. . . . They spoke with authority, conviction, confidence, and power, shouting playful duties reminiscent of 1950s black radio disc jockeys. The most frequent style of rap was a variation of the toast, a boastful bragging, form of oral storytelling sometimes explicitly political and often aggressive, violent, and sexist in content."[10]

In her important book *Noises in the Blood,* Jamaican author Carolyn Cooper points out that although Bob Marley's first album *Judge Not* was recorded as early as 1963—a year after Jamaica's independence from Great Britain—the roots of reggae and thus some early attributes of rap are traced to the contributions of the original Wailers and not to Bob Marley. She claims that it is difficult to ascribe authorship to songs that emerged prior to 1972 because of the cooperative manner in which the group produced songs. That is to say, "while Bob strummed and brooded, Perry would croak out catch-phrases and Doggerel" worked to match the percussion sounds being developed. With so much going on, and each member adding to the mix, it is difficult to know who actually wrote the songs. Cooper concludes that while some songs are distinguishable as being by Bob or someone else, "most likely they were written by both men and the band, improvising in the studio."[11] The verbal spontaneity of the group, coupled with their commitment to improvisation, is attributed to the shaping of the reggae lyrics prior to 1973. Considering the commitment to group improvisation, it is fitting to speak of reggae as a group project.

Reggae artists are committed to a belief structure:

> Rastafarianism, whose roots are in Africa, in Jah, Haile Selassie, the Emperor of Ethiopia. The themes of their messages are rooted in their despair of dispossession, their hope is in an African or diasporan solution. As a result, their messages emerge as an ideology of social change.[12]

In essence, because reggae emerged in a social context in which the main players were edged out to the periphery and treated as social outcasts, they turned to a religious faith that was itself outside the main stream, Rastafarianism. Don Taylor points out that as early as the 1960s, Bob Marley turned to Mortimer Planno of the Divine Theocratic Temple for guidance and an interpretation of the Rastafarian faith. Most reggae singers do not only make a connection between Rasta and Reggae but are themselves of the Rastafarian faith. Regarding Marley, "Planno took Bob through the stages of Rastafarianism, taking him to the settlements deep in the interior of the country where he learnt about the grounation ceremonies, and the all night convocations which meant feasting on coconut meat, rice and peas (ital cooking)." Furthermore, in this context, Marley began the process of thinking through "chants of the traditional Bongo Man and the Humba and Nyabinghi chants" and applying the ensuing aesthetics and sensibilities to his musical interests.[13]

Reggae and Rastafarianism

Because of the indissoluble relationship between Rastafari and reggae it is important to consider briefly the history of Rastafari and the importance of the Bible both for Rastafari and reggae. In fact, observation of Reggae lyrics reveals both theological and biblical warrants for their desire to "Chant down Babylon."

The Rastafarian religion was founded in the 1930s in Jamaica. According to Leonard Barrett, the economic and political situation in Jamaica during the 1930s and the coronation of Rastafari (Haile Selassie) as Emperor of Ethiopia were the triggers that led the Rastas to search the Bible for the meaning of these events. That is to say, within the context of the "decade of despair" beginning in 1930, political powers showed insensitivity to the situation of those struggling for existence. While some prospered, "the average wage for a full day of unskilled labor was twenty-five cents for men and fourteen cents for women." It is within this socioeconomic and political framework of great need that Haile Selassie was coronated in Ethiopia. This political development in Africa marked for many Jamaicans the fulfillment of a biblical prophecy that would end their oppressive situation. Those who looked to scripture "remembered a pronouncement of Marcus Garvey: 'Look to Africa where a Black king shall arise. This will be the day of your deliverance.'"[14]

It may not surprise readers that a great deal of reggae music is steeped in the scriptures and in African history. This is because the Rastas look to Africa and the Bible, and are convinced that Ras Tafari is none other than Jesus Christ returned to redeem Africa and people of African descent. The Rastas find conclusive evidence in the Bible that their messiah was black in Song of Solomon 1:5–6: "I am Black, and comely, O ye daughters of Jerusalem, as the tents of Kedar, as the curtains of Solomon. Look not upon me because I am black, because the sun hath looked upon me." According to the Rastas, the color of God is also made clear in Jeremiah 8:21: "For the hurt of my people am I hurt; I am black; astonishment hath taken hold of me." As the Rastas look to the Bible and at what is happening on the world stage in Africa, it is clear to them that the redemption of black people is at hand and reggae music is one way of making this a reality. Bob Marley, for one, saw growing turmoil and change in Africa and called for a new vision, one premised on the emergence of Haile Selassie:

> How good and pleasant it would be
> Before God and man
> To see the unification of all Africans
> As it's been said already let it be done
> We are the Children of the Rasta man
> We are the Children of the Higher man.[15]

The twin concepts of the divinity of Haile Selassie and the redemption of black people have distinguished Rastafarians from other Afro-Caribbean faiths seeking to promote an awareness of Black consciousness in the Caribbean. The discourse concerning the divinity of a black man, Haile Selassie, and the articulation of biblical passages to justify these claims, are made in a sociopolitical context in which the vast majority of Rastafarians, and indeed many reggae artists, are at the base of the social and economic ladder. However, the Bible is read and put to song in a cultural and social setting in which many Jamaicans value those with lighter complexions more highly than their darker fellows. In this context, to sing about one's God being in one's image is a meaningful way of redeeming the image of Black people from disrespect and indignity. Having one's God ("Jah") in one's image fosters self-confidence and self-esteem because the blackness of Jah ensures the dignity and sanctity of black people everywhere. Blackness is thus no longer seen as a curse but is taken up into the divinity of Jah and becomes the basis for singing or talking about humanity.

Increasingly, reggae artists have become aware that music is not just for entertainment but has a higher focus and purpose—letting the world know of the divinity of the black man who as God lives among us in the here and now. "During his tours Marley was often asked by the press about his music and his motives. He took every chance he got to turn such questions to his meta subject, Rastafari. 'Religion is just a word like politics,' he told his interviewers, 'Religion is just war. It's a warfield. The only good sign I see is Rastafari. Rasta mean head. Fari mean creator. Rastafari is head creator. Head creator is God. What does God mean? Rastafari! Haile Selassie is the Christ who them speak of, Him come again.'"[16] Leonard Barrett makes the connection for us between religion and reggae, tying reggae to the yearnings, inner needs, and demands that are typically associated with religion as an orientation for life. This music, reggae, entails a complex and thick blending of Africa and the African diaspora, "soul, nature, sorrow, hate, and love." It provides a complex and hopeful message of "oppression in exile, a longing for home, or for a place to feel at home. Reggae, like its earlier counterpart calypso, quickly became a medium of social commentary."[17]

> Old pirates yes they rob I
> Sold I to the merchant ships
> Minutes after they took I from the
> Bottom less pit
> But my hand was made strong

> By the hand of the almighty
> We forward in this generation triumphantly
> All I ever had is songs of freedom.[18]

While the religious sensibilities differ in terms of doctrine, it seems clear that rap music has, in some of its genres, benefited and learned from the praxis orientation and social critique stemming from the epistemological and aesthetic links it has with politicized reggae. This mirroring of the sociopolitical sensibilities of reggae (as one of its progenitors) in rap's own religious orientation, however, is often expressed in unusual and underexplored ways.

Rap, Theology, and Religion

In his recent book *Holler If You Hear Me,* Michael Dyson asks whether there is "theological space in Rap." He answers affirmatively at two levels: at the basic ontological level, and when the rap artist assumes the role of prophet and preacher in the community. At the ontological level, the central question addressed is not merely, where do you stand in relation to blackness? But, how do you get back to your black self? The bottom line here is to affirm the spirituality of the self in the search for black selfhood. "Hip-hoppers who address thug life, gang culture, and ghetto existence view themselves as urban poets whose job is to tell the truth about poor black life on the streets."[19]

Rap theology, which is also discussed elsewhere in this book, is intimately linked to notions of how society functions and who operates the levers of control. In rap theology, God takes sides and identifies with rappers in their attempt to confront violence with counterviolence. Their God is the God of the Old Testament who uses violence as midwife to give birth to new possibilities and realities. "For many thugs, God is the great accomplice to a violent life style. Big Syke, Tupac's mentor in thug heuristics, states a belief that may shock outsiders. 'God is a killer too,' he says, 'Don't get it twisted. God kills a lot of people. He wipes them out in masses. God is real.'"[20] Underlying the notion that God kills on behalf of the offended and wronged is the perception that God understands "all about their struggles and trials." And because God understands that their violence is in response to a prior violence inflicted by society and the brokers of power, God forgives. Rappers make a pact with God, asking God to forgive them because sometimes killing is unavoidable. What we find in the search for "theological space in rap" is not only the quest for authentic selfhood undergirded by God-talk but the rapper emerging as preacher and prophet. At Tupac's funeral the Reverend Wilson eulogized him by saying: "He was their preacher, if you will, who brought a message that [young people] can identify with, related to what was real, that spoke to the reality of the circumstances, situations [and] environments they have to deal with every day."[21] Regarding Tupac's obsession with God, Dyson states:

> In "So Many Tears," he asks God to intervene in his suffering, "God can you feel me?/Take me away from all the pressure and all the pain." In "Only God Can Judge Me," Tupac seeks an answer for his existence and his friends' deaths, and in "I Wonder If Heaven Got A Ghetto" Tupac declares his sympathy for Thug life Pondering his destiny. In "Staring At The World Through My Rearview," Tupac questions the divine presence when he says, "Go on baby scream to god, he can't hear you." In "Are You Still Down?" Tupac pleads for Salvation: "Please God come and save me/Had to work with what you gave me." On "Picture Me Rolling," Tupac wonders if God's forgiveness is forthcoming as he asks, "Will God forgive me for all the dirt a nigga did to feed his kids?"[22]

While many rappers like Tupac are venerated in the community by youth in search of direction, the standard response of the church is epitomized by the thoughts of Bishop T. D. Jakes. He acknowledges that while Tupac's messages are prophetic, they reveal the pathos and pain of the community but fail to provide clarifying direction. According to the bishop, we should not confuse the cry of despair for prophecy or entertainment for leadership.[23]

Yet, is the bishop circumscribing prophecy? Are we to look for prophetic leaders in the church or temple, or shall we know them by their fruits? It seems to me that quite often in the history of the black religious experience, the saving word has not been limited to religious institutions. Quite often, the word comes from outside rather than from within those institutions, and from those who are truly on the margins. I suggest that paying attention to the presence and impact of women in rap music might speak in powerful ways to the religiously identified quest for meaning expressed in rap and in its musical relative, reggae.

Furthermore, I suggest that the struggle against sexism within the rap music enterprise marks a movement on the part of women to enliven the social critique and commitment to praxis—as religious quest—that marks the best of reggae and rap. I understand this process of critique and correction as a religious quest in keeping with the manner in which Anthony Pinn frames the nature of religious questioning and exploration in the introduction to this volume. It is also tied to the issues of "being" and ownership reflected in Leola Johnson's contribution to this book. Furthermore, the following argument is also linked in subtle ways to social critique as a critique of the religious institutions presented in chapter 4.

Reggae, Rap, and Women: Social Critique and Black Religion

The congruencies between reggae and rap are real. Not only is there a common ethos in which these musical expressions are used as conduits in African American and African Caribbean cultural expressions, but the response to women and the role of women as purveyors of these art forms are also rather similar. In *Rastafari Women,* Obiagele Lake's discussion of women's role in reggae music speaks of "repression in the midst of revolution." She agrees that reggae music is revolutionary in its critique of Western lifestyles and the presence of imperialism in Jamaica; yet when it comes to the portrayal of women, misogynist ideas are inescapable. Women are portrayed as sex objects and dependent, and when they deviate from these norms they are regarded as undesirable. But just as we observed in the case of rap, this penchant to keep women in their place is a reflection of the cultural ethos. Lake puts it this way:

> In the 1990s women continue to be the main, and often sole, members of the household who are washing clothes, cleaning house, cooking, ironing, and child care. Women are obliged to work just to survive with little time to upgrade their skills or that of their female children. These economic constraints are exacerbated by the cultural validation of these roles in music. Females are raised to believe that their virtue, as women, lies in their physical bodies. The lyrics in "Duppy Laugh" imply that this woman, who lacks in these virtues, is compelled to do absolutely anything for her mate in order to keep him.[24]

There are some hopeful signs for women's liberation in reggae lyrics such as "No Woman No Cry," and "One Love." But even an artist as revolutionary as Bob Marley was ambivalent in his assessment of women: "Me never believe in marriage that much. Marriage is a trap to control man; woman is a coward. Man is strong. Dat woman in America . . . Angela Davis, a woman like that who defends something: Me can appreciate that."[25] It took Rita Marley in "*Who Feels It Knows It*" and Judy Mowatt in *Black Woman* to begin to change the ethos and to use reggae as a medium of women's liberation and positive self-affirmation. Ultimately, these women indicate for us the possibilities of using rap and reggae as a medium for the uplift of community.

With respect to rap, in the early years there were not many women who broke into the male-dominated world of beat-box innovators, because women are virtually absent from the area of music production. "Although there are female DJs and producers, such as Jazzy Joyce, Gail 'Sky' King, and Spindarella, they are not major players in the use of sampling technology nor have they made a significant impact in rap music production."[26] Women are at a distinct disadvantage for a number of reasons. On the one hand, they are not encouraged to learn about mechanical equipment either formally through the public school curriculum or informally through socialization. During the early years in which rap emerged, there was gender segregation in regard to these mechanical and technical skills. A female DJ in the early 1970s was an anomaly. On the other hand, women have also not been welcome in the male social spaces where technological skill is shared. Some of the early DJs speak of visiting the homes of male friends who were knowledgeable in the requisite technological skills and these visitations continued until their skills were acceptable.

Because these social spaces are typically occupied by males, women are less likely to spend extended periods of time learning the necessary technological skills.

> Today's studios are extremely male-dominated spaces where technological discourse merges with a culture of male bonding that inordinately problematizes female apprenticeship. Both of these factors have had a serious impact on the contributions of women on the contemporary rap music production. Keep in mind, though, that the exclusion of women from musical production in rap is not to be understood as specific to rap or contemporary music, it is instead the continuation of the pervasive marginalization of women from music throughout European and American history.[27]

Women have not always accepted the status quo. In spite of the odds, black women rappers are emerging to give voice to issues around economic opportunity, sexual issues, and the pain of racism and sexism. Like male rappers, these women critique the powers that be. Unlike their male counterparts, black women rappers focus on sexual politics.

It is often perceived that while male rappers are sexist, female rappers are antisexist. "Female rappers have been uniformly touted as sexually progressive, anti-sexist voices in rap music. Given the prominence and strength of these black women's voices in the popular terrain, it is not surprising that they have been heralded as rap's politically correct underdogs."[28] Rose further indicates that there are three dominant themes present in female rap music: "heterosexual courtship, the importance of female voice, and physical and sexual freedom." Rose suggests that it is more helpful to view female rappers as being in dialogue with male rappers rather than being in opposition to them. The dialogue is both with the male rappers' sexist constructions of black women and also with "the larger social discourse, including feminism."[29]

The dilemma for women rappers is twofold: they want to signal their displeasure with the explicit sexism in rap lyrics, but they are also aware that the mainstream press may use their remarks as a political weapon to punish male rappers rather than to affirm women's rap as a means to question the role of sexism and its effect on black women. Anyone who listens to rap cannot mistake the negative portrayal of women in many of the lyrics. This is regrettable because women who are often already at the bottom of the social ladder and whose dignity is seriously threatened do not need to hear from male rappers that women are "hos" and "bitches." Black women who are already attacked from outside their community due to their race and gender and class prejudice should not have to face within their own community an ethos that demeans and diminishes their self-respect.

This troubling ethos is not found only within the African-American rap community: it is also true of the black church. Ever since the founding of the African Methodist Episcopal Church by Richard Allen in the late eighteenth century, for example, women have been denied a central role in its leadership. The same became true in black churches that developed in subsequent years, with the message being that women are inferior to men. While the African Methodist Church has made some progress in this regard, having recently elected its first female bishop, other black churches have not been as progressive. I mention the place of women in black churches because rap, as a mode of critique and correction, should provide an alternative space where those on the margins can learn to accept their beautiful black selves. But much of rap reinforces the negative values voiced by churches and the larger society. Could it be that many rappers belittle and diminish women because they have been influenced by the troubling positions some of these churches take, as well as the attitudes of the larger society?

The way forward seems to entail a rethinking and reconstitution of community. Both forms of musical expression represent voices from the margins, articulating an alternative community through a new language. Rap and reggae artists arrogate to themselves the power of definition. They provide a musical score that reflects a new social and cultural reality, with societal change and the emergence of a new consciousness as its goals. In his song "Open Your Eyes and Look Within," Marley asks if his people are satisfied with the life they are living. He calls for "Exodus" and the movement of Jah's people. In the same vein, rap's "Prophets of Rage" tell us that knowledge of self does not originate in the books we read but rather from participating in healthy community. In the book, *Fight the Power,* Chuck D of Public Enemy unfolds the three vital elements of sustaining and creating black community. Education, economics, and enforcement, he writes, are an integral part of rap and reggae's mission:

> During my years of crisscrossing throughout major and minor cities in America I've developed a theory with regard to the Black community. I call my theory the "Plantation Theory." The Plantation Theory states that Black people don't really have communities; what we have are clusters of plantations. A community is an environment that has control over the three E's: education, economics and enforcement. Without control of these vital aspects of our existence, we're like robots existing in an environment with no real control.[30]

His assessment of the role of education, economics, and enforcement as pillars of a viable community is incontestable when one examines the context from which rap and reggae emerge. Yet, explicit in the work of artists such as Chuck D and Bob Marley is a fourth element necessary in the building of community—religion. In both cases, whether the Islamic vision put forth by Chuck D's Public Enemy or the Rastafarianism promoted by Marley, religion provides an important mechanism for the development of a fuller sense of individual humanity within the context of community. Using these four pillars of community-building, we cry "exodus" as we move from plantation life to true community. This is a metaphorical and real movement from Babylon for "I and I," Word!

NOTES

1. Tricia Rose, *Black Noise: Rap Music and Black Culture in Contemporary America* (Hanover and London: Wesleyan University Press, 1994), 11.

2. Don Taylor, *Marley and Me* (Kingston, Jamaica: Kingston Publishers, 1994), 23–24.

3. Ibid., 24.

4. Rose, *Black Noise,* 11.

5. Ibid., 18–19.

6. Errol A. Anderson, "Black Nationalism and Rap Music," in *Journal of Black Studies* 26, no. 3 (January 1996): 310.

7. Rose, *Black Noise,* 2

8. Ibid., 34–35.

9. Ibid., 52.

10. Ibid., 54, 55.

11. Carolyn Cooper, *Noises in the Blood* (London: Macmillan, 1993), 119.

12. Ibid., 120–121

13. Taylor, *Marley and Me,* 26–27.

14. Leonard E. Barrett, *Soul-Force* (New York: Anchor Press, 1974), 182–183.

15. Bob Marley, "Africa Unite" on *Survival,* Polygram Records, 1979.

16. See Roger Steffens, "Bob Marley: Rasta Warrior," in Nathaniel Samuel Murrell, *Chanting Down Babylon* (Philadelphia: Temple University Press, 1998), 259.

17. Leonard Barrett, *The Rastafarians* (Boston: Beacon Press, 1997), vii–viii.

18. Bob Marley, "Redemption Song" on *Legend,* Tuff Gong/Island Records, 1984.

19. Michael Eric Dyson, *Holler If You Hear Me* (New York: Basic Civitas Books, 2001), 210.

20. Ibid., 211.

21. Ibid., 202.

22. Ibid., 203.

23. Ibid., 208.

24. Obiagele Lake, *Rastafari Women* (Durham, N.C.: Carolina Academic Press, 1998), 127.

25. Cooper, *Noises in the Blood,* 131.

26. Rose, *Black Noise,* 57.

27. Ibid., 58.

28. Ibid., 147.

29. Ibid., 147, 148.

30. Chuck D with Yusuf Jah, *Fight the Power* (New York: Dell, 1997), 31.

4

"Handlin' My Business"
Exploring Rap's Humanist Sensibilities

Anthony B. Pinn

There is a strong and persistent link between religion as a response to the absurdity and terrors of life and forms of cultural production such as music. The arts—or cultural production in more general terms—are shaped by a concern with "thick" issues that have ontological and existential weight, thereby providing commentary on religion and religious expression.[1] Put another way, "pictures, poems, and music" are significant with respect to the study of religion in that they express "some aspects of that which concerns us ultimately, in and through their aesthetic form."[2]

Not every form of cultural production undertakes this religiously informative exploration with the same level of intentionality and intensity, nor with the same level of accomplishment and long-lasting value. To make such a claim would entail denying those in the study of religion and other disciplines the ability to assess and adequately critique cultural production. This would mean negating the viability of "criticism and the question of artistic excellence."[3] We must be mindful of the power of interpretation, that is, what the viewer or listener makes of a particular art form. But we must also be sensitive to the artist's intent: What does the artist hope to invoke? Both the interpretation of the art form and the intent of the artist are conditioned by historical realities and concerns. Both artist and "consumer" are touched by the human attempt to make sense of our past and present in ways that speak to the future in urgent and moving ways.

Related to the desire to make meaning within the context of historical conditioning, rap music, for instance, maintains an "ontological stance" by which it suggests a certain way of being.[4] Even more questionable rap artists (those who are as well known for misogynistic attitudes as for progressive activism) maintain in their corpus of work a sensitivity to the "thick" questions of human existence. This is certainly the case with Tupac Shakur, whose "religious ideas were complex and unorthodox."[5] Furthermore, rappers such as Ice Cube have reflected on the ultimate meaning of life and placed this in the context of socioeconomic realities faced by African Americans. This interpretation is plausible in songs such as "When I Get to Heaven," in which Ice Cube argues for a space free of racial stigma.[6] Examples from various Islamic perspectives on this "ontological stance" abound, particularly those from the 1990s expressed in the rather apologetic and ideological work of groups such as Public Enemy and Poor Righteous Teachers. Such groups, with varying degrees of success, seek to illuminate and map out "the complexities of our experience" while suggesting a new direction for life.[7]

Most will think of rap's engagement with religion strictly in terms of traditional practices such as Christianity and Islam. However, to do so is to miss the more subtle and nuanced modes of religiosity present within rap and other forms of cultural production. This chapter is concerned with humanism as one of these more subtle forms of religion that influences rap music.

African American Humanism Defined

Religion's basic structure, embedded in history, is a general quest for complex subjectivity in the face of the terror and dread associated with life within a historical context marked by dehumanization, objectification, abuse, intolerance, and captured most forcefully in the sign/symbol of the "ghetto." The quest for complex subjectivity that is the elemental nature of religion involves a desired movement from life as corporeal object controlled by oppressive and essentializing forces, to life as a complex conveyer of cultural meaning with a detailed and creative identity. This subjectivity is complex, holding in tension many spaces of identification by making them vibrant components of a larger and tangled reality.[8] In this sense, it is the struggle to obtain meaning through a process of "becoming."

This basic impulse, the push for subjectivity, is manifest historically in a variety of forms, including but not limited to Christian churches. I suggest that another, but seldom considered, manifestation of religion's elemental nature is humanism—a nontheistic form of life orientation that relies on human ingenuity and creativity to achieve greater life options and a greater degree of subjectivity. As I have stated elsewhere, African American humanism as a mode of religious orientation is based on five central themes:

1. Understanding of humanity as fully (and solely) accountable and responsible for the human condition and the correction of its plight.
2. Suspicion toward or rejection of supernatural explanation and claims, combined with an understanding of humanity as an evolving part of the natural environment as opposed to being a created being.
3. Appreciation for African American cultural production and a perception of traditional forms of black religiosity as having cultural importance as opposed to any type of "cosmic" authority.
4. Commitment to individual and societal transformation.
5. Controlled optimism that recognizes both human potential and human destructive activities.[9]

These themes, or principles for life, were expressed early in the thought of enslaved Africans who rejected the Christian church and its teachings because neither provided a means for a greater range of life options. Frederick Douglass, who embraced above all else "perfect freedom of thought," for example, writing about his life in slavery and his escape to the North and freedom, avoids talk of a transcendent reality at work in the historical movement toward liberation.[10] Rather, he speaks in terms of the struggle for *More* premised on human ingenuity and activity. Douglass restricts his attention to the mundane because it is only through "those faithful men and women, who have devoted the great energies of their soul to the welfare of mankind" that one gathers a sense of felt change.[11] Humans become the measure of all things, so to speak.

As alluded to in the introduction to this volume, a similar turn to humanity over against supernaturalism is expressed in much of the blues. Take, for instance, singer Son House's critique of traditional perceptions of heaven as a response to earthly suffering:

> Yeah
> It ain't no heaven now and it ain't no
> Burning hell
> Said I
> Where I'm going when I die can't no
> Body tell.[12]

While most African Americans during the first half of the twentieth century did not express their humanist principles through public activities, some worked through progressive organizations. A clear example of one who expressed humanist principles in public as part of progressive organizational work is civil rights activist James Forman, a high-profile figure who linked his public activities to his humanist leanings. Speaking of a period during the 1950s, he notes: "The next six years of my life were a time of ideas. A time when things were germinating and changing in me. A time of deciding what I would do with my life. It was also a time in which I rid myself, once and for all, of the greatest disorder that cluttered my mind—the belief in God or any type of supreme being. . . . God is a myth; churches are institutions designed to perpetuate this myth and thereby keep people in subjugation . . . the belief in a supreme being or God weakens the will of a people to change conditions themselves."[13] Different versions of Forman's perspective have been held by many African Americans throughout the twentieth century who have a desire to enliven and further develop the individual's subjectivity within the context of healthy community.[14]

Concern with human progress can also involve a humanizing process that incorporates elements of theistic religion. But this should not be confused with human progress as the goal of a humanist orientation. The former embraces relationship with God as a dimension of human fulfillment, and the latter rejects transcendence as harmful supernaturalism. Because of the intersections between religion and cultural production discussed earlier, a clear understanding of the humanist sensibilities in rap music requires determining what humanistic rap is *not.*

Humanity and Humanitarianism—Not Humanism

I want to make a clear distinction between *humanizing* rap music and *humanist* rap music. The former entails being attentive to the full development of human potential, though not necessarily bringing into question traditional modes of theistic orientation. A clear example of this approach is the corpus produced by KRS-One (*K*nowledge *R*eigns *S*upreme *O*ver *N*early *E*veryone). Born in Brooklyn, New York, KRS-One (Lawrence Parker) became a major figure in hip-hop culture through socially and politically conscious rap done in collaboration with Boogie Down Productions. Recognizing his interest in theological and philosophical concerns that were often ignored by rappers, several commentators have labeled KRS-One's collaborative work and his solo projects humanistic in nature. Mark LeVine, for example, in an Internet article titled "KRS-ONE: Hip-Hop Clergy," categorizes KRS-One's style as "a philosophically and even religiously 'humanist' perspective in hip hop."[15] What LeVine alludes to is a critique of Eurocentric readings of scripture found in "Why Is That?" This critique, however, does not contain the basic suspicion of transpersonal realities inherent in humanism as defined earlier in this chapter. What KRS-One offers, rather, is a human-centered theistic orientation. Such an approach involves tension between divinity and humanity whereby the accountability shouldered by humans for the furtherance of human fulfillment is highlighted—but within the context of a divine presence in the world. In "Take It to God," for example, in which KRS-One provides an embodied theology, he still recognizes God as a transpersonal, transhistorical, and final source of meaning. Why else would listeners be told to "run to God, and let him in your heart?"[16]

There is ambiguity in KRS-One's philosophical stance when one considers his construction of hip-hop as a "new" religion, complete with the understanding that rappers are godlike because of their ability to create through the spoken word. Language becomes a creative process similar to what the first several chapters of the Book of Genesis seek to portray: "In the beginning God said. . . ."[17] Turning again to the Internet, where much of the conversation concerning rap music takes place, this perspective on rappers as godlike is alluded to by a commentator who writes: "The storyteller assumes the role of evangelist, and the rap becomes a chronicle of the messiah. These songs are at one and the same time 'about the rapper' and 'by the rapper,' in the same way that the Bible is both 'about God' and the 'Word of God' simultaneously."[18]

KRS-One understands the performance of rap as a "sacred" act. It grows out of and extends to a new audience his commitment to the best of the Christian faith.[19] This is not necessarily a faith tied to religious institutions, but one that is more in line with a general sense of Christian "spirituality," or a connectedness to the divine that is hampered by most institutions. KRS-One spoke to this perspective during a recent interview:

> From day one we came in with a deeper level of consciousness and discussed God and Christianity on each and every album. But most people when they look from a critical eye, they don't believe you could be a Christian and question the Bible or the Church. They think being a Christian

> means keeping your mouth shut, be quiet or apathetic in the face of injustice and blatant lies. I don't think Jesus intended that for any of us.[20]

In light of this self-description, one should understand KRS-One's project as radical humanitarianism, based on a fundamental appreciation for humankind, as opposed to humanism.

A similar humanitarianist praxis is central to rap artist Queen Latifah's work. For her, the development of self-consciousness, the type that promotes a determination to make the most of our opportunities and to demand respect based on a recognition of our human worth, is vital. Queen Latifah's appreciation for black humanity, the importance of the sensory experience, also shares a rhythm and sensibility notable in the work of humanist author, Alice Walker. Walker's hermeneutic of womanist reflection, however, promotes an appreciation for the human body, but her epistemological basis is different from that of Queen Latifah. A connection between humanity and the rest of creation is existentially and ontologically endemic to Walker's conception of human life. It is this connection that we must nurture and celebrate. In a very real sense, nature (and the universe) can be understood as God: "God is everything that is, ever was or ever will be."[21] Yet, for Walker, this does not promote a typical theism—recognition of and allegiance to a supernaturalism hitched to a transhistorical and transpersonal reality, a cosmic personality guiding the universe from a distance. Rather, her perspective is better described as a modality of humanism by which humans act in accordance with "a belief in their own judgement and faith in themselves."[22] In contrast, Queen Latifah's is not a humanistic perspective. Her honoring of the black female's spirit and body is tied to a reverence for the Christian God as the source of humanity's authority and meaning.

Queen Latifah raps about the "divinity" of the black woman, but this deification seems measured in terms of intrinsic beauty and worth and does not challenge the primacy of God.[23] The rapper is not seeking a Nietzchean removal of God from the throne. In fact, this divine being, God, is the prerequisite for self-understanding because "everything starts with God. . . . If I don't believe in God," Queen Latifah states, "I can't have faith in anybody else, including myself. If I can keep my connection to God—keep my faith—I can conquer everything."[24] For Latifah, a relationship to the Christian God is the elemental source of human fulfillment. Both Latifah and Walker would agree on the importance of reclaiming black bodies, but only for Walker is this in essence a humanist act.

Rap and Humanism: Critiquing Traditional Modes of Religion

Rap music is not marked by a group of artists or by a self-identified genre of rap that explicitly connects itself with African American humanism through a systematic presentation of its basic principles. Rather, there are strands of thought within certain forms of rap music that speak to a reliance on humanistic orientation, and they merit investigation.

In general terms, one can think that humanist sensibilities are expressed by some rap artists in order to reclaim the black body (as biochemical and physiological reality) within the context of history and culture. For example, the group Arrested Development advocates earth-based and African-derived modalities of spiritual development over against institutional modes of religious experience which fail to provide "thick" meaning and worth. Arrested Development provides an empirical method for exploring the nature and meaning of life by comparing the validity of traditionally theist claims regarding the human condition against the norm of liberation. A clear example of this movement is found in track 8, "Fishin' 4 Religion," on *3 Years, 5 months and 2 days in the Life of . . .* Speech, Arrested Development's leader, proclaims that his move outside the church is due to the church's flawed theology, which does not allow for social transformation, offering instead an overly spiritualized depiction of life that pacifies the oppressed. According to Speech, the church is "praising a god that watches you weep but doesn't want you to do a damn thing about it."[25] From Speech's perspective, "Baptist teachings' dying is the only solution."[26] There is a sense in "Fishin' 4 Religion" that social transformation or fulfillment of human potential must be designed and plotted within the realm of human interaction and experience. Transhistorical realities are held suspect, and soteriological considerations are earthbound. In this way, rap groups such as Arrested Development maintain the humanist leanings one finds in some blues tones: "I don't want to ride no golden chariot/I don't want no golden crown/I want to stay down here and be/Just as I am without one plea."[27] Human progress is not the result of superhuman assistance, and it is most solidly located in the realm of history without otherworldly considerations.[28] From the vantage point of some, this position is akin to nihilism. But consider Arrested Developments' "Fishin' 4 Religion" again, where the following words paint a different perspective, one marked by a measured and human-centered optimism and determination: "Passiveness causes others to pass us by."[29]

An appeal to a humanist ethic of the mundane is more tellingly played out in rap artist ScarFace's "Mind Playin' Tricks 94," which is an extension of the track recorded by the Geto Boys a few years earlier. Here, ScarFace acknowledges the existential angst resulting from a life of conflict and urban struggle. He flirts with the nihilism and self-destruction many associate with a godless existence, and he expresses the internal dilemma in ways reminiscent of writer Richard Wright's existential leanings: "Dear dairy, I'm having a little problem with my mind state. How many bullets would it take to change my mind quick? Sometimes I want to end it but I don't though."[30] ScarFace is encouraged, the story goes, to talk with his pastor, but to no avail because the church is marked by radical individualism and a gospel of greed by which ministers are guilty of "putting a price tag on the man's word . . . and they opening up these churches for some quick cash."[31] Theological and ethical shortcomings mark the church and only amplify the hardships and deadly "hustle" that define life as ScarFace knows it. His solution, to the extent it can be considered one, is to reject institutional religion and engage a humanist ethic of self-help by giving his "money to the most needy and never put it in the hands of the most greedy."[32] One can raise questions concerning the strength of this ethic as it is preached by a character whose life is marked by the traumas of a hustler. Yet, what is of significance is the mere advocacy of this humanist ethic, which moves beyond a theistic one. In this case, I would agree with what many Christians claim about those who fall short of a Christlike existence: that the practice, not the principle, is flawed. Practice of the humanist perspective is flawed in much of rap music, yet this deficiency is not an indictment of humanist principles themselves.

Artists such as ScarFace do not speak only of humanist principles, as flawed as such a conversation may be. On a more basic level, the music itself also affirms humanist sensibilities. There is a sense of rebellion at work, one that is expressed not only through the power of the lyrics, but also through the epistemological demands of the sounds and the "context" in which both lyrics and sounds manifest themselves. The importance of sound was recognized by rap's ancestor—the blues—as powerful and as the mark of ability. Why else would Robert Johnson allegedly sell his soul for musical ability? Rap, through these three elements—context, sound, and lyrics—forces a confrontation with traditional sensibilities and convictions. This is accomplished in part as the sound and context force a recognition of the body—its presence, "feel," and placement in the world of the senses. The lyrics extend this preoccupation with the physical form by affirming its primacy. They put the listener in touch with being, and, unlike Gospel music, for example, give no credence to connection with a transcendent something. But like the blues, rap celebrates creative and vibrant humanity—physical and cultural realities.

Moving from Critique toward New Sensibilities

Rap artist Tupac Shakur's attention to humanity's ethical ambiguity as well as his preoccupation with human accountability for transformation moves rap beyond humanism as critique. Take, for example, "Blasphemy," found on Tupac's *The Don Killuminati.* The ethical and moral outlook presented in this "thug" life lesson is bleak, marred by the breakdown of communal relationships and structures, and premised upon a somewhat warped individualism as the guiding principle of survival in the United States. Yet these developments are not presented as the result of some type of theological anthropology of original sin as cosmic stain. It is clear that humanity is prone to much moral and ethical destruction in part because "niggas gon' hate for whatever you do."[33] In other words, ethical and moral shortcomings just *are.*

But there is a tension between this depiction of human nature and a recognition of the ability of humans to act in more productive ways because, as Tupac notes, "ain't nothing free, give back what you earn."[34] No doubt there are legitimate questions one can raise concerning the significance of this proclamation within the given context of thug life. Yet, it seems Tupac attempts to respond, in subtle and metaphorical tones, through an embodied theology by which the nature of life as a thug is reimagined.

For example, on the track "Hail Mary," Tupac provides an alternative Christology, one in which the Christ figure and his energy are represented in the context of thug turmoil as the authentic ground of transformation. There is an almost surreal quality of redemption brought to social existence through the presence of the thug, exemplified by Tupac and his THUG LIFE (*T*he *H*ate *U* *G*ive *L*il *I*nfants *F*ucks *E*verybody).[35] Hence, the reality of the thug and thug life present an opportunity to restore order.

While this view might not include an ethical and moral sensibility that most people are comfortable with—and I certainly do not promote or justify the destructive elements of this ethic—it provides a necessary function. Tupac gives significance to the thug as scapegoat in a way that could be explored theoretically in terms of philosopher René Girard's work on violence and the sacred. One might also think in terms of existentialist philosopher Albert Camus' character Cain, or writer Richard Wright's existentialism represented by the character Cross Damon.[36] There is a constructive dimension to the scapegoating of "misfits" as the horrific and dangerous carriers of social dis-ease. Sacrificing them allows for the maintenance of a more "orderly" and socially beneficial system of relationships. Perhaps Tupac recognizes this sacrilizing and sacrificing of the scapegoat in "Hail Mary." Is the scapegoat innocent of crime?

The line between innocence and guilt and the meaning of this distinction is blurred, but it is clear that what one finds in "Hail Mary" is a sacrifice of some for the benefit of others. Isn't this a way to explain the image of "brothas" being crucified? Tupac seems to see it this way: "Tell me I ain't God's son." This linkage to sacrifice and its ramifications is the underlying premise of his embodied theology and its radical reformulation of the Christ event. Tupac draws on the New Testament's basic rationale of the presence of God in human flesh, but this time, alluding to himself, the purpose is to "lead the wild into the ways of *the man*." (This is hauntingly reminiscent of something Cross Damon might say.) The ultimate location of this work is not transhistorical in any sense, but is in flesh.[37] While this signifying of the Christ event is clearly a step toward Camus' critique of Christology, its hermeneutic sensibilities provide a blurred resemblance to existential suspicion of Christianity and the human alternative.[38] Tupac's "blasphemy" against traditional modes of religious expression—his radical humanizing of Christology—breaks the illusion of life provided by religious theism.

One might think of Tupac as a rather loose version of what Camus labels the "rebel." In a sense, Tupac answers the existential and ontological questions and commitments that mark the rebel and that litter the rebel's environment, which is "a society where a theoretical equality conceals great factual inequalities."[39] Put differently, there is an uneasy possibility for life marked by Tupac's (the rebel's) attitude, one that is firmly lodged on earth, in sensory experience:

> If we decide to rebel, it must be because we have decided that a human society has some positive value [in this case a "thug" society]. But in each case the values are not "given"—that is the illusionist trick played by religion or by philosophy. They have to be deduced from the conditions of liv-

> ing, and are to be accepted along with the suffering entailed by the limits of the possible. Social values are rules of conduct implicit in a tragic fate; and they offer a hope of creation.[40]

Tupac inverts or humanizes the story of the Christ event in ways that locate a parallel significance in human interaction. In this way, Tupac rebels, through a "thugafication" or blasphemy, against metaphysical responses to life. In his allusions to this event, there is no real appeal to transhistorical realities or transpersonal intervention in history. The laws by which Tupac lives in "Blasphemy" are not from Christian scripture but are humanity-derived lessons and stories about and from the streets. Historical developments appear to be the only reality worth addressing in any substantive way. His life is an emblem of true struggle as "the media be crucifying brothas severely. Tell me I ain't God's son." This flipping of the Christ event as trope, I believe, is the ultimate humanizing of theology in that Tupac locates all reality within flesh.

There is a theodical twist in Tupac's work. This involves a theological and religious mode of musical blasphemy revolving around the seeming paradox between the presence of moral evil in the world and the claims of a divine being of justice also present in the world. Tupac depicts this theodical twist in clear terms: "Is God just another cop waiting to beat my ass if I don't go pop?"[41] What does one do in face of the universe's silence concerning our predicament? According to Tupac, "God promised, he's just taking his time." Responses to such questions are not to be found in traditional religions because religious leaders and scripture do not address the realities of life in a "thug nation." To the contrary, through metaphor, signs, and symbols, Tupac suggests the answer to life's ultimate questions of meaning and place are found in a shift away from religious traditions, in an act of blasphemy and rebellion—aesthetics over against metaphysics.

While Tupac continues to make what is a rhetorical use of the God concept, the final answer to the absurdity of life is not found in a God silent, if present. It is found in human activity. At best, God is suspect because, in a thugged-out, Marxist twist, there is a link between deception and the presence of traditional Christian religion. For example, like Marx who spoke of religion as the "opiate of the people," Tupac metaphorically links the development of Christendom with the contemporary drug trade and drug-induced passivity in that the Christian faith is "God's words all crushed like crack." There is, then, little hope for social transformation to be found in theistic religions for those who search for "truth." Truth is "where it's hard to find God."[42]

In opposition to modes of institutionalized religion, Tupac offers another tradition, a new system of thought and practice, perhaps forged during his "exile" or prison term. It is, he argues, centered around "the saint for thugs and gangstas—not killers and rapists, but thugs. When I say thugs, I mean niggas who don't have anything."[43] The traditional, transcendent God is replaced in everyday dealings with the "Black Jesus" (or Black Jesuz), who he believes operates through—not against—the community of thugs. For Tupac, surviving a shooting and imprisonment speaks to the presence of this figure. According to Tupac, "I feel like Black Jesus is controlling me. He's our saint that we pray to; that we look up to. Drug dealers, they sinning, right? But they'll be millionaires. How I got shot five times—only a saint, only Black Jesus, only a nigga that know where I'm coming from, could be, like, 'You know what? He's gonna end up doing some good.'"[44]

There is a glimmer of hope, of possibility, implicit in the ethic promoted by Tupac because "by both rejecting and embracing suffering, Tupac offers a complex prayer that does not merely glorify violence but interrogates its meaning and howls at the pain it wrecks."[45] His twist on an ethic of human endeavor reflects an absurd hope in that "rebellion, without claiming to solve everything, can at least confront its problems." Therefore,

> Rebellion is born of the spectacle of irrationality, confronted with an unjust and incomprehensible condition. But its blind impulse is to demand order in the midst of chaos, and unity in the very heart of the ephemeral. It protests, it demands, it insists that the outrage be brought to an end, and that what has up to now been built upon shifting sands should henceforth be founded on rock. Its preoccupation is to transform. But to transform is to act, and to act will be, tomorrow, to kill, and it still does not know whether murder is legitimate. Rebellion engenders exactly the actions it is asked to legitimate. Therefore it is absolutely necessary that rebellion find its reasons within itself, since it cannot find them elsewhere. It must consent to examine itself in order to learn how to act.[46]

Tupac's theological formulations imply many of the basic dimensions of humanism, without the clear vision of transformation. But is this odd when one considers that after the Civil Rights movement we have given those of his generation only questionable resources and rhetoric with which to build a vision of a more liberated existence?

One might think of Tupac's perspective as a shift from a theistic orientation to a human-centered one, from a final appeal to transhistorical reality to comfort with sensory experience as the limits of reality. A last turn to Camus provides a concise depiction of this humanist turn one finds in Tupac's lyrics. Regarding the epistemological stance of the rebel, Camus says the rebel is one "who is on the point of accepting or rejecting the sacred and determined on laying claim to a human situation in which all the answers are human—in other words, formulated in reasonable terms. From this moment every question, every word, is an act of rebellion while in the sacred world every word is an act of grace."[47] The discomfort more traditional religionists experience with Tupac, then, speaks to the presence of humanistic principles, a perspective on humanity and human life that is often troubling. Nationally recognized minister and motivational speaker T. D. Jakes expresses this discomfort by portraying Tupac as representing "a generation that had trodden underfoot the principles of God, leaving their ideas over God instead of God's ideas reigning over theirs."[48]

Humanism and the Underground

If one thinks of ScarFace and Tupac as embracing humanism through a mode of rebellion premised on rejection of the objectifying dimensions of race and racial stigma, Sage Francis, as a white underground rapper, exhibits humanist sensibilities premised on a rebellion from within the structures of relative privilege.[49] But he is not just any white rapper in part because of a background in spoken word poetry and an interest in underground rap music, about which he says: "I'm so different. . . . I'm a real underground rapper. My tape quality sucks. My records are warped. My CDs skip."[50] Having won several important accolades as both a spoken word poet and rapper (e.g., winner of the 1999 Superbowl Emcee Battle in Boston and the 2000 Skirbble Jam Battle), Sage Francis is clear on the purpose of rapping. When developing material, he argues for the evocation of

> emotion and thought . . . I think it is important for people to do a good self-evaluation and understand why they are doing what they're doing. What's your purpose? If you don't live righteous, and you don't know what it is to be righteous, what the hell are you doing trying to tell other people how to live? Please be creative, get your brain working. Gather experience and then take people places with your words.[51]

Social commentary and critique are a necessary corollary of this perspective on the nature and meaning of rap, and Sage Francis seeks to model this approach through tracks such as "Makeshift Patriot." It draws on the sights and sounds of "9/11" to reflect on the content and aesthetics of terrorism:

> "Makeshift Patriot" was brewing in my head. . . . The TV was making me sick. The noise of the crowd in that song is actual audio I took at ground zero 5 days after the attacks. Which is an interesting fun fact. It was people cheering on the rescue workers. I had to go there and absorb some of the atmosphere. I couldn't stand the filter of the TV screen.[52]

The thick imagery seems to suggest the United States is implicated in the event, fueling a military mentality learned early. Hence, "The melting pot seems to be calling the kettle black when it boils over. But only on our own soil so the little boy holds a toy soldier."[53] Or, in more explicit and graphically troubling language, "We taught that dog to squat. How dare he do that shit in our own back yard!"[54] There is an archaeological process at work here, a digging through the layers of stigma, policy, and socialization into aggression, to expose the foundational elements of human life.

These filters, the easily digested bits and pieces of information concerning U.S. involvement in world affairs and the existential context for the terrorist strike against the United States, do not allow for a creative response to the world. What is required to actually "live" is confrontation with the repulsive elements of life and relationships—suffering, pain, anger, hatred, and so on—in an artful way, by pulling from them a thoughtful challenge to our assumptions and a troubling of our self-awareness. The objective, according to Sage Francis, is to extend the range of themes addressed in rap music, to become increasingly sensitive to the depths of human consciousness and interactions.

Personal correspondence imagery presented by ScarFace is also found in Sage Francis's work. ScarFace gave us his diary as the symbolized vehicle for his verses, and Sage Francis offers a similar vehicle—*Personal Journals.*[55] On this CD, he gives listeners no easy answers, no comforting clichés. The problems and absurdity of life remain strong. For some this perspective might promote a nihilistic orientation, but he does not find the situation that distressing, nor are humans that psychologically impotent. Others might find life's absurd nature a reason to embrace traditional notions of God to gain the comfort that cosmic arms might provide. This is not the direction in which he takes his listeners. In response to the idea of God, his words drip with sarcasm: "I believe that God is an old white man who lives in the sky. When he gets mad he shoots lightening bolts out of his finger. He hates gay people the same way he used to hate indigenous people. Plus, he is all-loving."[56]

In short, what is God? God is a contradiction in terms, or perhaps a human construct tainted with oppressive tendencies that harm the socially disadvantaged. This humanist-like critique of supernaturalism and transhistorical reality might be dismissible if it were not accompanied by a similar critique of religion in more general terms. When asked to define religion, Sage Francis uses less than flattering terms, depicting it as destructive: "Brain wash. Separatism. Easy answers. Crutch. Man-made. Sad. Scary."[57] There is, according to Sage Francis, no epistemological fixed source of truth, no ahistorical measure of correctness. Instead, *truth* involves coercion or persuasion, the ability, as he puts it in "Majority Rule," to "simply fool the masses. Attack them mentally with tools of power."[58] Sacred texts provide a good tool in this respect, as he remarks in "Next Textament." Confronted by a street evangelist's "book," the protagonist in this track finds not the proclaimed "peace, love, happiness" promised, but rather "pain, hate, ignorance, and false alternatives."[59]

The implications for a humanist interpretation of scripture are profound. For example, feminist scholars such as Sallie McFague who work in constructive theologies have sought to remove the sacred (hence untouchable) aura surrounding scripture, suggesting instead that biblical stories are just that—stories—or human constructs seeking to teach particular lessons. Sage Francis's humanist leanings allow him to take it even further. While many theistic theologians argue that scripture is an imperfect depiction of a divine presence or movement in the world, he poetically implies that even this is too grand a statement. We surrender too much to myth if we do not write our own testament. Taking the book from the street evangelist, he opens it to find it "blank . . . no deceptions." The protagonist is told to "look deeper," but where? In response, the evangelist remarks, "that's what the pen's for."[60] Write. The "pen" destroys myths, breaks deceptions.

Life involves struggle, and Sage Francis suggests, rap music at its best entails the relaying of this struggle in complex and detailed ways, raising new questions and possibilities. Theologically, however, these possibilities are expressed without reliance on a doctrine of God—there is no theistic response to the problem of evil that is worth recounting. Moral and ethical sensibilities and trajectories are based on human ingenuity and creativity. In a stance that ethicist Sharon Welch would approve, there is comfort with risk. As Welch argues, there is no foundation for moral action which guarantees that individuals and groups will act in "productive" and liberating ways. Acting in healthy ways is important but it is not guaranteed; ethical activity is risky.[61] Hence,

> ideals are far from realization and not easily won, that partial change occurs only through the hard work and persistent struggles of generations. Maturity entails the recognition that the language of "causes" and "issues" is profoundly misleading, conveying the notion that work for justice is somehow optional, something of a hobby or a short-term project, a mere tying up of loose ends in an otherwise satisfactory social system. Within an ethic of risk, maturity is gained through the recognition that evil is deep-seated, and that the barriers to fairness will not be removed easily by a single group or by a single generation. Maturity is the acceptance, not that life is unfair, but that the creation of fairness is the task of generations, that work for justice is not incidental to one's life but is an essential aspect of affirming the delight and wonder of being alive.[62]

In this system of ethics, the goal of social activism, or struggle, is not the ending of all forms of oppression. It is concerned with fostering space, broadly defined, in which we can undertake the continual process of rethinking ourselves in light of community and within the context of nature. Ethics in this sense is a commitment to rebellion, a rejection of reified and truncated identities, an endless process of struggle for something *More*. There is in this system no certainty, no assumptions of teleological movement. In fact, Sage Francis speaks of the inevitability of disillusionment—"disappointment plagues our existence"—with the "coolness" with which humanists, at their best, approach this absurd world.[63] But this does not cause social paralysis; rather, it solicits a measured movement through the world, described by Sage Francis in this way: the purpose of living is the accumulation of "experiences, emotions and to deal with the confusion in a way that is fair to others."[64] Anything else, according to Sage Francis, would amount to "easy answers. . . . Sad."[65]

From Arrested Development, to ScarFace, to Tupac Shakur and Sage Francis, we have seen that there are humanist sensibilities and assertions to be found in rap music—explicit and strong. While these rappers may not provide a complete humanist system of orientation, they point in a direction, raise questions, advance a critique, and in the process speak a late twentieth century and early twenty-first century word of appreciation to human-centered accountability, responsibility, and opportunity. To quote Sage Francis again, anything else would involve ridiculously "easy answers."

NOTES

1. Gerald H. Hinkle, *Art as Event: An Aesthetic for the Performing Arts* (Washington, DC: University Press of America, 1979), 6.

2. Bernard Schwarze, "Religion, Rock, and Research," in *Sacred Music of the Secular City: From Blues to Rap,* a special issue of *Black Sacred Music: A Journal of Theomusicology* 6, no. 1 (Spring 1992): 85.

3. Clive Marsh's review of *Good Taste, Bad Taste, and Christian Taste: Aesthetics in Religious Life* by Frank Burch Brown, *Reviews in Religion and Theology* 8, no. 5 (November 2001): 533.

4. Michael Eric Dyson, "Rap Culture, the Church, and American Society," in *Sacred Music of the Secular City: From Blues to Rap,* a special issue of *Black Sacred Music: A Journal of Theomusicology* 6, no. 1 (Spring 1992): 269.

Future writings on rap music and hip-hop culture in more general terms must give attention to the nature of production and the manner in which market forces impact the music produced and the figures elected to produce it. I am grateful for my conversations with my colleague Allen Callahan during which we debated this dimension of the music industry—a step beyond lyrical and musical analysis. William Banfield addresses issues related to the production of rap music but, as Callahan noted during our conversation, still more must be said about the issue.

5. Michael Eric Dyson, *Holler If You Hear Me: Searching for Tupac Shakur* (New York: Basic Civitas Books, 2001), 203–204.

6. Ice Cube, "When I Get to Heaven," on *Bootlegs & B-Sides,* Priority Records, 1994.

7. Nicholas Davey, "The Hermeneutics of Seeing," in Ian Heywood and Barry Sandywell, eds., *Interpreting Visual Culture: Explorations in the Hermeneutics of the Visual* (New York: Routledge, 1999), 25–26.

8. I give detailed attention to religion as quest for complex subjectivity in *Terror and Triumph: The Nature of Black Religion* (Minneapolis: Fortress Press, 2003).

9. Anthony B. Pinn, *Varieties of African American Religious Experience* (Minneapolis: Fortress Press, 1998), chapter 4.

10. Frederick Douglass, "An Unpublished Frederick Douglass Letter," edited by Herbert Aptheker, in Anthony B. Pinn, ed., *By These Hands: A Documentary History of African American Humanism* (New York: New York University Press, 2001), 77.

11. Ibid., 79.

12. Son House, "My Black Mama," in Eric Sackheim, compiler, *The Blues Lines:*

A Collection of Blues Lyrics from Leadbelly to Muddy Waters (Hopewell, NJ: Ecco Press, 1969), 204.

13. James Forman, "God Is Dead: A Question of Power," reprinted in Anthony B. Pinn, ed., *By These Hands: A Documentary History of African American Humanism* (New York: New York University Press, 2001), 269.

14. Alice Walker, "The Only Reason You Want to Go to Heaven Is That You Have Been Driven Out of Your Mind," reprinted in Anthony B. Pinn, ed., *By These Hands: A Documentary History of African American Humanism* (New York: New York University Press, 2001), 298.

15. Mark LeVine, "KRS-One: Hip-hop Clergy," Beliefnet Celebrity Interviews and Profiles, <www.beliefnet.com>.

16. KRS-One, "Take It to God," on *Spiritual Minded.*

17. <http://www.patricdaily.f9.co.uk.DOGGYS.htm>.

18. Ibid.

19. "KRS-One and the Temple of Hiphop." Found at <http://www.gospelcity.com/interviews/0202/krs-one_2.hph>.

20. Ibid.

21. From *The Color Purple,* cited in Walker, "The Only Reason You Want To Go To Heaven Is That You Have Been Driven Out Of Your Mind," 289.

22. Ibid., 290.

23. "Latifah's Law," on *All Hail the Queen.*

24. Queen Latifah (with Karen Hunter), *Ladies First: Revelations of a Strong Woman* (New York: William Morrow, 1999), 109.

25. Arrested Development, "Fishin 4 Religion," on *3 Years, 5 Months & 2 days in the Life of . . .* , Chrysalis Records, 1992.

26. Ibid.

27. For a discussion of humanism as expressed in the blues, see Anthony B. Pinn, *Why, Lord? Suffering and Evil in Black Theology* (New York: Continuum, 1995), chapters 5–6. Contrast the discussion in this text to that offered by Jon Michael Spencer in *Blues in Evil* (Knoxville: University of Tennessee Press, 1993).

28. Sterling Brown, "Negro Folk Expression: Spirituals, Seculars, Ballads, and Work Songs," in Anthony B. Pinn, ed., *By These Hands: A Documentary History of African American Humanism* (New York: New York University Press, 2001), 105.

29. Arrested Development, "Fishin 4 Religion," on *3 Years, 5 Months & 2 days in the Life of . . .* , Chrysalis Records, 1992.

30. ScarFace, "Mind Playin' Tricks 94," on *The Diary* Noo Trybe Records, 1994.

31. Ibid.

32. Ibid.

33. Tupac Shakur, "Blasphemy," on *The Don Killuminati.*

34. Ibid.

35. Malcolm Venable, "Missing You," *Vibe* magazine, March 2000, 99.

36. As the following discussion will make clear, I have in mind Albert Camus' *The Rebel: An Essay on Man in Revolt* (New York: Vintage International, 1991); René Girard, *Violence and the Sacred,* translated by Patrick Gregory (Baltimore: Johns Hopkins University Press, 1977); Richard Wright's *The Outsider* (New York: Library of America, 1989).

37. Tupac Shakur, "Hail Mary," on *The Don Killuminati.*

38. I apply a rather loose and limited interpretation of Camus here. Readers may be interested in analyzing the lyrics of "Hail Mary" and "Blasphemy" in light of, for example, "The Sons of Cain" and "Rebellion and Art" in Camus' *The Rebel,* 26–35, 253–277.

39. Camus, *The Rebel,* 20.

40. Herbert Read, "Foreword," in Camus, *The Rebel,* vii.

41. Tupac Shakur, "Hail Mary," on *The Don Killuminati.*

42. Tupac Shakur, "Black Jesus," on *Still I Rise.*

43. Rob Marriott, interview with Tupac Shakur, "Last Testament," *Vibe,* November 1996, T7.

44. Ibid.

45. Michael Eric Dyson, *Holler If You Hear Me: Searching for Tupac Shakur* (New York: Basic Civitas Books, 2001), 230.

46. Camus, *The Rebel,* 10.

47. Ibid., 21.

48. Dyson, *Holler If You Hear Me,* 208.

49. It is not clear how Sage Francis will fare outside the "underground" of rap music. However, it strikes me that he avoids many of the trappings of questionable appropriations of the form in that, unlike "Vanilla Ice," Sage Francis speaks out of his existential reality and does not attempt to consume and regurgitate a mythic understanding of blackness. That is to say, his work does not eradicate blackness by attempting to claim stereotypical depictions of it through a process of "whiteface." See Armond White, "Who Wants to See Ten Niggers Play Basketball?" in William Eric Perkins, ed., *Droppin' Science: Critical Essays on Rap Music and Hip Hop Culture* (Philadelphia: Temple University Press, 1996), 182–208.

50. Sage Francis, "Different," on *Personal Journals,* Anticon, ASIN: B00063Y38.

51. FuseOne, "Interview with Sage Francis #1, September 2000." Found at <http://www.hiphopinfinity.com/Articles/SageFrancis_Interview.htm>.

52. Hugo, "Interview with Sage Francis, January 30, 2002." Found at <http://www.non-prophets.com>.

53. Sage Francis, "Makeshift Patriot," on *Personal Journals,* Anticon, ASIN: B00063Y38.

54. Ibid.

55. I must thank my research assistant, Kwame Phillips, for bringing Sage Francis to my attention and for providing me with his lyrics and numerous descriptions of his work.

56. Jamie Boulding, "Interview with Sage Francis, August 2001," on <http://www.hiphopinfinity.com/Articles/SageFrancis_Interview3>.
57. FuseOne, "Interview with Sage Francis #1."
58. Sage Francis, "Majority Rule," on *Still Sick . . . Urine Trouble.*
59. Sage Francis, "Next Testament," <www.nonprophets.com/lyrics>.
60. Ibid.
61. Sharon Welch, *An Ethic of Risk* (Minneapolis: Fortress Press, 1999), 70.
62. Ibid.
63. Boulding, "Interview with Sage Francis, August 2001."
64. Ibid.
65. Ibid.

Part II

Rap and Issues of "Spirit" and "Spirituality"

5

Bringing Noise, Conjuring Spirit
Rap as Spiritual Practice

Mark Lewis Taylor

Rap music has inspired me . . . it's the spirit attempting to escape entrapment.
—Sister Souljah, Abyssinian Baptist Church, 1991

Bringing together rap and religion may seem to some a dubious undertaking. When hearing of a book on rap and religion, a young devotee of hip-hop in Philadelphia said to me, "That's so weird."

People may suspect, understandably, that the freestyles and pleasures of rap will be overly burdened by the seriousness associated with religion. Religion and spirit are often seen as dealing with weighty matters that are not easily adaptable to popular-culture phenomena like rap music.

Nevertheless, the intersections between rap and religion are many. They are historical, cultural, and they exist in many forms. In this chapter I will propose that rap music can be interpreted as a spiritual practice. I will base my argument primarily on studies of rap music and anthropological studies of religious and spiritual traditions. In so doing, I hope to make it possible to speak of rap music's "spiritual economy," that is, the way spirit can work and be worked upon in the world. Rap music's spiritual economy is not an otherworldly alternative to what some have called music's "political economy."[1] On the contrary, rap's spiritual economy emerges, as I will show, in dynamic interplay with the political and social dimensions of its contexts.

When it "brings the noise"—as in the expression popularized widely by Public Enemy's song (with Anthrax) "Bring Tha Noize"—rap music does more than play music. It goes deep into noise and redeploys its sounds in a way that brings something new and important—a "noize" that gives pleasure, yes, but that also has social and political impact and performs and awakens certain spiritual functions. When it brings noise, then, rap music also conjures spirit.

The word "conjure" is rich and appropriate when considering rap music's "spiritual economy." Conjuring evokes the magic and mystery that is, as we shall see, so central to musical emotion. Emerging from the Latin root, *conjurare* ("to swear together"), the term also suggests that when rap music conjures spirit, it is engaged in a process that is both serious and communal. Even the definition of conjure that most dictionaries describe as obsolete—"to conspire," from *conspirare* ("to breathe together")—may be appropriate given rap music's capacity to encode the winds of resistance that blow and sometimes swirl among people struggling to survive and flourish amid states of disorder and deadly regimentation.[2]

It is important to note that I will be giving emphasis to the whole musical character of rap, and not just to its lyrics. In fact, my primary focus will be more on the functioning of the entire musical event (context, audience, sound, and lyrics), and less on meanings of lyrical texts. Although it is true that rap is rooted in powerful oral traditions of the African continent, to view rap as only "a direct or natural outgrowth of oral African-American forms is to romanticize and decontextualize rap as a cultural form."[3] Thus, I will explore the interaction of rap and religion, and interpret rap as spiritual practice, by attending primarily to its music and how its music works on its listeners. Only in that context will I touch on some lyrical issues.

I will begin with a proposal for understanding "music's noise," and with a theory of the "musical emotion" offered by French anthropologist Claude Lévi-Strauss. Second, I will examine ways in which rap music intensifies some of the powerful dynamics of the musical emotion. Third, I will present rap's complex musicality in its present U.S. social context, since this context shapes significantly how rap musicians "bring tha noize" and affects what motivates "the bringing." Only at this point, then, will we be ready finally to clarify how rap music is a "spiritual" practice—how bringing the noise is a conjuring of "spirit."

Music: A "Supreme Mystery"

In spite of his primary interest in what is usually termed "Western classical music" and his own lifelong passion for Richard Wagner, the French anthropologist and mythologist Claude Lévi-Strauss offers a helpful orientation for understanding how any music works in our physical and cultural lives. Lévi-Strauss sums up his respect for musical modes of expression by saying it is "the supreme mystery of the sciences of man." All other disciplines can find in music's unique expressions a key to progress in all other fields of life.[4] Why is this so? A full answer would require that we range across Lévi-Strauss's four-volume work, *Introduction to a Science of Mythology*, and other writings in his voluminous corpus. Let us take just two major points that are crucial for understanding the mystery of music.

First, music works on us simultaneously, according to Lévi-Strauss, through two important matrices in which we all live, two kinds of webs or textures. He says that music operates as "two grids" in our lives.[5] One of these grids is physical. The rhythm of music works on us by engaging our organic physicality. In utilizing organic rhythms, music is of nature, having to do with our pulsing, pounding, breathing being, exploiting the regularities of bodily existence that are at work during rest, work, or dance. The other grid is cultural. Here, Lévi-Strauss does not mean words and lyrics, but the way musical sounds, along with rhythm, tend to be organized in terms of a scale. From his intercultural perspective on music, he stresses that the intervals between sounds, and the number of those sounds parceled out to various beats, are particularly important, for the number of intervals vary from one culture to another and carry distinctive meanings in different cultures.

When we listen to music—and whatever the lyrics may connote to us—we are caught up in an experience that is simultaneously physical and cultural. Our bodies and minds are played together on these two intersecting grids, and it is part of the power of music to engage and enliven the listener on both. But this is only the first point of Lévi-Strauss's discussion on the mystery of music. The second point concerns his understanding of "the musical emotion." Lévi-Strauss's description of the musical emotion need not be taken as the universally valid one for all peoples and contexts. He reminds us, however, of another trait of music, which will be of special importance for understanding rap music's power.

Recall that music listeners are being operated on, so to speak, in both their physical and cultural matrices, along those two grids. Musical emotion arises from the way that composers and players of music work those grids, seeking to promote pleasure, beauty, and intrigue in listeners. In particular, composers withhold or add more or less than listeners anticipate on the basis of patterns they think they can guess, but which they are "incapable of wholly divining."[6] There is a tension, in other words, between the expected and the surprising. Sometimes the surprises are minor, other times they are more dramatic. This play between expectation and surprise goes on because the players or composers can exploit what Lévi-Strauss calls the listener's "subjection to a dual periodicity."[7] Lévi-Strauss's notion of periodicity recalls his first point about the physical and cultural being integrated in music. The first periodicity to which listeners are subject is set by their respiratory systems, which is determined by their physical natures. The second periodicity is set by the scale of sounds, which is more determined by their cultural training.

Lévi-Strauss, then, elaborates the musical emotion as a play between the composers sometimes withholding more than we listeners expect, and sometimes less. In spite of its length, we do well to give a careful reading to a crucial passage in which he articulates all this:

> *If the composer withholds more* than we anticipate, we experience a delicious falling sensation; we feel we have been torn from a stable point on the musical ladder and thrust into the void, but only because the support that is waiting for us was not in the expected place. *When the composer withholds less,* the opposite occurs: [the composer] forces us to perform gymnastic exercises more skillful than our own. Sometimes [the composer] moves us, sometimes [the composer] forces us to make the movement ourselves, but it always exceeds what we would have thought ourselves capable of achieving alone. *Aesthetic enjoyment is made up of this multiplicity of excitements and moments of respite, of expectations disappointed or fulfilled beyond anticipation.*[8]

Musical emotion that thrives in this interplay of expectation and surprise, through repetition and the skill of composers and players, exposes listeners to changes in their physical and cultural experience. Not only is the experience of periodicity, and hence the temporal, involved, but so also is a new experience of space. The listening self, through the temporal interplay between the expected and the unexpected, finds the boundaries of self-changing in relation to the whole musical event and its various parts. The self is expanded, often by coming into itself in a new relationship to composers and players and their creations. To capture this self-change, Lévi-Strauss offers his famous observation about the transformation worked by music: "Music has its being in me, and I listen to myself through it."[9]

When the self is listened to, in this expanded way, there is a change not just in time and not just in the self, but in social space. This is part of music's power. It is appropriately called "mystery" by Lévi-Strauss because the new space or time is not completely controllable. Here is an important part of music's conjuring: even though the physical and cultural patterns presuppose certain expectations, even though the well-honed skills of composers and players are needed to exploit (and creatively transgress) that expectation, and even though discipline and skill are often demanded of the listeners themselves—even though *all* of these are contributing parts, the resultant transformative experience seems more than the sum of them all.

This conjuring event, however, takes on its distinctive character because of its relation to context, its working in the world. Thus, music, in Lévi-Strauss' view, can never simply be bracketed off and confined to a separate domain of "the arts," to some space at the margins of culture. Music is a transformative mode of expression, shaping and shaped by other experiences—temporal and spatial, physical and cultural. This means that Lévi-Strauss has not only given us one kind of theory about how music works upon us, but he has done it in a way that enables us to link the musical emotion to its broader settings in nature and culture. This link will be important when we look more closely at the effects of rap music, the genre to which we now turn.

Rap Music: Intensifying the Mystery

Lévi-Strauss was hardly thinking of rap music in the formulations cited above, at least if we take our cues from his declared favorite, Richard Wagner. Yet, because rap is a mode of music (which must be maintained against all those who declare it "non-musical"),[10] some key elements of Lévi-Strauss's explanations of the power of the musical emotion apply to it. Indeed, I suggest that the mystery—the way music works upon listeners and conjures them into a new state—is even more powerfully at work in rap.

To be sure, there are marked differences between Afrodiasporic forms of music and what is usually referred to as "Western classical music." Tricia Rose strikes the contrast well in her superb text, *Black Noise: Rap Music and Black Culture in Contemporary America* (1994). The difference between the two genres is in their placement of musical complexity. Western classical music represents complexity more in its melodic and harmonic structures. If Lévi-Strauss writes of a "delicious falling sensation" and patterns both expected and not expected, Western classical music usually develops this sense in the complexities of melody and harmony. For African-derived musical expression, writes Rose, the complexity is concentrated more in "the rhythmic and percussive density and organization."[11] Here she is drawing on studies such as John Miller Chernoff's *African Rhythm and African Sensibility* (1979).[12] The emphasis falls not just on rhythm, but on "polyrhythmic layering," a point underscored also by literary critic and historian Antonio Benitez-Rojo in *The Repeating Island* (1996).[13] Benitez-Rojo sees polyrhythm as a major trait of African-derived, Caribbean "peoples of the sea." Rose summarized the complexity of rap in this domain of the polyrhythmic:

> Dense configurations of independent, but closely related, rhythms, harmonic and nonharmonic percussive sounds, especially drum sounds, are critical priorities in many African and Afrodiasporic musical practices. The voice is also an important expressive instrument. A wide range of vocal sounds intimately connected to tonal speech patterns, "strong differences between the various registers of the voice even emphasizing the *breaks* between them," are deliberately cultivated in African and African-influenced musics.[14]

It is in this dimension of complex polyrhythm that one will find not only rap music's complexity, but also its potential to intensify the mystery, the heating up and greater elaboration of the new time and new space created by music, about which Lévi-Strauss wrote.

Before looking at that kind of reconfiguration of time and space in rap, let us note some other key features of this musical expression. Two inventions of rap must be understood in order to comprehend the full force of rap music and as the "spiritual practice" I will interpret it to be. These two inventions are scratching and sampling. Both are polyrhythmic practices in which rap musicians seek to excel. "Scratching" is a technical skill executed at the turntable, wherein a DJ plays a record back and forth with the hand "by scratching the needle against and then with the groove."[15] When two turntables are used simultaneously, "one record is scratched in rhythm against the rhythm of another record while the second record is played." This skill also involves "back-spinning" and creating "back-beats."

Highly skilled DJs repeat phrases and beats in ways that create slightly varied, but repeated rhythmic patterns, "creating the effect of a record skipping irregularly or a controlled stutter effect." "Breaking" the beat creates a sensation of suspension in listeners (intensifying, perhaps, Lévi-Strauss' "delicious falling sensation"), but at that moment DJs may also insert other phrases and sounds from other places on the record, or from other records flipped dexterously onto one of the tables. This process of insertion, or a borrowing from other records and songs, is called "sampling." Sampling is often done by samplers, "computers that can digitally duplicate any existing sounds and play them back in any key or pitch, in any order, sequence and loop them endlessly."[16] This intensifies still further the already complex dynamics going on in the polyrhythmic expression created through rhythm and scratching. The complexity achieved by sampling involves folding in phrases as well as alternative musical sounds, so that the oral and the musical interact in ever greater and unexpected ways. Music critic and author Nelson George offers a good description of this process as carried out by DJ Grandmaster Flash, one of the earliest and most skilled DJs. He describes Flash's techniques in one of his performances:

> It begins with "you say one for the trouble," the opening phrase of Spoonie Gee's "Monster Jam," broken down to "you say" repeated seven times, setting the tone for a record that uses the music and vocals of Queen's "Another One Bites the Dust," the Sugar Hill Gang's "8th Wonder," and Chic's "Good Times" as musical pawns that Flash manipulates at whim. He repeats "Flash is Bad" from Blondie's "Rapture" three times, turning singer Deborah Harry's dispassion into total adoration. While playing "Another One Bites the Dust," Flash places a record on the second turntable, then shoves the needle and the record against each other. The result is a rumbling, gruff imitation of the song's bass line. As the guitar feedback on "Dust" builds, so does Flash's rumble, until we're grooving on "Good Times." Next, "Freedom" explodes between pauses in Chic's "Good Times" bass line. His bass thumps, and the Furious Five chant, "Grant-master cuts faster." Bass. "Grandmaster." Bass. "Cut." Bass. "Cuts . . . cuts . . . faster." But the cold crusher comes toward the end when, during "8th Wonder" Flash places a wheezing sound of needle on vinyl in the spaces separating a series of claps.[17]

Note here that both lyrical and musical forms and meanings are broken apart and reconstructed. Moreover, there is a striking diversity of musical genres, a deconstructive/reconstructive process that poaches from Queen, the Furious Five, and Blondie's Debbie Harry.

There are many other examples of the power of a polyrhythmic performance. The grids of physical and cultural domains, to recall Lévi-Strauss's language, are so broken down and reconstructed, so dramatically ruptured and reoriented, that it is probably inaccurate to speak of grids at all—surely not just two of them. "Rap music," says Tricia Rose, "conjures and razes in one stroke." It is both "deconstructive" and "recuperative."[18]

Although the polyrhythmic intensity of rap is more developed than the music examined by Lévi-Strauss, Rose's description of the net effect of a rap music performance shows marked similarities to the musical event Lévi-Strauss described. The response of the crowd, worked by Grandmaster Flash through the polyrhythmic dexterity just described, is portrayed by Rose as "building intense crowd anticipation,"[19] especially as the break-beats and backspinning increase in number and are repeated in surprising ways. This, again, plays with the dialectic of the expected and the unexpected in music that creates novelty and sustains mystery.

The polyrhythmic complexity of rap music and performance may bring about a new event of transformation far more dramatically than Lévi-Strauss ever envisioned. Again, however, Rose's language about the effect of rap music on audiences is similar to Lévi-Strauss's description of music's mystery. She describes, for example, the effect of complex cross-rhythms, as having "a function in time which is the reverse of (Western) classical music—to dissolve the past and the future into one eternal present, in which the passing of time is no longer noticed."[20] I use the term "intensify" to capture the difference between rap music and "Western classical" music. The breaks are more multiple, pushed to the form of rupture. The new satisfaction, the fulfillment of expectation, is located close to the deconstruction. Again Rose is eloquent when she summarizes the impact of rap's multiple musical strategies: it "systematically ruptures equilibrium," and the break beats are "repositioned as repetition, as equilibrium inside the rupture."[21]

Rap offers, then, a much more intense mode of the mystery of musical emotion. It is no mere resolution of tension between the expected and a surprise by withholding more or less of what was expected. It is a more radical creation. Finding "equilibrium inside the rupture" comes close to being a "coincidence of contraries," as some traditional mystics have reflected.[22] We do not need to take wing into the ethereal domains of a full-blown religious mysticism: I make reference to the mystics only to accent the deep mystery of rap music, how its noise/noize has a conjuring power.

Before we wrestle with rap music's conjuring power, and with notions of spirit and the spiritual, we need to come to terms with its context.

Amid a "Thirty-Years War": A Theater of Pleasure and Resistance

Rap music is not fully understood unless it is seen in its dynamic connection to contexts of struggle, especially of African and Afrodiasporic communities throughout the Americas. The relation to context is obvious from a simple reflection on rap's sound-making apparatus. Its performative practices of scratching and sampling, its use of the mike for projection of voice and audio effect, all show a dependence on the wider society's advanced technological devices. Many rap performers and producers originally functioned as caretakers of these devices, repairing and maintaining the "new technologies of the age for the privileged."[23] Nevertheless, the relation of rap music to the devices of current technology is not only one of dependency, it is also one of creative subversion and invention. This is nowhere more clear than in the practices of scratching and sampling, in which sound and technology are retooled for expression of sonic effects that are alternatives to the messages and effects that usually circulate in mainstream technological channels.

This dual relation to the technology of its era, of dependency and creative retooling, is just one key feature of rap music's relation to context. The use and retooling mirrors rap's relation to its times, as Rose suggests, both *reflecting* the times and *contesting* them.[24] We should not romanticize rap here. It does not always do both. Especially in high-market, commercialized rap forms, the reflection of the technological era and all its values results in a celebration of that era and even of some values that are often detrimental to the communities where people of color have played a primary role in producing rap music. But in its origins and at its best, rap has a strong element of contestation amid suffering. Knowledge of the context of the South Bronx, where Jamaican sounds and sensibilities ran up against the acute social suffering of African and Afrodiasporic peoples, is therefore crucial for understanding rap. The South Bronx, and later the similarly traumatized world of South Central Los Angeles, would understandably fuel the rise of rap sensibility, discourse, and musicality. Tricia Rose reminds us of this when she recalls that the origins of rap music emerged in the "de-industrialization meltdown of social alienation, prophetic imagination and yearning."[25] Bakari Kitwana, in his recent study of rap among "hip-hop generationers," keeps his discussion in touch with those origins by elaborating on the fundamental challenges faced by black youth, such as unemployment, police brutality, and the U.S. criminal justice system.

How are we to understand these fundamental challenges in relation to hip-hop generationers today? More needs to be said, especially because the music of Afrodiasporic peoples has long functioned as a resource for survival and resistance. Throughout slavery, the spirituals, work songs, and blues were resources for not just getting by, but for dreaming and, at times, making one's way through and out of slavery.[26] What, then, is distinctive about the hip-hop generationers' context within which youth have embraced rap?

There is, indeed, continuity between the present use of rap and the legacy of Afrodiasporic peoples' use of music for resistance and survival. What distinctively marks the last three decades, across which rap has developed, is the operation of a special kind of social "pincers movement" against black youth. In a military maneuver, this refers to an attack on a group that takes place from two flanks as well as from a major front.[27] Black youth and African American communities have almost always been on a major front—a front where they must absorb, survive and resist forces spun by centuries of slavery and discrimination, many of which persist into the present.[28]

Black youth in African American communities today, however, have had to live on this historical front *and* deal with two other developments that we can perceive as flanking attacks. One is a process of economic traumatization beginning in the 1970s; the other is the rise of a new punishment regime that has taken a special toll on youth of color. This thirty-year period clearly is the era of the hip-hop generation, whose birth years, according to Kitwana, range roughly from 1965 to 1984.[29]

The *economic traumatization* of this thirty-year period has been well documented, even if the media and many U.S. citizens gave little thought to it during the alleged boom years of the 1990s. During those years, Kevin Phillips in *The Politics of Rich and Poor* (1990), William Julius Wilson in *The Bridge across Our Racial Divide* (1999), and others have attempted to sound an alarm about a racially marked and growing divide between the rich and poor in the United States. In 1990, the already wealthiest 1 percent (those making $174,000 or more per year) were seeing an increase in their incomes by over 74.2 percent, while the lowest 10 percent were experiencing a drop of 10.5 percent in income.[30] William Julius Wilson also documented that the growing inequality, combined with the loss of manufacturing jobs and urban economies' transition into a service economy, had an especially devastating impact on black urban communities.[31]

Along with other affected communities of this time, black youth felt the forces of rising wage inequality, growing household debt, and a middle class that was among the fastest shrinking among industrialized nations. Communities in New York, as in the South Bronx, which became the midwife in the birth of rap music, suffered acutely and were forced to spin out their own alternative communities for survival. In this urban metropolis, the thirty-years war was played out in an especially brutal divide between the affluent crafters of technology and globalization and the neighborhoods of the poor.[32]

During this thirty-year period, too, came *the rise of a new punishment regime,* constituting the second flanking attack within which black youth of the hip-hop generation have been caught in a pincers movement. The new punishment regime consists of increased police funding and the modeling of inner-city police action after military and paramilitary operations used in wartime. By 1999, Amnesty International was portraying the problem of U.S. police brutality as so severe that the U.S. government was found in violation of its own citizens' human rights.[33] While cops of color also brutalized their own people, the majority of brutality, according to sociologist Joe Feagin, involved white cops against victims of color.[34] Furthermore, the startling rise in the number of prisons marks the new punishment regime most visibly. Between 1980 and 2000, the U.S. prison population nearly quadrupled. This has been "the most frenetic and rapid prison build-up of any nation in world history."[35] In the 1990s, prison construction became a $7 billion industry.[36] So extensive has the prison industry become that both street-talkers and scholars have referred to the United States at the turn of the century as "Gulag America," "Lockdown America," or "Big House Nation."[37]

The prison system also has a role in institutionalizing the U.S. nightmare of racism. The criminal justice system, which is the prisons' context, is fraught with what many studies term "cumulative racial bias."[38] Over 70 percent of the imprisoned are now people of color. As many as 50 percent are African American.[39] Moreover, the use of the death penalty is forcing its way back with U.S. Supreme Court approval in 1976, after a short period of abolishment. There are now more than 3,700 inmates on death row USA. While the rates of execution have slowed from the nearly one hundred per year in 1999 and 2000, we are still executing, on average, about one person every other week. In the United States, the death penalty is used almost exclusively against the poor, and disproportionately against people of color. While whites make up the greatest *number* of all those who have been executed since 1976, blacks and other peoples of color go to death row far out of proportion to their percentage of the U.S. population. Most tellingly, 81 percent of all executions occur as punishment for the murder of white victims (who make up only 50 percent of all murder victims). Whites who kill blacks are far less frequently punished, and blacks who kill blacks are least often executed.[40]

It is in this kind of context that rap music developed. Rap became a "contemporary stage for the theater of the powerless," especially for youth of color who have struggled on that historic front long occupied by people of color in the United States. Today they are also caught in the pincers movement of economic traumatization and the rising punishment regime. "Pincers" are also a grasping tool consisting of a pair of jaws and handles that work to facilitate the grasp. Black youth—on the front against white racism in the United States, now stuck in the double jaws of economic trauma and the criminal *in*justice system—have taken a stage under pressure to craft an art and to achieve self-expression in their group for dealing with the pincers movement that marks their time.

We do well to return to Tricia Rose, whose words capture how rap music functions in the context of the "thirty-years war" in America: "On this stage, rappers act out inversions of status hierarchies, tell alternative stories of contact with police and the education process and draw portraits of contact with dominant groups in which the hidden transcript inverts/subverts the public, dominant transcript."[41] In providing a theatric of resistance, rappers not only ride the globalizing technology available to them, but they are also at least potential critics of the structure of globalization that debilitates so many on its underside.

Rap Music and Spiritual Practice

It is on stage amid the thirty-years war in the United States that rap musicians not only "bring the noise" for resistance and pleasure, but also "conjure spirit." In taking the stage with music's power and the unique musical properties of rap music, these musicians occasion the happening of something new, something, which in the context of social pressures and social need, becomes enabling in various ways. They conjure. What is conjured, I suggest in this final section, is "spirit."

In many popular audiences today, "spirit" is often contrasted with "religion." Amid the eclectic and hybrid terrain of global religious phenomena, people often refer to themselves as "spiritual but not religious." What is meant by "spiritual" is highly varied. The meaning of the statement lies less in what is meant by spiritual and more in what is meant by the contrast with religion. In making the contrast, speakers are usually distancing themselves from official religious organizations and hierarchies that often have claimed sole propriety to public senses of mystery or the sacred.

Claiming to be spiritual enables those same speakers to cultivate their own discursive and ritual experiences of mystery, to construct or join alternative religious communities and movements, and thus seek to avoid the more established religious orders. The need to make this contrast becomes even stronger if established religions are seen, as they often are, to be ineffective communicators—silent about social trauma or actively complicit in systematic dehumanization. The Catholic Church's sanctioning of and profiting from the slave trade and powerful Protestant American churches' justifications for slavery are just two dramatic examples.[42]

I have argued elsewhere that popular culture in the United States tends to give to the terms "spirit/spiritual" three kinds of meaning in social context: "liberatory," "liminal," and "integrative."[43] Rap music is an active conjuring agent in each of these domains of meaning, and, from that perspective, it is a kind of spiritual practice. I conclude by showing how rap music intersects these domains, and how this positions rap music in a dynamic discourse of spirituality and religion that is often not acknowledged.

1. *Rap as liberatory*. Perhaps Sister Souljah expressed most directly this function of rap music when, at the Abyssinian Baptist Church in 1991, she explained that rap music inspired her, and that "it is the spirit attempting to escape entrapment."[44] Rap music is a contestation with entrapment. It is a struggle for liberatory experience amid entrapment.

This has been a strong theme in many spiritual and religious traditions. For example, in many Christian forms the Exodus traditions are used to articulate the need for freedom from oppression and exile. Recall Jesus of Nazareth's linking the "Spirit of the Lord" to "release for the captives" (Luke 4:18); Gospel writers espousing a truth that makes one free (John 8:32), or Swiss Protestant theologians writing of the "sovereign freedom" of a gracious god who makes freedom.[45] One might also consider the "liberation theologies" of Latin American, South African, and U.S. freedom struggles.[46] Whether it is hungered for, dreamed about, or celebrated in rituals new or old, a drive toward liberation is one of spirit's key characteristics. When rappers tell alternative stories while facing police brutality or prison warehousing of the racially stigmatized poor, depicting the struggle, survival and flourishing of oppressed communities, they conjure spiritual practices for these communities. When they challenge power inequalities and material oppression, deploying polyvocal discourse (again, with all the power of music's mystery and the special technological noise that rap is) that destabilizes dominant discourses and patterns, then rap musicians constitute a spiritual practice.

Afrodiasporic people and movements have often deployed religious and spiritual symbolics to articulate and strengthen their drives for liberation. This is especially evident in the ways West African spirituality gave rise to Vodou in the Caribbean. Vodou comes from the word *vodun,* meaning "mysteries," and refers to a speaking by African deities, particularly in Abomey.[47] It is a religious practice that is embodied in dance and music and became, in part, a survival strategy in the sinister system of chattel slavery entrapment. There was perhaps no more challenging place to forge such a music than the island called Hispañola, into which 864,000 Africans were imported in the eighteenth century alone, for transport to the U.S. mainland, usually through New Orleans.[48] Consequently, West African spirituality impacted the spirit and music, always integrally connected, that spread across the popular landscapes of the United States. This fusion of spirit and music occurred due to the need of a liberatory drive beyond the time of slavery. Ventura summarizes the power of African-based *vodun* spirituality as an aesthetic forged amid the liberating struggle from slavery:

> Vodou is the African aesthetic shattered and then desperately put back together. More than simply "put back together," it has been recreated to serve its people under the shattering impact of slavery and poverty. Vodou is not so much Africa in the New World as it is Africa meeting the New World, absorbing it and being absorbed by it, and *re-forming* the ancient metaphysics according to what it now had to face.[49]

Not just Vodou, but also Yoruban religiosity, myths associated with the African trickster figure, Anancy the Spider, and others have been part of music traditions in the Americas for communities wrestling with oppression.[50]

It should come as little surprise, then, that, in the context of the thirty-years war afflicting the U.S. body politic, African and Afrodiasporic music would function as a kind of liberative spirituality. Hence, the contestation and performance on stage, seeking to subvert hierarchies and domination, are not just for aesthetic show at the margins of power. In spite of many commercial co-optations, it can often fuel aestheticized action, where pleasure and resistance come together for liberatory intent.

A key example of this is that of the "Raptivism" movement. Raptivism is a hip-hop music label that issues its music and sponsors various rappers as part of the Prison Moratorium Project (PMP). It is designed to mobilize youth and others around the problems posed by today's prison industry, and the entire nexus of problems involving economic injustice and overspending on crime control at the expense of education. The PMP was founded in 1995 when progressive students met with former prisoners in the Harlem-based Community Justice Center. The PMP has become a youth-led grassroots organization dedicated to halting prison expansion, empowering youth and other constituencies, and advocating for a fair, effective, and more humane social and economic system. In 2000, the Raptivist tour visited forty cities and announced in the magazine *Rap Pages* that "this will be the spark that re-ignites a conscious movement." In summer 2002, the PMP and the Raptivism label promoted Shabaam Sahdeeq's *Never Say Never,* Danny Hoch's *Jails, Hospitals, and Hip Hop,* and Tahir's *Homecoming.*[51] Interestingly, significant respect is given to spirituality and the sacred on the Raptivist Website, where churches are invited to transcend their frequent aversions to rap music and join with the Raptivists. "Getting real" about organizing to transform the oppressive terrain of today is portrayed as entering "a real place" that is also, say the Raptivists, "a *sacred* place" where rap musicians, hip-hop generationers, and black churches might all work together.[52]

This way of interpreting rap music, as a spiritual practice because of its conjuring of liberatory practice, is fully consistent with a large literature in the anthropology of religion linking spiritualities with liberating action. In his new *Reader in the Anthropology of Religion,* Michael Lambek observes that religion and its rituals (with dimensions of the carnivalesque, the transgressive, festivals of mocking and parody, etc.) are often meaningful and effective by being about rebellion, reversal, or inversion of compulsory social norms that cause disorder.[53] In the language of Roberto da Matta, the religious can be understood as the festive practice of "licensed release," that is, a release from the pressures of multiple and systemic oppressions. Religious language and symbolics, in many ways, then, seek to redress the disorder and suffering borne by subordinated people on the underside of hegemonic power.[54] Rap music is a spiritual practice in its capacity for conjuring festivals of release and emancipation, *and* for situating those conjurations amid social movements. Again the Raptivism movement is exemplary.

2. *Rap as liminal.* Another powerful interpretation of spiritual and religious experience comes from theories that view religion as liminality, a state of being betwixt-and-between, in the margins, on the threshold. Religion was most systematically presented as an experience of liminality by

anthropologist Victor Turner. The liminal (from Latin, *limen*, "threshold") is a time of chaos, a state of the opportune in which ambiguity and danger are specters, where, especially under the influence of conjuring agents, intensified experiences of boundaries produce, according to Turner, "a moment in and out of time."[55] In this kind of "time" people tend to be clothed by themselves and their communities with the languages of danger, taboo, magic, the sacred.

In a way, any discourse that is liberatory, as rap music was portrayed above, will by definition also be liminal, that is to say, betwixt-and-between, on a threshold, here, between entrapment and liberation. Speaking and rapping from that place of transition, articulating the inversions desired for the future but without the yearned-for liberation, makes rappers' musical discourse a liminal activity and, as such, a mode of spiritual practice. In this liminal space, however, there is not just the simple in-betweenness posed by a tension between the "now" of oppression and the "not yet" of some liberation. "The now" is itself constituted by divided groups and divided selves, double and sometimes triple consciousnesses[56]—so divided and multiple that rappers' voices often give expression to that confusion, that experience of belonging and not-belonging, of needing to be multiple, even if that multiplicity means being caught up in some of the very practices from which liberation is sought.

This complexity of the oppressive now helps account, in part, for the fact that rappers pressing for liberative justice and peace (Wyclef Jean: "We want equal rights and justice")[57] often present representations that remain violent and oppressive from some angles. Rappers' calls for justice can be vitiated by their compromises with contemporary misogyny, heterosexism, or nationalist patriotism. (Wyclef has imbibed much of the post-9/11 patriotism, decking himself out in a full red-white-and-blue U.S.–flag suit for some performances.)[58] These representations are the rappers' own fault and have been challenged within rap culture itself. These contradictions must also be viewed in relation to the complex worlds within which rappers live and work. The reality of the landscape of the present will always be complex, and even a vision of some emancipatory future does not always entail a lack of ambiguity and contradictions.

This situation is a frequent challenge for black cultural artists in particular. The often contradictory and polyvalent present has to be dealt with. In Ralph Ellison's epilogue of his book *Invisible Man*, the lead character ruminates: "I lived a public life and attempted to function under the assumption that the world was solid and all the relationships therein. Now I know that men are different and that *all life is divided and that only in division is there true health*."[59] He comes to this conclusion after a significant part of his life had been committed to the revolutionary agenda of a socialist organization, which was flawed not so much for its socialism as for its wooden agendas that failed to address the white supremacist ideology driving many blacks into the labyrinthine netherworlds of invisibility.

Black artistic representation, I suggest, especially in today's rap music, will never be able to re-present a clean and clear "liberatory" future. Even when liberation is the aim of politically conscious rap musicians, "the now" from which liberation is sought is so complex, so fraught with manifold meanings that subordinated people especially (as is true of most of humankind) are often forced to embrace contradictory meanings in order to survive the present and keep moving toward liberation. This does not mean that the goal of liberation need be eclipsed by a need to deal with complexity. Not at all. But the drive to liberation must be represented in a way that deals with liminal ways of navigating division, multiplicity, and complexity.

Polyvocal and polyrhythmic features—hallmarks of rap music, to recall Tricia Rose's analyses—represent the polyvalence of that liminal state, the experience of subordinated peoples being torn between the contradictory segments of the present. I repeat, the liminality here is not only between the now of oppression and a liberated future, but between the many voices and meanings that operate *in* the now and which segment the lives of people in struggle. Black cultural experience, as represented in rap music's efforts to stay true to this painful polyvalency, is liminal music par excellence, and as "liminal" it is intensely spiritual. Its liminality is just as vibrant with religiosity as anything that anthropologist of religion Victor Turner describes as religious. The music is a practice for opening oneself to that polyvalency and its tensions, enabling one to use it not only for subverting brutal systems sustained by more simple dichotomies, but also for incorporating complexity, ambiguity, and diversity into the listeners' more expansive and flexible being.

3. *Rap as integrative.* One of the fruits of liminality's embrace of polyvalence is its tendency not only to represent divisions and multiplicities, but also to suggest new alliances and unity for the liberatory struggle. This marks another way in which rap music is a spiritual practice, in its penchant to make unity, to press for the integrative search for some whole vision. Many of the established religions often have an elaborate narrative or story that puts the many parts of life into some kind of sequence with a beginning

or an end. Or the religious system may offer a cosmology that relates all of existence into several tiers of existence, which are then brought into some relation. Anthropologist of religion Clifford Geertz saw this penchant for creating wholes as part of the religious sensibility.[60] It is in the search for systems of meaningful paradigms, that is, comprehensive networks and worldviews, where the religious is to be found. Here, the religious sensibility is, above all, integrative, involving the making of connections.

Rap musicians rarely deploy a system—a fully cosmic scenario—especially one on the order propounded by the many formal religious systems. There usually does persist, however—and it is significant—a penchant for the whole, a wonder about the fullness of things. Sometimes the sense of the whole is sustained by a notion of humankind's organic connection to "nature"; at other times, it is the felt need for coalitions and a more unified community to represent "one humanity."

Perhaps Arrested Development, an alternative rap music group from the early 1990s, ably demonstrates this integrative reach. At the beginning of their hit song "Tennessee" on the first album, main lyricist Speech asserts in discourse directed to God: "Let me understand your plan." Then when the song crescendos into its key bridge, a female vocalist reissues the request: "Won't you help me?/Understand your plan."[61] This is a kind of cathartic lament in the form of a railing before the sacred for some perspective, here in a song about death and lynching in the United States. Arrested Development also displayed an integrative reach in the ways by which they advocated revolutionary practice. They called for a "unity of minds," a united front drawing from representatives of Africa, the Caribbean, Europe, Asia, and Australia. "It's not just race, we're all in this together." This call for united action is issued by Speech from "a mountaintop so I can better see/step back and see the whole mighty picture."[62]

Black nationalist, Islam-influenced, and other movements can also help shape rappers' integrative reach. In these ways, rap links into that long history and frequent practice of religious symbolics, providing its devotees some experience of what is yearned for—that is, restored unity with all humanity and all creation.

Each of the spiritual functions identified here as deployed and released by rap music can be said to be at work in a very powerful song from Wyclef, *The Ecleftic* (2000). His song "Diallo" steps forth as an aesthetic intervention into a cultural and political context of police brutality. Amadou Diallo was the young Guinean man slain in 1999 by New York City police in a hail of gunfire—forty-one shots, nineteen of which hit his body. The officers were found "not guilty" of all charges. Wyclef's commemorative song for Diallo, featuring vocals by Youssou N'Dour and MB2, came after a court exonerated the policemen. The song deploys a host of religious imagery, from biblical psalms to Rastafarianism, to African ancestral remembrance, spirit-return, and Christian apocalyptic. It is not the mere presence of this traditionally religious imagery that imbues the song with its spiritual strength, but the way that this language is crafted into the whole work and working of the song—the economy of the song. Again, what is crucial is that listener sensibilities are engaged by meanings that are liberatory, liminal, and integrative.

As *liberatory,* the song intones a clear challenge to the repressive social order that the police represent and defend, and it offers a call to people to seek liberation from that guarded order. Wyclef rejects the police's words of sorrow and their explanation of believing that Diallo was reaching for a weapon when in fact he was extracting his wallet. Police are charged with being "vampires" and murderers, killing innocents, and "suckin' on human blood." As Erksine's chapter notes, there are strong links between reggae and rap; and Wyclef displays this connection in that the vampire imagery he employs recalls Bob Marley's well-known "Babylon System," where established orders are portrayed as sucking the blood of sufferers and children. Wyclef demands flat out that the call is now for equal rights and justice. And, from the belly of the U.S. beast, he places Diallo with Steven Biko, and says he can hear Diallo's spirit now calling for ten thousand chariots, on their way to America to set things right. At this point, the hip-hop beat is overrun by fierce African drumming and soaring voices, finally settling into the deliberate sound of a simple snare-drum march, leaving listeners, at song's end, in the presence of a rally speaker who reminds everyone how the recompense will come: "Now there ain't but 20,000 police in the whole town. Can you dig it? Can you dig it? CAN YOU DIG IT?!?"[63]

As emphatic as the liberatory discourse is in the song and in the music that carries it, the song also illustrates the *liminal* function of spirit. Wyclef bluntly utilizes liminal, threshold imagery in locating police as coming into peoples' view as an "enemy" appearing "on the borderline." In the song, the borderline is not just a place where Diallo dies at the hands of his murderers, but also where many are portrayed as living only to die, dying in order to live, only to be the next in line to die once again. Wyclef's listeners are described as like him, part of a subordinated community, living betwixt and between life and death, with forty-one shots always likely to come from the borderline. The aura of taboo and magic, which, according to Turner, liminal situations have, is well captured in Wyclef's simple poetic rendering of life at the border: "Night is in the air."

The eclectic character of the music especially represents the polyvocal and polyrhythmic complexity of the song, which is so typical when seeking to express liminal situations. Wyclef's voice captures this polyvocality, ranging from lyricizing like a hardcore rapper, to mimicking Diallo's final, careful thoughts, intoning prayers like a Baptist preacher, shouting, "Jah! Ras-tafari!," lamenting as in R & B, and more. All these vocal modes are spoken over the music.[64] Wyclef also pulls in a variety of musical modes to join the hip-hop beat, for example R & B female background singers, African vocals, organ chords, and march music (the snare drum). All these musical modes are prefaced by the staccato salvo of police gunshots that opens the lyrical segment of the song. All of this constitutes the polymusicality of the song, enabling the piece to vibrate in a host of in-between states, deep in a liminal consciousness.

There is also the *integrative* impact. There is no appeal here to a common shared nature, nor any simple call, "People unite, come together, now!" There is something more powerful than that, however, just as integrative and unifying. Wyclef artfully situates his listeners in a variety of sonic spaces, finally creating a remarkable unity of self with others. First, he sets listeners in the doorway with Diallo muttering his thoughts as any human being might when first seeing the police, in the fervent prayer-life of a believing Christian or Rasta trying to sort out all the pain and injustice before their gods. He then moves on from this scenario to situating listeners in the power of his own vocalized rage and despair, denouncing the wrongs done, announcing coming recompense.

In the longest stanza, Wyclef invites listeners themselves to speak into the song, thereby integrating listeners into the song's quest for meaning. He asks *them/us* directly, "Have you ever been shot forty-one times? Have you ever screamed and no one heard your cry? . . . Have you ever lived only so you can die again, . . . from these enemies, on the borderline?" In short, have you stood, or do you now stand, in a place like the one in which Amadou Diallo found himself? "Have you ever been held against your will, taken to a dark place . . . ?," Wyclef asks again, later in the song, and this time grafts in still others, invoking thoughts of the 2 million imprisoned in the American Gulag.

It is when Wyclef unites listeners with many others who know the forty-one shots are "by their side" that he positions the listeners in readiness for the tribal singing and dancing that comes at the end, complete with words in Haitian Creole invoking Martin Luther King, Jr., before listeners are sent off to receive the rally speech's call to action.

As Wyclef and others demonstrate, rap songs and their musical genres will weave together the liberatory, the liminal, and the integrative in a myriad of different ways. Thus, they will play out in our times a spiritual economy of rap.

NOTES

1. Jacques Attali, *Noise: The Political Economy of Music* (Minneapolis: University of Minnesota Press, 1985).

2. See the book-length study by Theophus H. Smith, *Conjuring Culture: Biblical Formations of Black America* (New York: Oxford University Press, 1994).

3. Tricia Rose, *Black Noise: Rap Music and Black Culture in Contemporary America* (Hanover, NH, and London: Wesleyan University Press, 1994), 95.

4. Claude Lévi-Strauss, *The Raw and the Cooked: Introduction to a Science of Mythology*, vol. 1 (New York: Harper and Row, 1975), 18. First published in France as *Le cru et le cuit* (Paris: Librairie Plon, 1964).

5. Ibid., 16.

6. Ibid., 17.

7. Ibid.

8. Ibid.; italics added.

9. Ibid.

10. Rose, *Black Noise*, 80–84.

11. Ibid., 65.

12. John Miller Chernoff, *African Rhythm and African Sensibility: Aesthetics and Social Action in African Musical Idioms* (Chicago: University of Chicago Press, 1979).

13. Antonio Benitez-Rojo, *The Repeating Island: The Caribbean and the Postmodern Perspective*, 2d ed. (Durham, NC: Duke University Press, 1996), 16–17, 21, 27, 36.

14. Rose, *Black Noise*, 66, quoting Marc Dery, "Rap!," *Keyboard*, November 1988, 34.

15. Rose, *Black Noise*, 53.

16. Ibid., 73.

17. Nelson George et al., eds., *Fresh: Hip Hop Don't Stop* (New York: Random House, 1985), 67. Cited from Rose, *Black Noise*, 54.

18. Rose, *Black Noise*, 65.

19. Ibid., 53.

20. Ibid., 66. Rose is citing the words of Christopher Small, *Music, Society, Education: An Examination of the Function of Music in the Western, Eastern and*

African Cultures with Its Impact on Society and Its Use in Education (New York: Schirmer, 1977), 54–55.

21. Rose, *Black Noise*, 70.

22. See Nicholas of Cusa (1401–1464), for example, in Ray C. Petry, ed., *Late Medieval Mysticism* (Philadelphia: Westminster Press, 1957), 352–391.

23. Rose, *Black Noise*, 63.

24. Ibid., 22.

25. Ibid., 21.

26. Angela Y. Davis, *Blues Legacies and Black Feminism: Gertrude "Ma" Rainey, Bessie Smith, and Billie Holiday* (New York: Pantheon, 1998), 70–71, 167–168.

27. "Pincers," in *Webster's II: New College Dictionary* (Boston: Houghton Mifflin, 1995), 836.

28. Derrick Bell, *Faces at the Bottom of the Well: The Permanence of Racism* (New York: Basic Books, 1992), and Marcellus Andrews, *The Political Economy of Hope and Fear* (New York: New York University Press, 1999).

29. Bakari Kitwana, (New York: Basic Civitas Books, 2002), xiii.

30. Kevin Phillips, *The Politics of Rich and Poor: Wealth and the Reagan Electorate in the Reagan Aftermath* (New York: Harper Perennial, 1990), 14. Phillips confirmed his study with another one, *Wealth and Democracy: A Political History of the American Rich* (New York: Broadway Books, 2002), xii.

31. William Julius Willson, *When Work Disappears: The World of the New Urban Poor* (New York: Alfred Knopf, 1996), 29.

32. On what the South Bronx felt like and looked like through the eyes of youth of color, see Jonathan Kozol's book, *Amazing Grace: The Lives of Children and the Conscience of a Nation* (New York: Crown, 1995). For additional background, see Robert Fitch, *The Assassination of New York* (New York: Verso, 1993), 161, 215–217.

33. Amnesty International, *United States of America: Rights for All* (London: Amnesty International USA, 1998), 87–98. Cf. Jill Nelson, ed., *Police Brutality: An Anthology* (New York: W. W. Norton, 2000), and Allyson Collins, *Shielded from Justice: Police Brutality and Accountability in the United States* (New York: Human Rights Watch, 1998).

34. Joe Feagin, *Racist America: Roots, Current Realities and Future Reparations* (New York: Routledge, 2000), 147–148.

35. Steven Donziger, *The Real War on Crime: Report of the National Criminal Justice Commission* (New York: HarperCollins, 1996), 31.

36. On this and other aspects of the economics of prisons, see Mark Lewis Taylor, *The Executed God: The Way of the Cross in Lockdown America* (Minneapolis: Fortress Press, 2001), 19–20.

37. Christian Parenti, *Lockdown America: Police and Prisons in the Age of Crisis* (New York: Verso, 1999).

38. "Developments in the Law—Race and the Criminal Process," *Harvard Law Review* 110, no. 7 (1988): 1473–1641.

39. For sources, see Taylor, *Executed God*, 25–28.

40. Statistics from the Department of Justice and the NAACP, cited in "Race of Defendants Executed since 1976," Death Penalty Information Center, http://www.deathpenaltyinfo.org/dpicrace.html#inmaterace.

41. Rose, *Black Noise*, 101.

42. On the Vatican and slavery, see Molefi K. Asante and Mark T. Mattison, *Historical and Cultural Atlas of African-Americans* (New York: Macmillan, 1992). Concerning Protestants in the United States and slavery, see Forrest G. Wood, *The Arrogance of Faith: Christianity and Race in America from the Colonial Era to the Twentieth Century* (New York: Alfred Knopf, 1990), 197ff.

43. Mark Taylor, "Tracking Spirit: Theology as Cultural Critique in America," in *Changing Conversations: Religious Reflection and Cultural Analysis*, ed. Sheila Greeve Davaney and Dwight N. Hopkins (New York and London: Routledge, 1997).

44. Sister Souljah, "We Remember Malcolm Day," Abyssinian Baptist Church, Harlem, New York, February 21, 1991. Cited from Rose, *Black Noise*, 62, 197.

45. Karl Barth, *Theologian of Freedom*, ed. Clifford Green (Minneapolis: Fortress Press, 1991), 44.

46. Jose Comblin, *Called to Freedom: The Changing Context of Liberation Theology* (Maryknoll, NY: Orbis Books, 1998).

47. Michael Ventura, *Shadow Dancing in the USA* (New York: St. Martin's Press, 1985), 111.

48. Alfred N. Hunt, *Haiti's Influence on Antebellum America* (Baton Rouge: Louisiana State University Press, 1988), 9, 15.

49. Ibid.

50. See Timothy White, *Catch a Fire: The Life of Bob Marley* (New York: Henry Holt, 1983), 22, 25, 54–56.

51. http://www.raptivism.com/#.

52. No More Prisons! Web site: http://www.nomoreprisons.org/front.htm.

53. Michael Lambek, *Reader in the Anthropology of Religion* (London: Basil Blackwell, 2002), 243.

54. See Peter Stallybrass and Allon White, "Introduction," in *The Politics and Poetics of Transgression* (Ithaca, NY, and London: Cornell University Press and Methuen Books, 1986), 1–20. Abridged in Lambek, *Reader*, 275–87.

55. Victor Turner, *Dramas, Fields and Metaphors: Symbolic Action in Human Society* (Ithaca, NY, and London: Cornell University Press, 1974), 39. For Turner's earlier study, built on studies of religious and ritual process among the Ndembu, see his *The Ritual Process: Structure and Anti-Structure* (Chicago: University of Chicago Press, 1969).

56. The classic statement of "double-consciousness" of blacks in America is in W. E. B. Du Bois, *The Souls of Black Folk* (New York: Library of America Edition, 1990), 8–9.

57. Wyclef Jean, featuring MB2, Youssou N'Dour, "Diallo," on *The Ecleftic: 2 Sides II a Book,* Sony Music Entertainment, 2000.

58. Wyclef also produced the recent song by Canibus, "Draft Me," rapping about taking aim at "you all with bloody red turbans," and seeking to settle scores in war (see the album *C True Hollywood Stories,* Archives Label, 2001).

59. Ralph Ellison, *Invisible Man* (New York: Modern Library, 1994), 567.

60. Clifford Geertz, "Religion as a Cultural System," in *The Interpretation of Cultures* (New York: Basic Books, 1973 [1966]), 87–125, and excerpted most recently in Lambek, *Reader,* 61–82.

61. See Arrested Development, *3 Years, 5 Months and 2 Days in the Life of . . . ,* Chrysalis Records, 1992.

62. See Arrested Development, *Zingalamaduni,* Chrysalis Records, 1994.

63. Wyclef was himself brusquely arrested in Brooklyn recently at a hip-hop concert protesting cutbacks of funding for public schools in New York City. See Warren Cohn, "Wyclef Arrested, Hip Hop Artists Protest," *Rolling Stone,* July 25, 2002.

64. Recall Chuck D of Public Enemy who noted that rap is a vocal discourse that can be laid down over almost all kinds of music. See Chuck D with Yusuf Jah, *Fight the Power: Rap, Race, and Reality* (New York: Delacourte Press, 1997), 248–249.

6

Rap as Wrap and Rapture

North American Popular Culture and the Denial of Death

James W. Perkinson

[People] make their own history, but they do not make it as they please . . . but under circumstances directly encountered, given and transmitted from the past. The tradition of all the dead generations weighs like a nightmare on the brain of the living.

—Karl Marx, *The Eighteenth Brumaire of Louis Bonaparte*

The ultimate effect of white Europe upon Asia and Africa was to cast millions into a kind of spiritual void; I maintain that it suffused their lives with a sense of meaninglessness. I argue that it was not merely physical suffering or economic deprivation that has set over a billion and a half colored people in violent political motion . . . The dynamic concept of a spiritual void that must be filled, a void created by a thoughtless and brutal impact of the West upon a billion and a half people, is more powerful than the concept of class conflict, and more universal.

—Richard Wright, *White Man Listen!*

Yet, in 1976, the real Bronx was far from a cultural wasteland. Behind the decay and neglect was a cauldron of vibrant, unnoticed, and quite visionary creativity born of its racial mix and its relative isolation.

—Nelson George, *Hip Hop America*

In this chapter, I examine the performative effects of rap music in the context of postindustrial metropolitan social structure, racialization, and the denial of death. I argue that rap can be read as a peculiarly postmodern form of shamanistic communication, a ritualized refiguration of the actuality of mortality in the public sphere. I claim that twentieth-century America witnessed a sustained expulsion of the reality of mortality from public life in an uncompromising attempt to manage some of the more obvious "rearrangements and enforcements" of mortality (i.e., social structures that concentrate wealth, power, and life chances for some at the expense of others) through popular discourses of racialization and institutionalized tactics of racism, and a "return of the repressed" in various pop culture fascinations and mediations, emerging from the urban core, not the least of which is hip-hop culture and rap music.

Rap's rhythmic structures and ritual codifications, rather than its lyrical surface texts, will exercise our theoretical imagination in what follows. As the basic argument seeks to root rap innovation in its sociocultural conditions of production, the core discussion of the music will be developed only after first building up a relatively thick context of sociological, racial, phenomenological, and historical analyses. Rap refigures the denial of death, the racialization of context in black and white, the encounter with the grotesque face of colonial conquest. Only root-work in the murky depths of each of these facets of the modern project will suffice to adumbrate the intensity of hip-hop's percussive insurgency in the midst of our contemporary postmodern complexity.

The Great American Denial That Rap Denies

Postmodern culture emerged around the globe in the latter half of the twentieth century as, among other things, an increasingly intensified metropolitan culture structured (in part) in a profound denial of mortality. Those who study the phenomenon of cultural attitudes toward death have been unequivocal in their characterization. Philippe Aries works through the epochs of Western history to characterize the twentieth century as "death denied".[1] Elisabeth Kübler-Ross has thoroughly underscored the degree to which modern society uses its technology to flee the ubiquitous fact of mortality.[2] Sherwin Nuland explores (and challenges) the resulting sense of failure when the disease cannot be defeated by a medical profession driven by the imperative to "solve the Riddle."[3] Ernst Becker traces the way the general phenomenon of denial underpins specific practices, such as American funeral efforts to present the dead as merely sleeping. David Chidester details the shifts in language serving to mask death in euphemism, accompanied by increasing professional control over actual dying and dead bodies, removing death as a reality from ordinary experience and creating a "buffer between the living and the dead."[4]

It is this buffering effect that will especially occupy our attention—not only as interventions between the living and the dead, but as realizations of intervention in the parsing of social space into antiseptic middle-class enclaves of "normally" enculturated human and racially "othered" communities living closer to nature's predations and mortalities.

It is curious, however, that this euphemizing of death seems to operate by a law of compensation. Yes, as Aries has emphasized, death is now a hidden fact—the "dirty and ugly" secret of modern society that, in contravening the aseptic values of bourgeois hygiene, medicine, and morality must now be secluded and sequestered. The hospital indeed emerges as the new bureaucracy of ultimacy, advertising care, promising cure, and providing quarantine when the smells and sights and sounds betray the promise. Whereas at century's onset, 80 percent of North Americans died in company of family and friends at home, at the other end of the era, 80 percent now are quietly managed into the grave by the white-robed children of Hippocrates.[5] Death incarnate has largely left the community and added solitude to its repertoire of terrors.

At the same time, however, death as "eloquence" has gained a proportionate following.[6] At least in popular culture, the fact has reemerged in drag, offering its emoluments as both visionary experience and elocutory emphasis. Where it has become de rigeur to dress and address mortality in such soft figurements ("laid to rest," "called home," etc.), death has emerged as perhaps the most "dead on" intensifier of meaning or dramatizer of effect of our time (I am "dead certain," "dead tired," "a dead aim," etc.). On the other hand, it is extremely old news that death sells.[7] The media has marketed out-of-the-ordinary mortality (plane crashes, industrial accidents, war brutalities, drug overdoses by movie stars, etc.) as the bread and butter of its business. At the same time, the entertainment industry capitalizes on "splash and gore" in big-butted bottom-line figures.

But in any case, what is clear is the contradiction. Death is not allowed to offer its body in public except through a surreptition. It is not the slow accretion of death's small triumphs over a lifetime that fascinates (for "death as aging" we have reserved a great huge warehouse called "Florida"), but its sudden swift descent on still vigorous flesh. The horror of ruptured vitality is packaged as pleasure.

The other side of this masking of mortality is the elevation of adolescence to a heretofore unattained preeminence. Western industrial and postindustrial commodity cultures can indeed be partly analyzed as, representing a concerted attempt to marginalize and even eliminate (old age and) death as a meaningful constituent of metropolitan social life. Death is consigned to "nature" and to "older" forms of human existence—part of which has been left behind on the farm or screened away from the more developed metropolitan life-worlds in various strategies of bionic intervention. But in the very turn away from age and mortality, youthfulness has now been fashioned as the new fetish, marketed as the ultimate image of a humanity on the rise toward a biotech immortality, and sold as the constituting aim of middle-class leisure activity. The incarnate orthodoxy of this newly "christened" image of erotic youthfulness is a metropolitan lifestyle driven by the privileges and powers of accumulation, organized into exclusive enclaves of shared interests, and committed to forms of identity constituted in consumption.[8]

Rap will be seen to emerge as precisely the conflation of these two ramifications: a body of youth auguring the reality of death.

The Great American Denigration That Rap Displays

But this contemporary orthodoxy also has its necessary heterodoxy. The brokering of resources, opportunities, and statuses that allow for such a pursuit is partially moderated and manipulated by the assignments of race. To the degree poverty, high incidence of disease, unemployment, "illiteracy," uncollected garbage, abandoned buildings, and so on represent "specters of death" in social form, the racialization of lower-class urban experience in dominant-culture discourse has arguably functioned as a form of social *prophylaxis.* In simultaneously constructing and imposing irremediable forms of "difference" (e.g., "blackness," "Latin-ness," etc.), racialization and its accompanying structures of racism can be partly understood as forms of quarantine imposed by the dominant culture.[9] They function to reduce contact with the social "body" of death. Institutional practices (in the real estate, housing development, banking, and insurance industries, for instance) that function disparately to rearrange resources and opportunities (in part) on the basis of race are, in effect, so many processes of "ghetto-creation and maintenance." They forcibly concentrate in particular areas of the city and forcefully cordon off from middle-class lifestyle venues the forces of impoverishment that constitute an early, prolonged, and unmistakable encounter with death in manifold forms.

People racialized as "black," for instance, give evidence of the highest disease and mortality rates, whereas society's dominant "white" community lives longest.[10] A recent *New England Journal of Medicine* article offered evidence that racism continues to inflect the delivery of health services, directing more palliative and less radical therapies toward white recipients and more radical and invasive procedures toward darker-skinned sufferers of the same symptoms and disease-stages.[11] At the same time, demographic surveys indicate the greater concentration of toxic waste processing plants and polluted industrial properties in or near communities of color—a demography whose disease incidence is correlatively higher as well. Add into this mix the very evident stress accompanying the ongoing experience of racism, and a certain picture becomes evident.[12] Mortality is not simply "indiscriminately" distributed across class and race lines. It is "concentrated," to a degree, in certain social-class locations.

Quarantining of lower-income populations of color in areas of concentrated poverty targeted for various kinds of illegal drug and legal alcoholic beverage marketing has, in fact, *not* resulted in higher percentages of use when compared to white population segments. But it *has* translated into differential "policing tactics," known in polite society as "profiling" but more accurately described by its victims as "brutality." The profoundly racist operation of the criminal justice system—in effect using the so-called war on drugs as the neoliberal equivalent of enslavement, arresting black and Latino youth with virtual impunity in many urban centers, and contracting out the incarcerated populations as the new, cheap labor of the age (along with various migrant populations)—both directly and indirectly influence mortality rates.[13] It was no accident—nor is it at all outdated—when James Baldwin wrote in 1963: "White Americans do not believe in death, and this is why the darkness of my skin so intimidates them. And this is also why the presence of the Negro in this country can bring about its destruction."[14]

Baldwin perhaps embroiders on Hegel's master-slave dialectic here (or else gives Hegel true grounding in modern history). The human being (or perhaps more accurately, the male human being) is constituted in a freedom struggle that finally risks even death itself.[15] For Hegel, to emerge in truth one must insist on recognition even to the point of death. In the (inevitable?) struggle for survival, someone "wins" and enslaves another, who is then made to labor over nature to produce the substance of living for the winner. At the heart of that relationship between the master and the slave is death—a death risked, a death avoided, and, for the slave at least, a death reconfigured into a form of living death.

But Hegel's genius is to have hinted at a surprising reversal in the equation. The master who appears to be independent and "free" is, in the sublation of the dialectic operating between opposites in human language and experience, finally dependent upon the slave and the unfree. And the slave who has been reduced to a mere shadow of the master to a form of laborer for the latter that is, in reality, a mere delay of death or its elaboration into a mode of gradual demise is, in fact, the one who emerges into the truth of death defied and of "being" ramified. The slave, says Hegel, has been struck to the core by the terror of unremitting contingency, of the possibility of life being ended at any moment at the whim of the master. In the face of such, he has been forced to carve out from hard soil, by hand, a facsimile of human substance, an objectified version of subjective being, that, though owned by the master, nonetheless bears the stamp of the slave's own personal impress of work and wit. It is the slave who has descended into the void of nonbeing and has come up knowing truth. It is the slave who has looked the end in the eye and is still breathing, chastened, shivered, struck profoundly awake to the utter delirium of a life that is standing on the back of death. The slave *knows* what the master has managed to hide from. The death defiance involved in the original moment of struggle is masked and manipulated in the subsequent enslavement. The master lives mastery as untruth and "knows," in an unconscious gesture of denial, the reality of destiny only in the eye of the slave. The slave becomes, for such a one, both the prophylactic against, and the troubling sign of, the end that both share.

This, too, rap will adumbrate: a reversal, not of fates, but of fear and its fixations in a certain narrowness of experience.

The Great American Projection That Rap Protests

James Baldwin was not hyperbolic. "Black" skin, in North America, is the uncanny figuration of what lurks dragonlike and unfaced beneath white skin. ("Black" here is being used in a metaphorical sense for a complex and contested set of meanings and practices of exclusion that are also operated, with more or less similar effect depending on circumstance, by other ethnically specific forms of stereotyping.) "Blackness" projected onto darker hues by a desperately anxious dominant culture yields "white" skin as a structure of denial. To be white in North America (to date) is to be caught up in deep-seated cultural constructions—and contradictions—of the social meaning of mortality. Middle-class lifestyle is, in part, an imagination of life as antiseptic, ordered, upwardly mobile, volitionally amendable, protected from violence and chaos, and free of victims.[16] Suburban residence is assumed to be tranquil, tame, tidy, and untainted by the "problems" observed elsewhere. The "gated communities" that have come increasingly into being in recent decades by way of well-monitored points of entry and well-policed "exteriors" have successfully "exorcised" the sights and sounds and smells of death from their daily routines.

Such structures are constituted in contradiction. They represent profoundly powerful concentrations of "carrying capacity" gathered from beyond their borders.[17] They metabolize resources garnered from their "elsewheres" by means as diverse as gulf wars aimed at uninterrupted oil flows, NAFTA treaties opening up desperate labor situations and unregulated environmental conditions to instant exploitation by unrestricted investment, world and local banks whose loan strategies in final effect (not in publicized rhetoric) rearrange capital out of communities of poverty and into communities of plenty, large corporations whose financial departments realize $300 billion a year (in this country alone) in "legal" interest scams by way of alternative credit institutions in disadvantaged communities, a federal government whose tax concessions and subsidies amount to a $450 billion transfer payment in the direction of "wealth-fare" for hard-lobbying corporations and well-connected individuals, and so on.[18]

The favored lifestyles and residences carefully screen out the blight and the bluster left in the wake of their predatory "reach"—except when they want info-tainment relief from the pressures of counting money and courting power, or a quick adrenaline shot by way of the mesmerized eye with no risk attached. But the "inclusive" economics is obviously complemented by an exclusive sociopolitics. Such communities consume the living substance of others but refuse a shared sociality or a reciprocal exchange of spirit. And much of the rationale for the refusal goes by way of the tacit function of *racial* perception. Projected "otherness" ("blackness," "brownness," "redness," "yellowness," etc.) is the great unexamined "apology," in the cultural common sense, for the impoverished living and early dying that are structurally imposed on various "elsewheres" (around the world and on the home front) in the process of enhancing accumulation and longevity inside the gate.

And even as the gated community can thus be analyzed as a socioeconomic *structure of denial* of the decay and death "exported" elsewhere, so white skin serves as the individual correlation for that larger demographic prophylaxis. (In rap "crossover," as we shall see below, the prophylaxis is decisively broken.) In the operations of the racial imagination, whiteness emerges, in one sense, as the social artifact of a cultural quest for "clarity," "definitiveness," "intelligibility," "order," "form," "freedom."[19] It gains force as an elusive index of identity whose substance is largely that of a silent negation of imagined "darkness," a kind of lived denial of many of the social conditions imposed on communities of color.[20] As the "color" of a psychic gesture, whiteness abreacts "away from" the formless fact of mortality, the beginning of life in dark intimacy, the reproduction of life in a merging that muddles boundaries between bodies. It promises control; it organizes sight as "reflection," as light bouncing off a surface. It resists opacity, interiority, the density of contacting surfaces, the proximity of perishability, the permeability of the body to all other bodies, the wetness of exchange, the "surroundingness" of the ground of incubation and end.[21] The attributes listed above are not so much immediately obvious as the surrogates of white identity, but rather accumulate as the "epiphenomenon" of imposed darkness, in all of its powers of containment and quarantine. Projected color "identifies," contains in a category, ramifies an invisible wall around an impossible geography, mobilizes the policing eye on the street and highway, guards the gate against intrusion. All the silent attributions of whiteness are the payoff of that projection.

Such an understanding of "opacity" as a social hieroglyph, produced and reproduced in various forms of cultural discourse to reinforce a simultaneous exploitation and exclusion, need not imply that its significance is simply an imposition "from without" on communities of color. The "blackface" put on the institutional structures of violence giving valence to white desire and concreteness to white interest is not simply so much charcoal and elbow grease exercised by white imagination. The category has necessarily been taken up by communities of color in various forms of agency and been refigured in various forms of positivity.[22] The 1960s, for instance, especially witnessed a weariness with trying to sidestep white modes of categorizing African American "appearance" and a new tactic of reversing the valence. "Blackness" was taken up by Stokeley

Carmichael and SNCC, by Angela Davis and black nationalist groups, by Albert Cleage and black religionists, by Amiri Baraka and black artists, by James Brown and black musicians, by Gwendolyn Brooks and black poets, by James Cone and black theologians, and others as a public badge of pride precisely in counterpoint to its public purveyance in white media as a surreptitious sign of shame.

But that moment of explicit reversal of a contested category—that rap itself will also recapitulate and resyncopate with profound public effect—had a long history of reversal and revisionment behind it.

The Great American Transfiguration That Rap Transposes

Historian of religions Charles Long has provocatively sounded out the way slave communities refigured the violence of their enslavement. In his collection of essays entitled *Significations,* Long offers academic finesse in the key of vernacular redress. He signifies on the signification that seeks to mark and locate him as "non-white."[23] He does so by way of a History of Religions discourse, broken open on the anvil of colonial historiography, yielding, in the process, "strange fruit." The chain and shackle, the sardine packaging of the Middle Passage, the hulk of ship, the hurt of whip, the phallic burst of cannon, the fanatic thirst for conversion—Long reads all of these through the lens of mythic reconstruction. Colonized communities and enslaved sodalities the world over re-created themselves recurrently from the shards of ritual, and the ashes of story left them once they had been effectively metabolized in the growing world economy and reclassified in European taxonomies. They did judo on genocide, taking up their shattered cosmograms and refiguring "fate" in the fantastic shape of a Divine Grotesque.

Rudolph Otto's *mysterium tremendum et fascinosum* gives Long his academic ammunition.[24] The concept is cracked in two by Long to differentiate the religiousness of the experience of destruction from the mundane hollowness of the experience of conquest.[25] What, for the West, seemed to be simple "confirmation" of its own myth of superiority, was, for "the rest," a plunge into terror. The terror was not only physical, but primal. Indigenous myths of origin were peeled back to their articulations of the original rupture of creation, when sky separated from earth and deity from humanity. Here was the original faultline of chaos slipping again in seismic ferocity. This was the earthquake of beginnings all over again, when the Force behind the world made its potency palpable and its meaning incomprehensible. This was no tame experience of divine intention; this was a "fall" into utter contingency—the "taste" of the hard tooth of mortality crunching one's own bone.

The religions of the oppressed that resulted—the native Ghost Dance, the pacific Cargo Cult, the Rasta reiteration, the ring shout, the hoodoo root work, the voodoo *veve* revolt, all the riot of ritual ribaldry—are read by Long in terms of the *tremendum*.[26] "Fascination" with deification is the luxury and necessity of the culture of domination.[27] For those who lose history, however, "God" must be wrestled with in inchoate forms of darkness. It is this face of divinity that Long tries to render "thinkably unthinkable" in the cozy denials of the academy. Indigenous religion in general, and black religion in particular, cannot be grasped solely in terms of surface feature. The deep quest beneath the detail is a matter of touching unbridled terror. The Ultimate offers no decipherable physiognomy, only sheer opacity. And yet it is precisely this opaqueness that is given embodied dramatization in communal celebrations and there is rewrought into an intensity of vital identities. The possession cult of the colonized and the perishing is the vibrant taming of a two-faced force: God and the Devil, Life and Death in syncopated lockstep, where each is made to "sound out" and signify upon the other.

Numerous other scholars have worked this same angle. Paul Gilroy's writing is a virtual elaboration of these insights under the rubric of the "slave sublime."[28] Toni Morrison, again and again, manages to conjure the "unsaid unsayable" in her liquid prose.[29] From Jamaica Kincaid to Angela Davis, from Ellison back to Hurston, from Wright forward to Walker, the struggle is to write apocalypse under the twin sign of violence and "vibrance." What has been damnably suffered has also been astonishingly transfigured. The "deep throat" of ritual intensity must be read on many levels at once.

It is this that is also the deep-throat "word up" on contemporary rap. It is not surprising that young people on the contemporary scene of holocaust would innovate new "riffs" on the old theme. Folk forcibly "baptized into" an unavoidable encounter with mortality on a daily basis in our postindustrial landscapes of abandonment must either reinvent their world or resign themselves to despair and dismemberment. Hegel (by way of Fanon) offers a point of interrogation.[30] What rap constitutes can be partly explored as a peculiarly male mobilization of the "recognition economy" animating the master-slave dialectic.[31]

In our contemporary urban wastelands, the death-struggle definitive of Hegelian dignity and human "truth" has not ceased to define a necessary transcendence. B-boys and boasters, gangstas and other West Coasters, live crews and posses of every cry and hue, give continual exclamation point to the strange truth Martin Luther King, Jr., discovered after Watts erupted in 1965 in defiance of his own counsels of nonviolence: despite thirty-four dead bodies and a burned-up community, young blacks told King that they had "triumphed in the streets" because "we made them pay attention to us."[32] Malcolm had understood—better than King—that the first and most important step in the freedom quest of any community is "pride": the self-esteem that accrues to the first taste of beginning to decolonize one's own mind and demand a hearing. Early rap reverberated as a form of cultural self-exorcism writ large.

But the "devil" in global capital has learned quickly. Hegemony today resists resistance by way of capitulation: any gesture of opposition capable of gathering a following is quickly bought off with success. With rap music and hip-hop culture in general, the big label companies and fashion moguls rapidly got over their sense of offense once the smell of big money came around the corner. The dominant culture today is fat and absorbent. It enfolds with immediate comfort and cash. As Fanon lamented regarding the freedom "won" in French colonies in the 1950s, so too in turn of the millennium "AmeriKKKa": there is no opposing "eye of desire," no face-to-face challenge, auguring death, offering life, exposing the lie of mastery.[33] Instead, under the rhetoric of "rights," impersonal bureaucracy, indefensible brutality, and incomprehensible policy increasingly represent the blank face of control and containment. There is no hot form of struggle discernible, only a domestic "cold war."

In consequence, it is no surprise that, more often than not, the death struggle today is "black on black." (Or "brown on brown," etc., or a very complex slamming together/exploding apart of racialized identity: "black on yellow," as in African American/Korean American economic conflict in inner-city Los Angeles; or "olive on black," as in similarly structured Chaldean American/African American encounters in inner-city Detroit.) The resistant arm blow most frequently lands on a homeboy.[34] Kool Moe Dee, for instance, captures both the instinct for battle and the flip of resistant bombast back on itself in his one-liner from Stop the Violence Movement's antiviolence all-star jam *Self-Destruction:* "I never ran from the Ku Klux Klan/so I shouldn't have to run from a black man."[35] The bigger enemy of white supremacy and overclass hegemony is (seemingly) out of reach. But each of these forms of the "opposing other" are also mediums of projection. At another level, the bulls-eye is a mysterious "Something" just beyond consciousness, hovering, suffocating, unanswering, defiantly "not quite there."[36] The mortality and contingency that slave and ex-slave ritual arm wrestled into a kind of "body-knowledge" in the antiphonal sweat of a four-hour worship service, hip-hop now communalizes as a competitive contest.[37] "Knowing" oneself as alive is no longer codified in the trance breakthrough of conversion, but the break-dance of bodies and words on the concrete.[38] Ritual combat here mobilizes a new street-corner culture of rhyming recognition: words fly, rhythm cries, eyeballs see into the beyond on the horizontal plane of defiance and def-jam self-dependence. Robert Bellah is right when he underscores urban survival as a big daddy arena of resourcefulness at the turn of the millennium. In the "Hobbesian world" of late capitalism, he says, "far from breeding dependency, life in the ghetto . . . requires the most urgent kind of self-reliance."[39] In this world, rap can easily be read as the new recognition ritual of urban male "initiation."

Saying such is not to deny the frequently puerile cant of repetitious rap lyrics today. Nor is it to dissemble before its often misogynist preoccupations and adolescent grandiosity. But the interrogation here is aimed at a different trajectory. Where else in our death-denying culture is face-to-face confrontation with human contingency as rawly engaged in a ritual form? That these expressive modalities would find a huge cross-over market among middle-class youth of various cultures (including its majority market in this country among white suburban kids) as ritual significations engendering something like "religious response" is also not surprising. Hip-hop has become the adolescent "idiom of choice" the world over, today, for negotiating questions of identity and desire. Adolescence is a new wrinkle in the human life cycle. A definitive creature of capitalism's erosion of the family and simultaneous elaboration of technology, bureaucracy, and commodity, the teenager is a new phenomenon on the horizon. As a kind of living embodiment of temporal disjuncture, contemporary youth are a sign of the times. In them, we face our own dissimulation.

Adolescent Entropy

The adolescent body is a clear augury of capitalism's fundamental contradiction. It emerges in our pedagogy as physicality shot through with hormonal insurgency, enjoined to multiple and indeed continuous "orgasms of consumption" while simultaneously derided when it dares consummate "intercourse with the image" in actual physical copulation. A virtual crockpot of chemical potency—

> suspended between mom and the mall,
> heated daily in the commodified blaze of the social,
> tipped at every turn,
> dipped in the commercial,
> sipped in the sample,
> rippled in the visual river,
> slipped the trip of "ecstasy" everyday from five to twenty five

—and yet expected to hold back the fluid like a tantric hero. "Adolescence"—the long stretch of amplified arousal that is denied any real prospect of a "family values" form of satisfaction until social maturity somewhere around twenty-eight years of age on average in our culture—is a mirror of the impossibility of our society.

Youth are also a site where the surreption of death in our culture shows through. In their bodies, time disrupts its own capitalist codification as continuous, uniform, and infinite. It bulges with differing frequencies, aches with tumultuous temporalities, each demanding its own separate hearing. Without the necessary "concept" and ritual ramification, youth nonetheless "know" time possesses sharp edges and ends, social disjunctures, and physical dismemberments. They know the body of childhood has "died"; they know "death" in the body. They are made to live in such a space of death, in the gap between the child and the adult—the body of the carefree learner long dead, the body of the responsible producer still far ahead, offered consumption as their only solace, besieged with the siren-call necessity of reembodiment without release or prospect. It is no wonder that youth are fascinated not only by Eros but by the great, banished "dark" one of the West. They know what "we" adults have hidden—precisely in being unable to know.

Rap gives that subjugated knowledge of endings, and of death itself, a social body.[40] While much of hip-hop culture has indeed been subverted (from both within and without) into a preoccupation with machismo, misogyny, and predatory violence, there remains at its core a codification of death both "dared" and "defied" that continues to echo with transcendent and tragic power.[41] Jon Michael Spencer offers an analysis of the phenomenon under the twin rubrics of "mastery of form" and "deformation of mastery."[42] Applying these concepts, borrowed from literary critic Houston Baker, to probe the rhythmic structures of rap, Spencer also mobilizes Amiri Baraka's play, *The Dutchman,* Fanon's *Wretched of the Earth,* and Nietzsche's notion of "religion" to underscore rap's insurgent aggression.[43] Lyrics alone only tell a piece of the story. The driving base-beat, the syncopated production of "breaks" in the time signature, the sampling of the melodic harmonies of soul redeployed in service of percussive lower frequencies—all contribute to rap's hidden intentionality, according to Spencer and others.[44] That intention is one of "murder."[45] Much as Fanon read the release of muscular tension in rites of possession in colonial Algeria, Spencer reads rap's microstructures as a "canalizing of the impulse to kill."[46] Razor blades on throats can be heard in the undertones.[47]

Hip-hop does not simply gesture in idle boast, it both "places" and "displaces" death. Its aggressive modalities (of scratched vinyl and stone-faced denial) are not innocence but augury. Yes, they serve to contain what might otherwise break out in blood. They "release" the violence brought down on a community by invisible policy and all too visible policing. They "play out" what might otherwise remain "pent up," subject to sudden earthquakes.

For the dominant culture, such displays of musical mastery function like "religion" in the sense in which Nietzsche says religious belief is really a masked belief in the necessity of police.[48] The serrating sounds of rap both exhibit and allay fear of what is masked. In part, they "civilize" the severity of the eye that gazes back from the ghetto. Pull away the mask, however, and the grin is a cracked skull, likely to rise from the grave with war in its eye sockets. The cracked bone is just as likely to provoke living mourners to take up rocks like Palestinians. Or Glocks and Uzis. The dominant culture much prefers rap to its alternative; but it also hears and fears this alternative in the "allaying" tones.

But the rhythms of rap also "entertain." They "host," give physical form to a desire that does not just want to penetrate the other genitally.[49] They do not only mask; they make palpable. They partially "produce" what they placate. They are not far removed from South Central when the outrageous verdict of "innocent" comes back from Simi Valley. Literary critic Baker wrote, after that 1992 upsurge, that the voice of the violated on the street of the ghetto could not be heard by going directly to a Rodney King. There one only encountered the ventriloquized voice of "the massah."[50] The unvitiated verb has to be heard in the sounds of choice produced away from the scene of surveillance. Rap represented the kind of sound that could be "sounded out" by the articulate and attentive pedagogue. It had been hammering away at the deaf ear of the nation for long years prior to King's beating.[51] Yes, video supplied necessary evidence. But the eye by itself is deceptive. Human beings are complex creatures, requiring audition as well as vision. The voice is far more capable of nuance than the eye.[52] And hearing it demands attention to depth-resonance as well as surface-sonority. The depths of rap harbor a truth about America never yet heard by America. That truth is that it will not last forever. Empire never does. It will die. One day.

What Tricia Rose calls "Black Noise" is far more than meets the eye. Even when organized in terms of Spencer's "mastery of form," making use of hearer-friendly cadences and offering parent-friendly pacifisms, rap can still open the underworld. Underneath the "pirating" and repackaging by mainstream firms and the promotion and promulgation by major broadcast forums, DJ scratches still undercut MC moderation.[53] Middle-class premonitions of mastery are deformed. The beat breaks down the gate. The neighborhood is penetrated by a sonic intention. White youth sample a flavor they can't find at home. Affluent alienation finds not quite a voice, but a texture of pain and its posturing that catches the breath.

The death that haunts adolescence like a nightmare that can't quite be remembered suddenly re-presents itself. There is an edge that vibrates dangerously here, an abyss that opens, beckons, terrifies with its strange allure. The vibrancy and vitality that mark the inner resonance of rap that is not simply "wanna-be repetition" is compelling. What is it that compels? The power that is typical of all spiritual work. A "close encounter of the ultimate kind" at the threshold of nonbeing, looking over the cliff edge, stripped down to the essential realization of being alive in spite of destiny. Incomprehensibly, Life "is," in spite of, indeed, *because of,* the close proximity of Death. And it is so, right here, right now, in this body moved in-itself beyond-itself. There is, in rap that does "keep it real," that stays close to the bone and honest, a kind of inchoate transcendence, a form of rhythmic resurrection, potent precisely because it has one leg in the grave, a nascent knowledge of nirvana, on the cusp of extinction, still flaming in spite of the wind.

From Shamanic Healing to Prophetic Hardening

While such a construction can be read, in a modernist frame, as sheer romanticism, it can also be comprehended, in older indigenous idioms, as shamanistic work, opening a crossover point between "this world" and the "other side."[54] It begs to be comprehended as, in its most incandescent moments, a postmodern form of incantatory conjuration. It returns what the mainstream culture tries to hide: the grotesque grin of universal desire in the face of demise. But it does so in a *living* form of grotesquery—of artistry performed on the ugliness of destruction that renders it strangely beautiful and vital.[55] Rap, in this revelation, straddles life and death by refusing the quarantine. Something of the animation of human "being" in general—alive to its own paradoxical impermanence and improbability—is damnably and yet irresistibly revealed in this particular body of articulate aggression, gesturing under duress in a social topography of desperation, refracted in a sensibility rooted in (West and Central) African explorations of percussive polyphony, intensified in histories of enslavement and enghettoization (Long's *tremendum*), inflected in *griot* traditions of rhyming narration, spiced with the digital amplification of trance rhythms.[56] Rap growls with an aliveness common to every "awake" human existence. It is no mystery why it sells in the suburb. Ironically, it offers an intimation of wholeness. Rap's market crossover mimics an older instinct to facilitate passage between "upper" and "lower" worlds.

Historically, human healing has often involved flights of at least fancy, if not fact, to "other" realms. Trespass of boundaries—between human and animal domains, between living and dead bodies, between the temporal divisions of ancestors and offspring—is definitive of the shamanistic vocation.[57] Rap, in this compass, can be read as a raid on ultimate destiny for the sake of a proximate deliverance. It gives urgent expression to what can't be avoided if life is not to be lived in a state of somnambulance or "living death."

Many of death's urban signatures, for instance, were given haunting eloquence in Grandmaster Flash's early 1980s "Message" in the forms of sharp-edged sound, broken syntax, burned-out-building-and-vacant-lot imagery, and the intonations of street-corner predation. Hip-hop has certainly gone global in market and manner since, treating not just the savage inequalities of ghetto "realities," but softer topics like romance, finance, and free-lance humor. But its root remains the anger and attitude of a harsh confrontation. Young lives planning their own funerals; jail as school; gender as the jaded space of an intimacy war; education as an initiatory beating; home as hell; old age as twenty-five.

The "Death Row" label named the experience both figuratively and actually: rap is the tongue riot of the anteroom of ultimate negation, whether that room is called "prison cell" or "ghetto corner." Ice-Cube's *(AmeriKKKa's) Most Wanted* album and Public Enemy's self-signification underscored the outlaw ambience. The jail style of baggy pants halfway down the butt adopted by early 1990s urban youth faced with the decimations of crack and the defamations of drug arrests—whether dealing or not—defined the defiance.

Especially in the 1990s "high gangsta" period, rap refigured the elemental nihilism of a crack-sapped community, speaking far beyond its borders. It was able to do so because it reflected what writer Nelson George described as "the mentality and fears of young Americans of every color and class living an exhausting and edgy existence, in and out of big cities."[58] In figures like Tupac Shakur and Biggie Smalls, the country heard an impulse already coursing "deep in its soul."[59] For "poets of negation" like these, George says, "black male pride was a weapon and an attitude," both "an attack on the negative" and "a way to spin the negative on its head."[60] Their antiheroism took root in more than just urban concrete.

To the degree the social conditions giving rise to rap have not been altered, however, but actually in many situations worsened, the soil remains stone hard. The plant forced to grow in such conditions inevitably adapts to the hardness. Hip-hop culture is the "tag" on the American Dream, intimating the stark underside of the boom, blooming in black and red. For its own ghetto practitioners, this culture serves a sense of independence, of communal creation "in spite of." It is the equivalent of blues-song growling love-hurt into the joy of "still breathing."

For the suburb and other sites of consumption of urban desperation, however, rap is a young man's opium. Defiance and dare are packaged as rage, offered as sage commentary, staged as "revolution." The rhythmic structures "sound out" suburban alienation and wrap emptiness in a vibration of power. The result is a ritual experience of insurgency that portends, but does not deliver, revolt. Rather, the product is a blunt blend smoke of hallucinogens. The promised potency is impossible in the mode of consumption. White youth see a face of grimace that resounds in deep truths that have no social tangibility in the gated community. The video flash, the MTV finesse, belie the struggle observed. No site of contestation is identified. No connection is drawn between the "thump of baton on black back" that the music mimics in its pumped-up percussion and the middle-class lifestyle of living high on a hog raised and killed elsewhere.[61] The very dollar plunked down to purchase the sound is not innocent of the scent of blood on ghetto streets. The open maw of capital is the real grin behind the grimace. But the Mask remains intact. And Death is left laughing on the side, still unrecognized. And still triumphing *in* this life, not just at its end.[62]

If a collective effect of shamanistic healing was hip-hop's early possibility, its reality is real loss in the war of competing witchcrafts. White supremacy continues to infiltrate much of the private talk in this country. Capitalist intimations of unlimited accumulation and unbridled concentration of wealth continue to determine much of the social organization. And patriarchy continues to recruit new fists in its rapacious construction of woman as object.[63] Where rap's exploration of human resilience at the abyss-edge between life and death could have resulted in a new confrontation with the history of this nation, a new depth of encounter with all of our ancestral voices, a genuine "baptism" in our genuine possibilities, the result has been instead a deepening of the crisis. Healing "demand" has been swallowed up in harrowing denial. And the shaman's face has hardened into prophecy. Death increasingly dis-appears as the mysterious force behind ritual fantasy and is left ever more naked on the horizon as the sheer fact of our fate.

Postscript Summary in the Sound of Syncopation

> Hip hop has brought America a new language of rhythm, speech, and movement that has inspired a generation to take to verse to say what was too long unspoken about this nation. If rap went away tomorrow, would the discussion disappear too? Or would it just come coded in an alternative form? . . . *Hip Hop America* . . . chronicles a generation coming of age at a moment of extreme racial confusion—in these years since official apartheid was legislated out of existence and de facto segregation grew—that has been grappling with what equality means during the worst economic conditions for the underclass since the Depression. Hip hop is . . . the spawn of many things. But most profoundly, it is a product of schizophrenic, post–civil rights movement America.[64]

In the above, Nelson George is tracking a development that is quintessentially "American." It signifies on America. This is its object, its topic, its material condition. It speaks "out" of as well as "to." It represents the breaking open of a sealed space, the arising of a body locked away as terminal if not dead. It is the grave lid sliding back and the ghost stepping forth. But the body that is spoken through is not the ghost. Urban youth are very much alive. What emerges in their staccato gesture is a deeper truth. Their hard-staring eye does not simply codify their own reality. It unleashes a laser of dark light. They are the possession cult of the national history in the present, the place where America can be encountered in its own intention of violence, its own structure as supremacy beating the "inferior" to death, its own constitution as rape, as "rigid force of plunder" sanctified by a price tag, sold in a Benetton's ad.

And here responsibility falls on all of us to read rightly, to "be read," ourselves, irresistibly, to enter into an alternative economy of recognition. It is a national schizophrenia that appears here, a national confusion. Hip-hop speaks the unspeakable. Yes, it is immediately bought off. Yes, it is commodified in the icon, eviscerated in the visual facility, telemarketed into the medium of "more of the same." But its mediation as medium is not entirely lost. It augurs depth. It gives edge to what order wants to deny or deify, but not deal with: the fact of demise. The truth is in the base beat. The melody of American fatuity is stripped. It is the thump of the bottom, the vitality of being alive in the face of not being at all, that is coiled in on itself, intensified, interrogated, elaborated in a long growl of defiant irony. This is the face under the face.

In Zen terms, this is what the face of America looked like before America was born; this is the sound of one hand clapping. All manner of spirits fight for expression in this young body besieged with too much truth in too short a time in too small a space. Time and space are reconstituted here. This is not the mall. This is not the suburb. This is not the green lawn, the ripe vine, the waft of delicate scent of daffodil. This is the grunt of groan. This is the funk of fomenting brain on fire, the ice of hawk-faced wind without a coat, the slide of syncopated step avoiding the rat tooth. This America doesn't smile in high alto giggle. This America is "destiny" for all of us, a "guerrilla art" articulation of our ultimate deposition.[65] What will we answer in that final moment? Martin Luther King, Jr., went to the mountain, peered over into the Promised Land, and came back shouting. Hip-hop goes to the basement, peers over into the Other World, and comes back harsh. Both are the truth. America only believes in the former.

Rap, however, is the strange rapture of unwrapping the nightmare inside of the Dream without flinching. It is the embodiment of the other ancestor that Thomas Jefferson denied. It is the code of contemporary healing, offered in the key of challenge. The sample is the metaphor of the meaning of "America." The sharply tensed edge between the beats is the place where the past surges up, unrepentant and raging. Will it find us at home? Or only creating another structure of denial?

NOTES

1. Philippe Aries, *Western Attitudes Toward Death: From the Middle Ages to the Present,* trans. P. M. Ranum (New York: Knopf, 1974), and *The Hour of Our Death,* trans. H. Weaver (New York: Knopf, 1981).

2. Elisabeth Kübler-Ross, *Death: The Final Stage* (Englewood Cliffs, NJ: Prentice Hall, 1975), 7–11.

3. Sherwin Nuland, *How We Die: Reflections on Life's Final Chapter* (New York: Vintage Books, 1993), 223, 248, 255.

4. David Chidester, *Patterns of Transcendence: Religion, Death, and Dying* (Belmont, CA: Wadsworth, 1990), 280.

5. Charles A. Corr, Clyde M. Nabe, and Donna M. Corr, *Death and Dying, Life & Living,* 2nd ed. (Pacific Grove, CA: Brooks/Cole, 1997), 45.

6. Ibid., 86–89.

7. Ibid., 89–92.

8. Robert Bellah, *Habits of the Heart: Individualism and Commitment in American Life* (Berkeley: University of California Press, 1985), 71–75; and Thomas Dumm, "The New Enclosures: Racism in the Normalized Community," in R. Gooding-Williams, ed., *Reading Rodney King, Reading Urban Uprising* (New York: Routledge, 1993), 189.

9. Stephen N. Haymes, *Race, Culture, and the City: A Pedagogy for Black Urban Struggle* (Albany: State University of New York Press, 1995), 5.

10. Sherry Parker, "Making a Case for Personal Social Security Accounts," *Self-Employed America,* November–December 1999, 15.

11. Jack H. Geiger, "Race and Health Care—An American Dilemma?" *The New England Journal of Medicine* 335, no. 11: 815–816.

12. Cited in a talk given by Joe Feagin, entitled "Racism and the Coming White Minority," on April 20, 2000, at Wayne State University, Detroit; see Joe Feagin, *Racist America* (New York: Routledge, 2000).

13. Noam Chomsky, "Containing the Crisis at Home and Abroad," transcript of talk given at Loyola University, Chicago, October 18, 1994, made available through Alternative Radio, Boulder, Colorado, 6; Carl Rowan, *The Coming Race War in America: A Wake-up Call* (Boston: Little, Brown, 1996), 193–199; Eric Schlosser, "The Prison Industrial Complex," *Atlantic Monthly,* December 1998, 51–79. Mark Taylor addresses the prison system in his chapter.

14. James Baldwin, *The Fire Next Time* (New York: Dial Press, 1963), 106.

15. G. W. F. Hegel, *Phenomenology of Spirit,* trans. A. V. Miller (Oxford: Clarendon Press, 1977), 117–119.

16. Gloria Albrecht, *The Character of Our Communities: Toward an Ethic of Liberation for the Church* (Nashville: Abingdon Press, 1995), 113.

17. Larry Rasmussen, *Earth Community, Earth Ethics* (Maryknoll, NY: Orbis Books, 1996), 120–121.

18. Michael Hudson, *Merchants of Misery: How Corporate America Profits from Poverty* (Monroe, ME: Common Courage Press, 1996), 1–6; Mark Zepezauer and Arthur Naiman, *Take the Rich Off Welfare* (Tucson: Odonian Press, 1996), 6–13.

19. Richard Dyer, "White," *Screen* 29, no. 4: 44; Thomas Kochmann, *Black and White Styles in Conflict* (Chicago: University of Chicago Press, 1981), 16–42; Cheryl Harris, "Whiteness as Property," *Harvard Law Review* 108, no. 6: 1.

20. David Roediger, *The Wages of Whiteness: Race and the Making of the American Working Class* (London and New York: Verso, 1991), 12.

21. Charles Long, *Significations: Signs, Symbols, and Images in the Interpretation of Religion* (Philadelphia: Fortress Press, 1986), 133–157; Edward Bruce Bynum, *The African Unconscious: Roots of Ancient Mysticism and Modern Psychology* (New York: Teachers College Press, 1999), xxiii, 79; Mikhail Bakhtin, *Rabelais and His World,* trans. H. Iswolsky (Bloomington: Indiana University Press, 1984), 27, 29, 32–33, 53.

22. I am especially indebted here to the work of anthropologist Nahum Chandler both in *Callaloo* and in personal discussion. Nahum Chandler, "The Economy of Desedimentation: W. E. B. Du Bois and the Discourses of the Negro," *Callaloo* 19, no. 1: 88.

23. Long, *Significations,* 7.

24. Ibid., 163.

25. Ibid., 123.

26. Ibid., 167.

27. Ibid., 137, 169.

28. Paul Gilroy, *The Black Atlantic: Modernity and Double Consciousness* (Cambridge, MA: Harvard University Press, 1993), 37, 55.

29. Toni Morrison, "Unspeakable Things Unspoken," *Michigan Quarterly Review* 28, no. 1: 1.

30. Franz Fanon, *The Wretched of the Earth,* trans. Constance Farrington (New York: Grove Press, 1963), 216–222.

31. Hegel, *Phenomenology of Spirit,* 117–119; Nelson George, *Hip Hop America* (New York: Penguin Books, 1998), 184–188.

32. James Cone, *Martin and Malcolm and America: A Dream or a Nightmare* (Maryknoll, NY: Orbis Books, 1991), 99, 223, 292.

33. Fanon, *The Wretched,* 219–221.

34. Tricia Rose, *Black Noise: Rap Music and Black Culture in Contemporary America* (Hanover, NH: Wesleyan University Press, published by University Press of New England, 1994), 141.

35. George, *Hip Hop America,* 199.

36. Long, *Significations,* 116.

37. Ibid., 169; Gilroy, *Black Atlantic,* 102; Rose, *Black Noise,* 61.

38. Rose, *Black Noise,* 48.

39. Bellah, *Habits of the Heart,* xiv.

40. Nelson George characterizes hip-hop as a "society-altering collision" over the last two decades "between black youth culture and the mass media (George, *Hip Hop America,* ix). Underneath the crossover is conflict, below the level of the video is a "loud, scratchy, in-your-face aesthetic that, to this day, still informs the culture" (xi). At one point George notes its effect as that of "a deadly virus" (xi).

41. "It is essential to understand that the values that underpin so much hip-hop—materialism, brand consciousness, gun iconography, anti-intellectualism—are very much by-products of the larger American culture. Despite the 'dangerous' edge of so much hip-hop culture, all of its most disturbing themes are rooted in this country's dysfunctional values. Anti-Semitism, racism, violence, and sexism are hardly unique to rap stars but are the most sinister aspects of the national character" (George, *Hip Hop America,* xiii).

42. Jon Michael Spencer, *The Rhythms of Black Folk: Race, Religion, and Pan-Africanism* (Trenton, NJ: Africa World Press, 1995), 5, 136, 144.

43. Ibid., 136, 142, 145, 149; Fanon, *Wretched,* 52–57, 147.

44. Spencer, *Rhythms,* 165, 173; Rose, *Black Noise,* 75.

45. Spencer, *Rhythms,* 143–144.

46. Ibid., 145–146; Fanon, *Wretched,* 203, 220, 241, 291.

47. Spencer, 145.

48. Ibid., 149.

49. Ibid., 169–171.

50. Houston Baker, "Scene . . . Not Heard," in R. Gooding-Williams, ed., *Reading Rodney King, Reading Urban Uprising* (New York: Routledge, 1993), 45.

51. George, *Hip Hop America,* 143.

52. Berendt, *The Character of Our Communities,* 14–19.

53. George speaks of DJs in Jamaica giving "back-a-yard" parties where "the bass and drum pounded like jackhammers" in a dub style that "stripped away melody to give reggae's deep, dark grooves throbbing prominence" (George, *Hip Hop America,* 6). In rap, the "massive rumbling" of this "subterranean assault" is combined with disco's "magic art of mixing" and DJ "toasting" to form the unique synergy of hip-hop. Later hip-hop was reinvented in the image of the video, transliterating the underground vitality of beats and rhymes into the visual culture of TV and cinema.

54. Mircea Eliade, *Shamanism: Archaic Techniques of Ecstasy,* trans. Willard R. Trask (Princeton, NJ: Princeton University Press, 1964), xiv, 243, 259, 355.

55. Victor Anderson, *Beyond Ontological Blackness: An Essay on African American Religious and Cultural Criticism* (New York: Continuum, 1995), 129, 139.

56. Robert Farris Thompson, *Flash of the Spirit: African and Afro-American Art and Philosophy* (New York: Vintage Books, 1983), xiii–xvii.

57. Eliade, *Shamanism,* 6, 34, 89, 314, 376.

58. George, *Hip Hop America,* 49.

59. Ibid.

60. Ibid., 51.

61. Spencer, *Rhythms,* 143.

62. Kristin Hunter Lattany, "Off-timing": Stepping to the Different Drummer," in Gerald Early, ed., *Lure and Loathing: Essays on Race, Identity, and the Ambivalence of Assimilation* (New York: Penguin Books, 1993), 164.

63. The phrasing in these last three sentences is beholden to bell hooks's aphorism for the systemic reality defining the context of struggle as "white supremacist capitalist patriarchy." bell hooks, *Black Looks: Race and Representation* (Boston: South End Press, 1992), 153.

64. George, *Hip Hop America,* xiii–xiv.

65. Ibid., 11.

7

The Spirit Is Willing and So Is the Flesh

The Queen in Hip-Hop Culture

Leola A. Johnson

In this chapter, I build on the work of a new group of black feminist critics who look at hip-hop culture as a site of feminist struggle. These women, many of whom are young, have refused to follow an earlier generation of black feminists in denouncing hip-hop as a space of patriarchal domination.[1] These new young critics view the denunciations as too simplistic. They argue that hip-hop can also be seen as a place where black women oppose and take power away from men. One result of this new school of black feminist thought has been a growing body of literature that identifies the transgressive and oppositional elements of hip-hop's major female types, namely "The Bitch" and "The Ho." These types also dominate U.S. cultural discourse about Black women outside of hip-hop. In many ways, the "Matriarch" and the "Jezebel" of the nineteenth and twentieth centuries are just older versions of today's Bitches and Hos.[2]

Here, I look at a third type that is common in hip-hop representations as well, but one that gets much less attention than the other two. The Queen, like the Bitch and the Ho, has been a remarkably stable type through the years. Latifah, one of the most successful women in hip-hop, embodies the type of the Queen today, but she has followed in the footsteps of Aretha Franklin, the Queen of Soul; Dinah Washington, the Queen of the Blues; Bessie Smith, the Empress of the Blues; Marie Laveau, the Voodoo Queen of New Orleans; and a host of other Queens, Empresses, and Ladies who have reigned over black popular culture. What I hope to demonstrate in the pages that follow is that these black Queens, all "aristocrats of the street," have been celebrated in black culture largely because they would not abide by the strictures of hegemonic masculinity. I will show that the Queens have always been women who defied political, spiritual, sexual, and economic conventions associated with white capitalist male supremacy.

I begin with a discussion of Marie Laveau, the Voodoo Queen of New Orleans, who was an important symbol of opposition and transgression throughout the nineteenth century, largely because she refused to adhere to Eurocentric Christian ideas about spirituality and sexuality. I next talk about Bessie Smith, the Empress of the Blues, who is especially interesting as an icon of lesbian culture, but who also occupies an important place in antiracist and working-class discourses. I end with a discussion of Latifah, the Queen of hip-hop, an important contemporary symbol of transgressive sexuality and oppositional gender politics, although her symbolic importance is interestingly contained within the corporate practice of branding.

This discussion of the ways in which black Queens are constructed within culture—in texts ranging from news stories to poems—supports the argument that new black feminists are currently making about Bitches and Hos, namely that black popular music is not just a space of hegemonic masculinity.

What Black Women's Bodies Signify

Rana Emerson's work on black women's hip-hop videos, especially her study of the oppositional and transgressive elements of fifty-six music videos that featured women performers, exemplifies the new style in black feminist criticism. While all the videos privileged the male gaze in some way, most by focusing on the bodies of female performers, some also objectified men and made them the objects of the female gaze. And while all the videos were Eurocentric, in the sense that they privileged thin, light-skinned bodies, they also featured some large-bodied women as objects of the male gaze.[3]

The most clearly hegemonic aspects of the videos were their refusals to interrogate lesbian and bisexual themes, except in the case of Me'Shell Ndgeocello. In all other videos, women were constructed as sexually available only to men. Many treated women not only as the objects of the male gaze, the source of male visual pleasure, but also as the products of male sponsorship. Several included the male producers of the music more prominently than the female performers. On the other hand, many of these videos represented black women as active, vocal, and independent and as part of sisterhoods, partnerships, and collaborations. Videos that featured black female performers against a background of black female dancers illustrate some of the complexities of female representation in hip-hop culture. In these videos, the performers were represented as autonomous and willful, but the dancers were represented as sexual objects.[4]

Suzanne Bost points to this same sort of complexity in DaBrat's use of the Bitch and the Ho types.[5] Bost argues that DaBrat fuses the Bitch-Ho types, but only in order to subvert and critique them. On some of her album covers she is a Gangsta Bitch, adorned in oversized clothing and wielding guns, but on others she is portrayed as a Ho. Her most popular songs are Bitch and Ho narratives, but they are not just stories of victimization. DaBrat's Bitches and Hos are women in charge: Based on a close reading of the lyrics to "Unrestricted," a Ho story from DaBrat's year 2000 album, *Running Out of Time,* Bost argues that DaBrat "couples 'ho' with 'ferocious,' coding whore as gangster, giving the woman control over her own sexuality. She is her own pimp and her own protector."[6] DaBrat's postmodern practice of "subversion from within dominant modes of racialized and sexualized containment" mirrors the work of three black feminist performance artists. Sarah Jones, Ursula Rucker, and Dana Bryant perform the roles of Bitches and Hos in order to subvert those identities from within, by investing them with subjectivity, agency, and autonomy.

From DaBrat to Bryant, these women produce representations that affirm a black woman's power to control her own body in ways that not only challenge patriarchy, but also homophobia. In new black feminist criticism, the Ho and the Bitch are no longer products of the patriarchal, homophobic, Puritanical imagination, they are also embodiments of liberatory ideas about gender, sexuality, and spirituality. It is my argument that the Queen fits into this new black feminist framework; the Queens of black popular performance have long embodied transgressive and oppositional sexual and spiritual possibilities.

A Brief Note on Method

In this chapter I focus on representation and make no claims about the "real" Marie Laveau, Bessie Smith, Queen Latifah, or about any of the other Queens, Ladies, and Empresses of black popular culture. In this respect, my approach is similar to Farah Griffin's in *If You Can't Be Free, Be a Mystery,* a book-length study of the mythology surrounding Billie Holiday's life. Griffin's aim was to liberate Holiday from the tragic songstress narrative that had been disseminated by biographers, newspaper writers, and filmmakers. Griffin writes that she is "interested in the myths that surround Holiday. I think they continue to hold a great deal of interest and importance because of what they reveal about their creators and the audiences who consume them."[7] Like Griffin, I am interested in representations of the Black Queens more than in the Queens themselves because of what these representations reveal about their creators and consumers. I therefore base my discussion on representations of Black Queens, specifically newspaper articles, plays, poems, biographies, songs, and other cultural texts about Marie Laveau, Bessie Smith, and Dana Owens.

Marie Laveau: The Voodoo Queen

Marie Laveau generated a great deal of attention during her own time, the nineteenth century, and has also attracted a great deal of attention during ours. In New Orleans, where she and her heirs reigned as Voodoo Queens for more than a century, she was often mentioned in the newspapers and was widely known among whites as well as blacks.[8] Stories about her circulated nationally during the 1920s and 1930s, when WPA writers and academic ethnographers began collecting oral histories about black life in New Orleans. These writers treated Laveau as an important figure in the southern black religious experience because she ruled over an African religious practice popularly known as "voodoo." Her eighty-year reign over voodoo in New Orleans is still generating attention. Her tomb, which is near Homer Plessy's in St. Louis Cemetery 1, is New Orleans' most popular tourist attraction. An entire local industry is organized around producing Marie Laveau artifacts for tourists, and she is the subject of numerous local books and pamphlets. In 1993, St. Martin's Press published *Voodoo Dreams* by Jewell Parker Rhodes, a romance novel about Laveau's struggle with a powerful voodoo priest. This gave Laveau's story national exposure once again. All of these stories emphasize Laveau's spiritual gifts, her beauty, and her independence.

These stories have been remarkably stable across genres as well as authors. For example, the novel *Voodoo Dreams* essentially tells the same stories as the ethnographic *Voodoo in New Orleans*. Both these tales, as well as the stories Zora Neale Hurston collected in her travels through the South and the Caribbean, strongly emphasize Laveau's connections to West Africa.

Robert Tallant claims that many of her religious practices, especially her snake handling, originated in the area of West Africa that included Nigeria and Benin, and that she was actually a priestess as much as a Queen.

> It is said that the first gathering place of the Voodoos in New Orleans was an abandoned brickyard in Dumaine Street, where they met late at night for their dances and orgies. But the police soon drove them from this place, and it was then that they began to hold forth along Bayou St. John and along the shore of Lake Pontchartrain. Here the king and queen took their places. Here the bonfires blazed and the drums took up their beat. Here were the snake and the sacrifice and the bowl of blood. There are many versions of these ceremonies. In the original African rite the priestess lifted the snake from the box—it was a python, according to tradition—and allowed it to lick her cheek. From this touch she received vision and power and became an oracle. (According to a Dahomeyan legend the first man and woman came into the world blind and it was the serpent who bestowed sight upon the human race.)[9]

Lake Pontchartrain was the location of Laveau's most important public performance, the annual St. John's Eve festivities, about which many of Tallant's informants recounted truly spectacular tales. There is some debate among them about whether this festival was merely a party (and a money-making event) or a religious ceremony, but it was apparently one of black and white New Orleans' most well attended annual events. Whether the gathering was ultimately religious or secular, it was immersed in the visible symbols of a form of voodoo inflected by Catholicism. It was syncretic religious practice of the sort common throughout the African diaspora.[10]

In addition to linking Laveau with the African religious past, however, these tales also linked her to the capitalist present. Many of the stories that Tallant circulates are about Laveau's power as a businesswoman. She is said to have made money as a counselor, a healer, and a Madame, and also to have blackmailed members of the slave aristocracy with information gathered from a network of spying house servants. *Voodoo Dreams* adds to this tale by suggesting that Laveau used her position as a beautician to collect negative information about the planter class, which she used to her economic advantage. She was also known as a Madame who arranged liaisons between light-skinned girls and white men. This made her one of the most economically powerful black women of her day.

According to many witnesses, all of the Laveau women were the objects of sexual desire among black and white men alike. All were described as possessing light skin and long hair, two highly desirable traits, and were said to have the power and skill to possess any man they wanted. *Voodoo Dreams* tells their story with a Second Wave feminist flavor. Rhodes's Laveau is a freedom fighter committed to overthrowing the voodoo patriarchy, personified by Dr. John, the evil voodoo priest. Many of these stories are reproduced in the tours that are organized around her gravesite. In all of them, Laveau is represented as a woman possessed of extraordinary spirit, power, and will, attributes these stories share with those about Bessie Smith and other Queens of black popular culture. What's more, according to feminist jazz historian Sally Placksin, Bessie Smith and other Blues Queens may have taken their style from the "real" Marie Laveau and the other Voodoo Queens:

> Free women of color, glamorous and haughty show women, shrewd and clever business women, the queens began to accrue power in the early nineteenth century, after the Louisiana Purchase (1803) eased the formerly strict rulings against voodoo in New Orleans After 1817, New Orleans' Place Congo (or Congo Square) was the site where the most public voodoo ceremonies took place. On Sunday afternoons, slaves would gather to chant and to dance the tamer dances that represented six African tribes . . . Sidney Bechet had grown up hearing about the music played at Congo Square.[11]

The Blues Queens

The Queens who ruled the blues world of the 1920s have generated stories that have circulated through all the arts and through literature, and that are meaningful across boundaries of race, sexuality, and class. Stories about Bessie Smith, the Empress of the Blues, for example, have been used to affirmatively represent transgressive sexuality, antiracist politics, and feminism,[12] and Smith has been the subject of biographies, poems, and plays. These stories about Smith emphasize her power as an artist, although many also portray her as a victim of racism, sexism, and homophobia. For example, *Bessie Smith*, a 1997 biography/poem/celebration by the Afro-Scottish poet Jackie Kay, is filled with stories about the power of Bessie Smith's personality.

It represents Smith as so physically (at 6 feet tall and 200 pounds), sexually, and emotionally overwhelming that she dwarfed everyone around her. It tells stories about her refusal to follow other people's rules, about her many improprieties around members of Polite Society, and about her stopping a recording session with W. C. Handy, whom she considered a stiff, by saying she needed a moment to spit. Another story relates her knocking Carl Van Vechten's dainty and pretentious wife to the floor at the end of a high-society gathering.

Smith is also portrayed as charismatic. Kay, quoting Ruby Walker, Smith's longtime traveling companion and her abusive husband's niece, constructs the following picture of Smith's personality: "Bessie was a queen. I mean, the people looked up to her and worshipped her like she was a queen. You know, she would walk into a room or out on a stage and people couldn't help but notice her—she was that kind of woman, a strong, beautiful woman with a personality as big as a house."[13] Part of her royal presence, according to Kay, was her performance style, which owed more to the flamboyance of the Voodoo Queens than to the peasant style of the male blues stars:

> These old bluesmen are considered the genuine article while the women are fancy dress. The poorer the bluesman looks on that run-down porch, the more authentic his blues. The image of the blueswomen is the exact opposite of the bluesmen. There they are in all their splendour and finery, their feathers and ostrich plumes and pearls, theatrical smiles, theatrical shawls, dressed up to the nines and singing about the jailhouse. The blueswomen are never seen wearing white vests or poor dresses, sitting on a porch in some small Southern town. No, they are right out there on that big stage, prima donnas, their get-up more lavish than a transvestite's, barrelhousing, shouting, strutting their stuff. They are all theater. This combination of theatre and truth is at the heart of the blueswomen. They might be dressed up as divas, queens and empresses, but they are still telling it like it is.[14]

Kay also tells a number of stories about Smith's refusal to adhere to patriarchal, heterosexist, middle-class conventions, many of which came from another secondary source, and especially from the biography by Danish jazz critic Chris Albertson.[15] Albertson, in turn, got most of his stories from Ruby Walker. Kay talks about Smith's many and varied sexual and emotional relationships with men and women. She suggests that Smith was hedonistic, not only sexually, but in other ways as well. Kay even claims that Smith patronized "buffet parties," or sexual variety shows. Clearly, part of what has kept Smith interesting to artists and critics are the details of her private life.

Smith's position as a preacher's daughter who sang the blues, which had been termed the devil's music, has also been the subject of many stories. Her life in blues violated prevailing religious doctrines, as Angela Davis and others point out, yet Smith stayed engaged in black religion and spirituality throughout her life. Davis and others have pointed to Smith's periodic visits to churches while on tour, as well as her use of church-based performance styles, as evidence for her continuing connection to conventional black religion. But Davis also argues that Smith refused to accept the conventional separation of religion and the blues. "One of Bessie Smith's own compositions philosophically juxtaposes the spirit of religion and the spirit of the blues, and contests the idea of the incontrovertible separateness of these two spheres," Davis writes. To demonstrate this juxtaposition, Davis cites the following passage from "Preachin' the Blues," which Smith wrote in 1927: "Preach them blues, sing them blues, they certainly sound good to me. Moan them blues, holler them blues, let me convert your soul."[16]

Davis argues that these lines "turn the blues into a spiritual discourse about love . . . (revealing) an interesting affinity with West African philosophical affirmations of the connectedness of spiritual and sexual joy."[17] Another important story that circulated about Smith is that she played a pioneering role in the music industry. Although her career began on the street corners of Chattanooga, and in tent shows and on the vaudeville circuit, she signed with Columbia in 1923 and became the first African American ever to have a long-term contract with a white-owned record company. Over the next eight years, she recorded 160 songs for Columbia, helping it to become an industry leader. Her first record, *Downhearted Blues,* sold 780,000 copies in six months. She made a great deal of money for a black woman of her time and was able to support a large entourage that included her family, chorus girls, and musicians. After her recording career took off, she purchased a Pullman car for touring, painted it bright green, and furnished it with bedrooms, a kitchen, and a sitting room. The train car allowed her to tour through the South with decent accommodations, but it also gave her a traveling stage from which she could reach out to the southern black audiences that had originally made her the Empress of the Blues.

Kay and Davis are among the many writers who have been especially interested in the way Smith drew her power from the black working class, and Kay remarks on some of the ironies in Smith's role as the Empress of working-class life:

> All things are possible: the poor girl from Chattanooga can put on a silk gown and transform herself into an Empress; she can wear a lampshade-fringe-crown. There is a perception, on the one hand, of the blues as lowlife (the view of middle-class jazz fans and critics) and on the other hand, the blues as high-life, royalty (classic blues singers and their fans). This combination can't be bettered; the result is a black working-class Queen. No ordinary Queen who has inherited somebody else's lineage quite by chance, but a diva with style, daring, panache, imagination and talent. A queen who knows how to shimmy. A Queen who can send herself up. A Queen who can holler and shout. A Queen who knows what it is all about. A Queen of Tragedy; a Queen of Bad Men; A Queen of Poverty; a Queen of the jailhouse. A Queen who understands and has been through herself everything that other ordinary people, particularly ordinary women, have been through. A Queen of the Folk. No wonder that classic Bessie Smith and the other Queens were so loved.[18]

Today, Smith, like Laveau, has become a major character in a recurring affirmative story circulating in black popular culture—the story about a black woman who is powerful, talented and self-determined, but who also operates outside the norm.

All Hail the Queens

Dana Owens, also known as Queen Latifah, has taken on the mantle of earlier generations of Queens in the sense that she is an affirmative representation of a strong black woman. She stands out in large part because she operates in a culture filled with negative representations and stereotypes, in a world filled with Bitches and Hos. In fact, writers sometimes masculinize Latifah's power, showing that she is performing identities usually reserved for men. Keiro Mayo, writing for *Vibe*, says of Latifah that "No other female in the genre had the balls to challenge male supremacy."[19] An even clearer example of this perspective on Latifah suggests that "Latifah's introduction to the world via egocentric, boastful hip hop was only right—she needed a forum that would allow her to (excuse this) grab her dick. She was as powerful as any man."[20] Based on this "introduction to the world," adulation has come Latifah's way. Concerning this, Eisa Davis, in an essay on sexism in hip-hop, states that "Latifah in all her avatars—Afrocentric, introspective, and relationship-hungry; plain old Dana; Khadijah on 'Living Single'—isn't a model that was once useful for me and then thrown out; instead she has given me a foundation of bedrock to build upon."[21]

Latifah's status owes much to her skill as a "crossover" star. Her fans include people of all races, genders, classes, sexualities, and generations. She is skillful at packaging herself in ways that appeal to her diverse constituencies. Her book, *Ladies First,* which made the *New York Times* best-seller list, is an example of her crossover success. "Queen Latifah" is now a registered trademark displayed on products ranging from albums to a television sitcom. Her story, however, is also a "black" story that locates her within discourses of race rather than emphasizing her status as a commodity. She says that she became a Queen as a way of asserting her power as a black woman, not as a marketing ploy. She says that when she first started performing, as the lone female in a hip-hop crew, she was known as the Princess of the Posse. She became a "Queen" when she became the head of her own posse, during the anti-apartheid movement, as an homage to African women, especially the Queens of ancient Africa. Latifah insists that her title has nothing to do with European royalty or the desire for status in the white world, and has everything to do with Afrocentricity:

> My mom and I revered those African women we didn't know, because they seemed to be so close to the most royal ancestors of all time. Before there was a Queen of England, there were Nefertiti and Numidia. The African queens have a unique place in world history. They are revered not only for their extraordinary beauty and power but also for their strength and for their ability to nurture and rule the continent that gave rise to the greatest civilizations of all time. These women are my foremothers. I wanted to pay homage to them. And I wanted, in my own way, to adopt their attributes. So "Queen" seemed appropriate. Queen Latifah. When I said it out loud, I felt dominant. I was proud.[22]

Her story about her choice of the name Latifah suggests that her connection to Afrocentricity is deep, beginning in her family and neighborhood:

> My cousin Sharonda had a book of Muslim names with the meaning listed next to each one. So Sharonda and I went through the book to see if we

> could find something for us. Sharonda picked Salima Wadiah for her names. Mamoud was already her last name. So she became Salima Wadiah Mamoud. Then it was my turn. I was excited, turning the pages of the book. There was Aisha. Pretty, but not me. Kareemah. Cool, but common sounding. Then I got to Latifah. Sharonda's father, my Uncle Sonny, was a Muslim. He had a younger sister whose name was Latifah. I thought that name was beautiful. I loved the way it sounded, how it just rolled off my tongue. So I was already feeling that name, but when I read what it meant, I knew that was me. Latifah: "Delicate, sensitive, kind." Yeah, that was me. For me, Latifah was freedom. I loved the name my parents gave me. Dana Elaine Owens. But I knew then that something as simple as picking a new name for myself would be my first act of defining who I was—for myself and for the world. Dana was a daughter. Dana was a sister. Dana was a student, friend, girl in the 'hood. But Latifah was someone else. She would belong only to me. It was more than a persona. Becoming Latifah would give me the autonomy to be what I chose to be—without being influenced by anyone else's expectations of what a young girl from Newark is supposed to be. Or what she is supposed to do. Or what she is supposed to want.[23]

Latifah's style of dress was initially Afrocentric as well. Her first album features her standing upright and proud in clothing—pants, shirt, and crown—made from South African cloth. Another famous early image captures her crouching barefoot, looking up at the camera, also in African garb.

Not only does Latifah locate her story within a discourse of Afrocentricity, but she also locates it within a discourse of transgressive sexuality. Ever since she played Cleo, a lesbian character, in F. Gary Gray's 1996 film *Set It Off*, Latifah has been constantly asked about her own sexuality, and she has constantly refused either to affirm or deny the speculation that she is a lesbian.[24] In *Ladies First*, Latifah points out that she is not the only female in hip-hop to be enmeshed in rumors of lesbianism, and suggested that this was just the way sexist men dismissed powerful women. On the other hand, Latifah seems to welcome her following within the gay and lesbian communities. She was one of the featured artists, for example, at the 1999 concert, Equality Rocks, a benefit for gay and lesbian rights.[25]

Latifah's story, like Smith's, also has a location within feminist discourse as a story about a black woman opposed to patriarchy, but Latifah occupies this space by her own choice. She refuses to call herself a feminist, but her book is filled with feminist arguments about body image, self-esteem, identity, and independence. Furthermore, her first (and only) successful album, *All Hail the Queen,* is the anthem of hip-hop feminism and the most popular critique of sexism ever in the hip-hop generation. *Vibe,* for example, called "Ladies First," *All Hail's* most successful single, "straight-up revolutionary." This is because "Ladies First was the trigger finger firing off the first round of discussions about what was happening to the other half of the hip hop nation and how we actually saw our own world." And, in spite of the fact that it was cowritten by the person who also wrote the offensive "classic" of rap "Gangsta Bitch," "it ["Ladies First"] was the first song to openly address sexism in hip hop. It would not be the last."[26]

Nevertheless, Latifah (and other black women in hip-hop) refuse to associate themselves explicitly with feminism, especially of the Second Wave, because it is considered too white, too middle class, and too hostile to black men. Some writers locate Latifah's story in "Third Wave" feminism, as representing a race-conscious, sexually open feminism that rejects Second Wave white feminist elitism and racism, and also black sexism and homophobia. "When I discovered the Jungle Brothers, Queen Latifah and De La Soul shortly afterward, I realized that there was an alternative to gangsta rap," wrote Jeff Niesel, "these artists served much the same purpose as alternative rock had done in the mid-1980s—by blurring the boundaries between male and female and between black and white, they suggested that for political activism to be truly successful, coalitions must be built across the lines that divide people according to race, gender and class." Niesel continues by arguing that "for 'alternative' rappers, rap music had the most potential of any music to inspire social change, and, unlike gangsta rappers who separated racism and poverty from sexism, alternative rappers explicitly included women, demonstrating that for their work to be considered effectively political, race activists need to include rather than exclude feminists."[27]

Although Latifah's story crosses lines of race, gender, and sexuality, its most pervasive and stable quality is its focus on Latifah as a really good businesswoman. According to Latifah, "Too many contemporary female rap artists (and quite a few of their male counterparts) appear content to bask in the reflected shine of highend European fashion designers," but she is more concerned with promoting her own name, and she is committed to making certain "the QL logo with the crown will be there in the corner of your television screen for as long as her nationally syndicated talk show remains on the air."[28] Being a good businesswoman seems always to have been part of being a Queen, although Latifah seems to have taken it to new heights, as befits a Black Queen who must adopt her act to the dictates of the modern culture industries. In many ways, Latifah is like Laveau and Smith, but I cannot imagine these older Queens as commodities with the kind of crossover appeal Latifah has enjoyed.

The Spirit Is Willing and So Is The Flesh

The stories that are being passed on about Leveau, Smith, and Latifah share a number of common themes. They construct these Queens as complicated and powerful, not one-dimensional and tragic. They describe them as physically, intellectually, and emotionally larger than life, and at the same time, ordinary and plain. Smith is said to have been a very generous friend, but a really horrible employer who often left bands stranded on the road. Latifah, who is seen as a role model for young women, was once arrested for marijuana and gun possession. Laveau, who is celebrated for her ability to bend slaveholders to her will, is also said to have served them as a Madame. Nevertheless, what stands out about these stories, especially in relation to other possibilities, such as the stories of Hos and Bitches, is that all of the Queens are portrayed as being, relatively speaking, sexually, spiritually, intellectually, and materially in control of their own lives.

The stories emphasize these women's refusal to conform to racist, heterosexist, or patriarchal assumptions. This image is in contrast to stories about Bitches and Hos, who, no matter how cleverly they have been appropriated by black artists, were originally racist and sexist representations. The Black Queen is an affirmative representation who stands proudly outside of the mainstream. That is why Queens are so easily appropriated as icons of feminist and gay and lesbian culture, as well as symbols of black culture, all of which operate on the margins of sexist, heterosexist, and racist norms. Understanding the Queen thus requires a critical model that centers cultural categories that are typically marginalized.

Critics who work at the intersection of gay, feminist, race, and religious studies have developed models for identifying and analyzing affirmative representations, even when they fall outside the norms of heterosexual, patriarchal, Eurocentric norms. E. Patrick Johnson's essay on Aretha Franklin's song "Spirit in the Dark," for example, suggests that we look to performance studies for a way to affirmatively understand bodies that refuse to be confined by normative categories of identity. Johnson describes a scene he witnessed in a black gay night club where men dance to gospel music as the DJ testifies. What this scene represents is the fusion of body and soul, spirit and flesh, and also a "politic born out of necessity."[29] Furthermore:

> The "politic born out of necessity" is that of sexual expression and affirmation, the conjoining of the physical realities of being black and gay with those of being Christian. The performance "space" of the night club makes this union possible. Indeed, this performance environment . . . [allowed] us to experience our subjectivity in unusual ways as we celebrated our spirituality and our sexuality by publicly displaying our eroticized black gay bodies. As spectators of eroticized gay bodies that are simultaneously Christian bodies, black gay men in the night club space both witness and become witnesses for the union of body and flesh. In turn, this witnessing forges a sense of community and belonging among the night club patrons—a sense of community denied them in the performance "place" of the black church.[30]

The stories that are told about Laveau, Smith, and Latifah also speak to a politics born of necessity, namely, the necessity of finding a space for strong, sexually, and spiritually unconventional black women who are neither Jezebels nor Mammies, neither Bitches nor Hos. Black feminists who study hip-hop should look to the artists, novelists, playwrights, and poets who have circulated the stories of Black Queens. The identities associated with Voodoo Queens and Blues Women are also present among women in hip-hop culture, and it is time that the exciting new critical work on women in rap paid more attention to its Queens.

NOTES

1. See Kimberlé Williams Crenshaw, "Beyond Racism and Misogyny: Black Feminism and 2 Live Crew," *Boston Review* 16 (6) (December): 30, for an example of criticism that denounces hip hop's sexual representations as pure misogyny. Crenshaw famously wrote in that piece that "those of us who are concerned about the high rates of gender violence in our communities must be troubled by the possible connections between such images and violence against women. Children and teenagers are listening to this music, and I am concerned that the range of acceptable behavior is being broadened by the constant propagation of antiwoman imagery. I'm concerned, too, about young Black women who together with men are learning that their value lies between their legs. Unlike that of men, however, women's sexual value is portrayed as a depletable commodity: By expending it, girls become whores and boys become men" (p. 30). To be sure, Crenshaw's

analysis was in response to Gates's well-known intervention in the case of 2 Live Crew, in which he argued that the lyrics of that group merely reflected a standard form of cultural signifying that was not to be taken literally. See Henry Louis Gates, Jr., *The Signifying Monkey* (New York: Oxford University Press, 1988), 11–12.

2. For a general discussion of these types, see Patricia Hill-Collins, *Black Feminist Thought: Knowledge, Consciousness and the Politics of Empowerment* (New York: Routledge, 1994).

3. Rana Emerson, "Where My Girls At? Negotiating Black Womanhood in Music Videos," *Gender and Society* 16, no. 1 (February 2002): 115–135. "The most striking example of this is the lack of variety in body size and weight. This was surprising, considering the conventional wisdom that the Black community possesses alternative beauty standards that allow for larger body types. Many authors have concluded that these standards contribute to a more positive body image among Black women. . . . However, the majority of the videos I coded (30) featured artists who would be considered thin by most standards, while only 9 featured performers who would be considered overweight"(p. 122).

4. Ibid., 129.

5. "Hip Hop music gets a bad rap. Far too often it seems to be about the objectification of women, but hip hop artists position themselves around this topic in very complex ways. This complexity is missed when critics ignore the relationship between the verbal, musical, and corporeal levels of hip hop performance. Even as they make a show of their bodies—giving the audience 'something to look at' as Salt 'N Pepa do—female rappers often disrupt misogynist objectification by creating dissonance between the multiple layers of their performance. This dissonance reflects both a postmodern practice of resistance—subversion from within dominant modes of racialized and sexualized containment—and a long-standing tradition in African American cultures, from slave songs and quilts with hidden meanings to linguistic games and signifying stories. Within both traditions, artistic statements circulate about more than they seem to be. It is impossible to say just what they are 'about,' as word, body, rhythm, and melody often communicate divergent messages." Suzanne Bost, "Be deceived if ya wanna be foolish: Reconstructing Body, Genre, and Gender in Feminist Rap," *Postmodern Culture* 12, no. 1 (2001): 2. Posted on December 1, 2001, accessed on January 21, 2002: http://jefferson.village.virginia.edu/pmc

6. Bost, "Be Deceived," 32

7. See Farah Jasmine Griffin, *If You Can't Be Free, Be a Mystery: In Search of Billie Holiday* (New York: Free Press, 2001), xiii. Dyson also follows this method in his study of Malcolm X.

8. As Tallant points out, Marie Leveau, as described by his informants, was actually a whole family of women—grandmother, mother, and daughter—all of whom were Voodoo Queens. It was the Laveau family that reigned over voodoo in

New Orleans throughout the nineteenth century. Robert Tallant, *Voodoo in New Orleans,* 6th ed. (New York: First Collier Books, 1971), 62.

9. Ibid., 96.

10. See Zora Neale Hurston, *Tell My Horse: Voodoo and Life in Haiti and Jamaica* (New York: Harper and Row, 1990).

11. Sally Placksin, *American Women in Jazz: 1900 to the Present—Their Worlds, Lives and Music* (New York: Wideview Books, 1982), 41.

12. I use the term "affirmative representation" here to avoid the detritus of the term "positive representation," with its bias toward middle-class conventionality. An affirmative representation acknowledges an identity by making it visible and fluid (capable of being both good and bad). For a discussion of the pitfalls of thinking about representations as "positive." See, e.g., Michelle Wallace, "Negative Images: Toward a Black Feminist Cultural Criticism," in Lawrence Grossberg, Cary Nelson, and Paula Treichler, eds., *Cultural Studies* (New York: Routledge, 1992).

13. Jackie Kay, *Bessie Smith* (Bath, UK: Absoulate Press, 1988), 64.

14. Ibid.

15. Chris Albertson, *Bessie* (New York: Stein and Day, 1971).

16. Angela Davis, *Blues Legacies and Black Feminism: Gertrude "Ma" Rainey, Bessie Smith, and Billie Holiday* (New York: Pantheon Books, 1998), 130.

17. Ibid.

18. Kay, *Bessie Smith,* 66.

19. Ierna Mayo, "Queen Latifah: The Last Good Witch," in *Hip Hop Divas* (New York: Vibe Books, 2001), 53.

20. Ibid., 56.

21. Eisa Davis, "Sexism and the Art of Feminist Hip Hop Maintenance," in Rebecca Walker, *To Be Real: Telling the Truth and Changing the Face of Feminism* (Anchor Books: New York, 1995), 140. See also Kierna Mayo's "Queen Latifah: The Last Good Witch," in *Hip Hop Divas* (New York: Vibe Books, 2001), 52: "I think she changed the path for women in hip hop," says her business partner of twelve years, Sha Kim Compere. "There's a lot of female rap artists, like Eve, for example, that's not taking any shorts from any male rappers, and that's always been Latifah's vision. You can't call a woman a bitch in a record without thinking about Latifah."

22. Queen Latifah (with Karen Hunter), *Ladies First: Revelations of a Strong Woman* (New York: William Morrow, 1999), 18.

23. Ibid., 17.

24. Mayo, "Queen Latifah," 59.

25. Ibid.

26. Ibid., 54.

27. Jeff Niesel, "Hip Hop Matters: Rewriting the Sexual Politics of Rap Music," in Leslie Heywood and Jennifer Drake, eds., *Third Wave Agenda: Being Feminist, Doing Feminism* (Minneapolis: University of Minnesota Press, 1997), 239.

28. Mayo, "Queen Latifah," 5.

29. "'Spirit in the Dark' is one of many songs recorded by the 'Queen of Soul,' diva, Aretha Franklin, that blurs the boundaries between the sacred and the secular—both through its lyrics and its musical composition. Fueled with the vocal melismas and rhythmic syncopation found in gospel and blues, Franklin's song uses the sacred notion of 'spirit' as a metaphor for sexual ecstasy as she sings, 'It's like Sally Walker, sitting in her saucer. That's how you do it. It ain't nothing to it. Ride, Sally ride. Put your hands on your hips and cover your eyes and move with the spirit in the dark.' While some listeners might argue that the reference to spirit in this song is symbolic of the 'holy' spirit, those of us who hear the double entendre know that Franklin's use of this word is much more fluid. Indeed, she endows Sally Walker, the innocent and chaste little girl of the famous children's nursery rhyme, with sexual agency as Franklin encourages Sally to 'ride' the spirit in the dark." E. Patrick Johnson, "Feeling the Spirit in the Dark: Expanding Notions of the Sacred in the African-American Gay Community," *Callaloo* 21, no. 2 (1998): 404.

30. Ibid.

Part III

Rap and the Art of "Theologizing"

8

The Rub

Markets, Morals, and the "Theologizing" of Popular Music

William C. Banfield

> The genius of Black people is that you ain't seen rap coming. We keep reinventing ourselves through our expressions. The reality is the different styles that young people invent are an attempt to mark their own particular environments with the style they are accustomed to. And style is an attempt to put your stamp on your existence. . . . Black people keep inventing and re-inventing, asserting and re-asserting so that we can mark our own existence through the prism of style and give some sense to the weightiness of our existence. But we should not resist the edifying character of Hip Hop Culture as a tool of aesthetic, economic and social expression for young People.
>
> —Michael Eric Dyson, June 25, 2000,
> Mount Olive Baptist Church, Ft. Lauderdale, Florida

Searching for Theological Maps within Hip-Hop Music

Reinventing of self through artistic expressions, marking existence and all the while selling records is a complex formula. There is an intricate relationship between artistic desire and goals, communal expectations, and the larger market demand.

At the opening of a segment special celebrating twenty years of hip-hop on MTV, a long list of hip-hop artists presented a litany of their beliefs and hopes for what hip-hop is: a dance, a way of talking, freedom, a form of poetry, my culture, my womb, the mothership, the voice of America.

Hip hop artists, Dr. Dre, L.L. Cool J, Missy Elliot, Ice Cube, DMX, Nellie, and P-Diddy celebrated the mostly "good and plenty" of this worldwide popular phenomenon. What is most impressive is contemporary hip-hop artists' passion and belief in the music culture itself. We have not seen this since the seventies from a group of popular musicians who speak for a whole generation. As one host put it, "No other music speaks more directly and profoundly to young people all over the world."[1]

Hip-hop culture—its music, artists, ideology, and spirit—has had a profound impact on American culture. Above the fray of the opiate popular cultural form, media hype, and Hollywood's seductive imagery machines, there is something extremely powerful and meaningful in this music, and its appeal at deeper levels is telling. Anything of depth and with meaning in culture has such power because of sustainability. It sticks. Hip-hop as a cultural form has been with us for twenty-five years strong, and counting. And, like the blues some fifty years before, hip-hop is becoming a foundation for most contemporary popular music, from rap to rock, and contemporary jazz impulses in between. Its pervasiveness and longevity constitute its influence on the cultural marketplace. Furthermore, hip-hop's links to African functionality and African sociospiritual roots constitute the framework of its moral influence.

Popular culture in its various shapes and forms is the most influential human-driven agency in contemporary society. While we wait for and anticipate the "word," the church in its various denominational incarnations hardly says anything, nor does it move toward its prophetic role. Yet Paul Tillich, in his theology of culture many years back concerned himself with the relevance of "hearing" voices from outside the walls of the institution that were relevant and worthy of our attention. Herein lies the rub between the idea of music culture being an expression of morality or of marketism.

Artists in the past have "called up" spiritual, intellectual and aesthetic powers to represent authentic and vivid examples of human need and meaning. They have reflected and projected prophetic musical musings, which have moved us to consider who we are and who we are fast becoming. The last hundred years have seen extraordinary musical/historical movements from the Jazz Age, Harlem Renaissance, Bebop, Social Protest, and Social Action of the sixties and early seventies, to hip-hop, MTV, and the Internet. How are artists in popular forms continuing in the Black Arts' prophetic vein and moving us to self-reflective listening and action? Hip-hop culture provides a viable road map showing where contemporary music culture is heading. Hip-hop, like so many of its cousin forms in black popular music, also provides a road map for certain truths that are relevant to social, cultural, and theological interest and inquiry. But given the influences of contemporary commercial markets and ideologies (i.e., the emphasis on what sells), does such moral vision make sense today? What effect will such tensions between commercial market needs and a growing necessity for a moral-conscious culture have upon the artistry of contemporary popular culture? In order to explore some historical examples of how black musical forms have maintained a balance in addressing their relationship to the market, to community, to social accountability (or what I deem morality), and to artistic integrity, I will in this chapter do the following:

1. Point to necessary links in black music—aesthetically, historically, socially/theologically.
2. View hip-hop as a historical cultural form.
3. Define a possible black music theological perspective.
4. Suggest some ways to examine black contemporary culture by providing examples that can serve as models.

Overall, in this chapter I will examine possible maps of relevant inquiry pointed out by hip-hop music (and black cultural production more generally), despite hip-hop's potential to be suffocated and pulled continually downward into vacuous marketability.

Disconnected Discourses: Theological Inquiry in Modes of Popular Music

> The Depth of Music's integration into almost all of the various aspects of African social life is an indication that music helps to provide an appropriate framework through which people may relate to each other when they pursue activities they judge to be important and common place.
>
> —Jon Miller Chernoff, *African Rhythms and African Sensibility*

> Yo Hip Hop is a way of life. It ain't a fad, it ain't a trend. Not for those of us who are true to it. It's reflected in our slang, in our walk, and our stance. In our dress and our attitude. Hip Hop has a history, origin and a set of principles. . . . It's our way to release tension, to let out frustration that young people face in the world today. . . . It has evolved to represent what is happening now,

> the reality of street life. . . . Hip Hop is the Lifestyle, the philosophy and even the religion, if I may. It will remain for some of us as the raw essence of life.
>
> —Guru, "Hip Hop as a Way of Life," *JazzMaTazz*

Rap—a release valve, cry for help, CNN for the youth—and rage are terms we do not normally include in our theological discussions. Yet each of these terms actually relates easily to the spiritual ideas of prayer, redemption, gospel, the word, and revelation. The theological quest for exploring and hearing the work of contemporary artists is both compelling and important. Sometimes seen as disconnected discourses, dialogue between theology and popular culture deserves more serious time and attention. I had a theology professor in Divinity School whose definition for theology was "anything that illuminates the people and moves them beyond." That representation stuck with me. My own definition of theology is the conscious thinking, asking, probing, and activity that circles around illumination of the human condition so that revelation and enlightenment can come. Popular culture and expression are so important and compelling because they are ways in which people explore in vibrant and innovative ways their uncompromising push for life. Hence, contemporary popular music, rap for example, is the place within the framework of black American cultural mapping where we find the makings of relevant, rich theological "matters." As an ideology and cultural movement, contemporary music in general terms and rap in particular teeter on the edges of socially defined religiosity.

Anthony Pinn, in *Why Lord? Suffering and Evil in Black Theology,* effectively argues for "a hard labor, a strong and aggressive inquiry which must have the capacity to appreciate and respond to the hard facts of African American life."[2] His nitty-gritty hermeneutics presents a deeper understanding of black religious thought and its various discussions on the matter of the problem of evil. He speaks of a "guiding criterion" as the presentation of black life, couched in "black expressivity and linguistic creativity, a concrete orientation in which the raw natural facts are of importance."[3] Any exploration of cultural activity must happen from the inside where the participants set the rules for engagement and expression of the sort Pinn describes. While I am not suggesting that hip-hop entails some kind of "church service" where spiritual anointing is sought, an idea of shared community is relevant here. That is why it is plausible for a musical artist to speak of musical movement as a womb.

The role of culture in providing places where folks find healing and explanations for direction in their lives is paramount, especially as we turn to the functionality of rap. I think this is what Tricia Rose describes as the nature and function of hip-hop music to move among the folks who yearn for revelation. She writes: "Rap music and hip-hop culture are cultural, political, and commercial forms, and for many young people they are the primary cultural and linguistic windows on the World."[4] Elsewhere she writes:

> Rap music brings together a tangle of some of the most complex social, cultural and political issues in contemporary American society. Rap's contradictory articulations are not signs of absent intellectual clarity, they are a common feature of community and popular cultural dialogues. Cultural expression that prioritizes black voices from the margins of urban America . . . they speak with the voice of personal experience, taking on the identity of the observer or narrator.[5]

In this search for purpose and meaning, a point of human inquiry and a place of human activity are contained in the music. It is at the crossroads of these two points where music, culture, social progress, morality, and market demand meet. This point is, at the core, dialectic (sacred/social) and has been present in black music performance since the spirituals morphed into the blues (Charlie Patton), and race records morphed into gospel music (Thomas Dorsey, Sister Rosetta Tharpe). When these musical forms, which embodied questions, interests, artistic explorations, and sacred/social aspirations, became marketable, tension emerged.

Early rural blues singers were itinerant preachers. This blending of song and sermon is similar to the role played by the West African griots who, through song, impart myth, wisdom, family history, insults, jokes, and artistic virtuosity. The lines are continually crossed. When the Father of the Delta blues tradition, Charlie Patton, sang about love interests and morals, he rapped and preached over his blues licks, substituting words for musical runs and runs for words ("you gon' need a lawyer when you come around . . . King Jesus is his name").

Word and Revelation

One way to gain further meaning in this cultural dialogue from a moralistic point of view is to rely upon unmediated truth, that which is not powered by human authority, petitions, or actions. Instead, this unmediated truth appears despite human attempts to "reach" God, and revelation happens whenever lives are changed. And, music plays a role in this process. The belief in oneself that artists are able to elicit from their audiences is real. The role of the artist is to speak outside of reserved places of religious languages that may foster a revelation of sorts.

One has to ask what this form of creative expression—contemporary popular and hip-hop music—tells us about the human condition that the news, a preacher, a teacher, a theology, or market demographics cannot. There is an understanding that music moves people and speaks to certain "depths" that are unreachable by our more traditional modes of rhetorical redress. Popular culture has always provided young people with platforms, and hip-hop culture provides new and related questions and concerns for the following reasons:

1. It reports on today's young black males' relentless search for identity or place.
2. It explains some of the difficulty and frustration in living in a world defined by materiality that is only achievable for a select group.
3. It explores, in an "organic" language, the complex relationships that emerge among young, disadvantaged, angry, and disillusioned citizens.
4. It considers the reality of rejection by social institutions and structures (e.g., churches and schools).

Like its cousin forms before it, contemporary musical expression such as rap identifies sore points in our social constructs. Music and the arts rely on inner subjective experiences and are the outgrowth and reflection of the musician's thinking about those realities in relation to the world. Furthermore, music creates a value system, values about what we want and hope for, about our identities, about our love relationships, about our ethnic/cultural "names." Thus, it is helpful to consider musical expressions as a metaphor for a kind of theological probing. Getting to the music may allow us to get closer to the people who are screaming or celebrating various aspects of life. The work of popular artistry is essential to spiritualizing the world. The music, the lyrics, the performance as ritual, even as a televised, video medium, become carriers of important statements regarding our being. The trick is to transpose our everyday, veiled understanding of this activity as entertainment and to see it unveiled as meaning-full. There is a kind of theologizing that is essentially decoding and interpreting the work of artistry.

Music is public expression, a ritual, a quest to find meaning in community. And while a critique can be made of motives, behavior, and suspect ritualistic manifestations, the fact remains that there is within every period of musical movement a cultural synergy laced with a significant and committed meaning. Every ten years or so, a generation of young people adopt and/or create a musical/cultural, even spiritual, identity represented through artistry. Hip-hop culture is thus connected to four hundred years of musical and cultural development.

Music artistry gives shape and voice to ideas that "everyday" people feel and have. These deeper dimensions get at a kind of spiritual or inner experience that music informs. In short, music is the language of our emotions. Spirit—our deep and inner ideas—does not live in the realm of the aggressively rational, spoken word.

White suburban parents in the late 1950s and 1960s rallied to keep white American children from listening to black American music. Their protests were ignored, especially when the industry found the music profitable, so much so that they invested in white artists to trade on the aesthetics and sensibilities of black musical expression. This, in subtle ways, points to the ability of music to reach beyond socioeconomic, political, and "racial" markers to reveal deep impulses and meanings. By reaching into the inner depths, music informs what might be understood as "secular" and "sacred" dimensions of life. One gets a sense of this crossing of boundaries from what black musicians have said: the only difference between a gospel song and an R&B song is the singer changing "Jesus" to "Baby."

Music is the "appropriate framework," as Jon Miller Chernoff has pointed out, through which identity, values, community expression, and teaching are mediated. The African saying, "The Spirit will descend with a good song," comes to mind. Thus, when the whole community is "feelin' it," when the care and concern of our worth is being realized, God(s) give blessings and descend among the people. This kind of spiritual ritual in the black public domain was evident in the civil rights period when song, as Bernice Reagon has pointed out, moved the people to righteous activity and gave them principles and a way of life that cut across various dimensions of historical reality. Some artists hold on to the spiritual and deeper dimensions no matter how diluted they are by the industry. It is near impossible to play convincing music without this deeper performance dimension. This is why people respond so passionately, in such a spiritually instinctive way, to the experience of music.

Meaning in the Marketplace: Black Music as Significant Cultural Form

In his *African Music: A Peoples Art,* Francis Bebey writes: "Music is an integral part of African life from cradle to the grave and covers the widest possible range of expression including spoken language and all manner of natural sounds."[6] "Griot" is a word used throughout West African society to designate a professional musician. Music making is at the heart of all the griot's activities. The griots' work is the culmination of long years of study and hard work under the tutelage of a teacher, and so these cultural leaders are looked upon as "the inventors of melodies, poems and rhythms and their role is essential to ceremonies, that are the combination of philosophy, mythology, technique and art."[7] Bebey notes that "the African musician is an artist who dedicates himself to the service of the community at large."[8] Hip-hop music, in terms of musical performance function, is very closely tied to the roots of all black music in the diaspora, be it Europe, the West Indies, New York, or New Orleans. The line of artistic and cultural evolution is very clear: griot, plantation fiddler, slave preacher, blues singer, preacher who sings, Last Poet (Black Arts Movement), and, finally, rapper. Even the line, "It don't mean a thing if it ain't got that swing" (Duke Ellington, 1932), is the same as, "It don't go if it ain't got that flow." African retentions are prevalent in every black style that has developed in the American public marketplace. The griot is an artist as well as an important carrier of traditions of marked significance. Hip-hop and contemporary popular artists are modern-day griots, albeit sometimes misguided.

As a market force within popular culture, rap became a big practice among youth and turned into big money for the industry. We saw this with rock and roll as well: music becomes a place for assigning an identity that is culturally defined, constructed, then packaged, marketed, and commodified. A *New York Times* writer reported

> Rap like most everything from the Blues to alternative rock before it has been officially embraced by those who originally ostracized it, avariciously consumed by those from whom it sought independence. White young people (who make up 80% of hip hop sales) are listening to and using elements of rap not for theft but because they relate to it, because the music is a legitimate part of their cultural heritage. Black and White fans are flipping back and forth between the local rock and rap radio stations, simply in search of the best song.[9]

The market sells a product that appeals to consumers, but at this point the concern and responsibility of the industry stop. It is the artist's job to provide "meaning" in the marketplace. The market is not interested in morality but marketability and materiality—selling products. It exists to provide a forum for making sellable commodities and popular artists, and their products are hugely profitable. They have struggled happily with the dilemma of creating work that sustains a core audience while making music that illuminates and moves people. In his book *Life and Def, Sex, Drugs, Money + God,* record mogul Russell Simmons addresses the tension between meaning and market forces. He says the record industry is a multipronged business that only responds to core audiences. The core audience seeks identification with a product that meets pertinent needs. Being "true" to one's core audience, he argues, is the first rule for an artist wishing to be successful.[10] Russell argues that culture is the construction of image, and that image is contained in music, film, fashion, magazines, television, comedy, and politics. He writes, "My whole career has been about cultivating understanding and expanding this core audience for hip-hop culture and watching the impact ripple out into the mainstream."[11] Hence, if one takes Russell seriously, the role of artists in the marketplace is to allow, by conscious construction, their gifts to move a core audience with joy, and to lift and even entertain.

Artists, through their musings, provide a space in which people are "moved," touched, and inspired. Rapper, hip-hop producer, and now elder cultural statesman Chuck D, in his autobiography *Fight the Power: Rap, Race and Reality,* speaks to this point. He writes, "Educating through music is what I was meant to do."[12] But there is a rampant street or market ideology that says education is knowledge of self and "keeping it real"—including the correct gear, car, and so on—is the marker of authenticity. Unfortunately, in an attempt to keep a "real" façade and appeal to market forces, the carriers of hip-hop rhetoric (*Vibe, Source,* MTV, BET) have in some ways diminished the intelligent portrayal of the art form. Too often rap is reduced to the market trappings of styling and high profiling with no serious content. Brothers "be vibin'" to the beat with a flexible neck and nothing in the head. The extremes expressed in an effort to keep it real can be deadly, as market-driven rhetoric takes on a life of its own.

The tragic deaths of Tupac and Notorious B.I.G. served as a vivid portrayal of dramatic irony and a sad reminder of how fragile life is, and how deadly the "game" can be. Two great artists and beautiful souls: lost. But, Biggie's "Juicy," as a song and video piece, is so very powerful in what it conveys. Despite its obvious immersion in a full range of material idolatry, the message that comes through to Biggie fans is that you can make a change in your life—both within and outside the complex of market forces and motivations. "Juicy" presents a world in which one plays it close to the edge, toying with the images of market materialism. Similar wrestlings with the nature of life and market forces are present in the work of Mary J. Blige's "No More Drama." Mary J. Blige, referred to as a hip-hop queen, has been described by many serious musicians and musical insiders as "Mary who is just so real," referring to her sincerity. This quality, whether a belief system or dramatized in the emotion of song performance, is the single most arresting quality of musical arts; it is where much of the hip-hop community lays its trust in terms of accepted value systems. The song-writing team of Jimmy Jam and Terry Lewis (of multimillion dollar Janet Jackson pop formulas) chose to sample appropriate portions of the theme from the TV drama, *The Young and the Restless* for Blige's song. And, Blige's video for the song focuses on Mary in a violent and physically abusive relationship. The visual underscores a young woman at the end of her wits and pushed to her limit as she declares, "No more Drama."

The power of artistry to make plain by singing the deeper realties of our existence and to illuminate thousands of individual life stories at once is the greatest gift of popular culture and song writers. The point here, in short, is that there are numerous examples of artists whose musical poetry and action provide examples of consciously spun, plotted maps for cultural/social travel. In these maps are wisdom, reality and revelation waiting to be cast. These works and workings are extremely visible symbols and performance texts that are being taken seriously by a significant segment of our society.

Our inquiries, our theological probes, our missions for morality in the market must take this public expression into account when assessing the impact and effect upon popular music and its rub with market.

Conclusions

The soul era stands out as a period in black artistry when music communicated a refusal to accept the undesirable and a determination both to illuminate despair and to create a better future. "A Change Is Gonna Come" (Sam Cooke/Otis Redding), "Wake Up Everybody" (Harold Melvin and The Blue), "Higher Ground" (Stevie Wonder), "What's Going On" (Marvin Gaye), "Yes We Can" (Pointer Sisters), "Ain't No Stopping Us Now" (McFadden and Whitehead), and "I Will Survive" (Gloria Gaynor), are titles suggesting a comfortable alignment of strong moral and community commitment and great commercial artistry. Related to the best dimensions of this soul tradition, the entire wave from the new R&B movement out of Philly with Jill Scott, The Roots, Erikah Baduh, MusicSoul Child, and others are examples of hip-hop style and old-school sentiment colliding in the marketplace. Concerning such developments, Cornel West has written that the future of our artistry may hang on the quality of the response to our contemporary social challenges depending on not just the talents, but moral visions, social analyses, and political strategies that highlight personal dignity.

Black artistry is steeped in the tradition of telling human stories for the purpose of uplifting by examining the pain and working toward wholeness. Singing and performing are just two strategies employed by creative artists to manage the madness and provide a lifted spirit in the face of the consequences of "the everyday." By doing this, as Paul Gilroy suggested, we can continue to present our lives, our arts, our communities, and our nation as living symbols of the value of self-activity.

The more positive rhetoric from hip-hop griots involves self-knowledge, speaking the truth, keeping it real, and giving a shout out to one's "peeps." These are all significant markers for meaning, performance practices with an emphasis on revelation—dislodging negativity and moving the ritual participant toward enlightenment.

NOTES

1. "MTV Celebrates 20 Years of Hip Hop," MTV, Summer 2001.
2. Anthony Pinn, *Why, Lord? Suffering and Evil in Black Theology* (New York: Continuum,1995), 116.
3. Ibid.
4. Tricia Rose, *Black Noise: Rap Music and Black Culture in Contemporary America* (Hanover, NH: Wesleyan University Press, 1994), 19.
5. Ibid., 2.
6. Francis Bebey, *African Music: A Peoples Art* (New York: Lawrence Hill Books, 1975), 17.
7. Ibid., 26.
8. Ibid., 33.
9. *New York Times,* August 22, 1999.
10. (New York: Crown, 2001), 83.
11. Ibid.
12. (New York: Delta, 1998), 5.

9

Rap, Religion, and New Realities

The Emergence of a Religious Discourse in Rap Music

Ralph C. Watkins

Rap music is experiencing an emerging religious discourse founded on the rhymes of artists who claim to speak on behalf of God. This chapter looks at a few of the archetypes and prototypes of these God-conscious rap artists and their work. They create a dialogue among the faithful who listen to, and repeat, the rhymes in their daily lives, allowing the lyrics to influence their religious worldview and how they understand God.

Tupac Shakur in many ways serves as the precursor or prototype of this genre. Rappers like Tupac are fast becoming defined as preachers/theologians by a generation who listens to them and accepts their claim that they speak for God. A subtle discussion of this phenomenon appears in Michael Dyson's book *Holler If You Hear Me*. In "But Do the Lord Care?" Dyson recalls the death of Tupac Shakur and the reaction of one pastor who responded to the cry of the Washington, D.C., community as it asked him to do something to help deal with its grief. The Reverend Willie Wilson held a memorial service for Tupac, in which he clearly recognizes the role of God-conscious rappers in the lives of their listeners. Dyson writes:

> Hip-hop artists in many instances are the preachers of their generation, preaching a message which, too often, those who have been given a charge to prophetic words to the people have not given, Wilson said in the service. "The Tupacs of the world have responded and in many instances reflected . . . Scripture that comes to mind: 'If you don't speak out, then the rocks will cry out.'" I think in a very real sense these pop artists are the rocks crying out with prophetic words. About Tupac's role in what might

> be termed a postindustrial urban prophecy, Wilson was clear: "He is their preacher, if you will, who brought a message that [young people] can identify with, related to what was real, that spoke to the reality of the circumstances, situations [and] environments they have to deal with every day."[1]

Reverend Wilson is on to something of great significance. He sees young people entering into dialogue with rappers, discussing and defining issues that have historically been associated with traditional religious institutions.

Was Tupac a preacher? Yes! Not only was Tupac a preacher, but he has motivated a plethora of rappers to follow in his footsteps. They are new thinkers and theologians who give hope and earth-based answers to those facing the absurdity of postindustrial America. The God-conscious music produced by these artists is defined by explicit referencing of God within the context of questions related to the ultimate questions of life and being. Listeners respond to the message offered by these new preachers with "amens" couched in the organic language of the streets.

Does rapper DMX see himself as a preacher? His view is made clear in his interview in *Vibe* in 2001. The interviewer asks if he will become a "real" preacher. DMX dismisses the interviewer's qualifier—"a 'real' preacher"—as it is evident in his response that he already considers himself one. "Yeah I think so," he says "in the past maybe 10 years, I've been told that. That people see me as a preacher. I believe it. The Lord didn't keep me around this long for nothing."[2]

Within rap music this new religious discourse is received and massaged by many inner-city African American youth, most of whom do not attend formal institutionalized religious services. In fact, William J. Wilson has found that fewer than 29 percent of those living in the inner city or "ghetto" claim only a tangential relationship with formal, institutional religion.[3] But the lack of a relationship with black churches or other institutionalized religion has not stopped the yearning for a religious encounter. Life raises questions that these young people seek to address in nonconformist ways: How can a just God who loves humanity allow the injustices and oppression that frame life in the ghetto? Theirs is a new theological language, lexicon, and grammar. Before moving on, it must be noted that rappers provide this theological language in their lyrics and support it visually through the appropriation of religious signs and symbols such as the crucifix in videos and compact disc art.

The Critique of Church: The Answer from the Streets

Rappers are challenging the religious hegemony of the Black Church because they perceive this institution as having failed to respond to the pain, despair, and struggles of the inner-city working poor. While social scientists and others condemn the 'hood and its lifestyle, rappers affirm it. They claim that God is in the 'hood, and God has a special way of showing love for it. In the words of Tricia Rose, "Rappers are constantly taking dominant discursive fragments and throwing them into relief, destabilizing hegemonic discourses and attempting to legitimate counter hegemonic interpretations. Rap's contestations are part of a polyvocal black cultural discourse engaged in discursive 'wars of position' within and against dominant discourses."[4]

Rappers are engaged in a culture war. They are reinterpreting, reframing, and reconstructing a social and religious worldview through lyrics and rhymes that provide an alternate ultimate orientation, to borrow a phrase from theologian Paul Tillich. In short, they are constructing a theology. Yet, this is not a traditional and systematic theology. Rather, it entails the type of theological project Anthony Pinn has in mind when saying "theology is deliberate or self-conscious human construction focused upon uncovering and exploring the meaning and structures of religious experience within the larger body of cultural production. . . . Conceived in this way, African American theology's obligation, then, is the uncovering of meaning and providing of responses to the questions of life that explain experience, assess existing symbols and categories, and allow for healthy existence."[5] In light of this definition of theology, God-conscious rappers are constructing a theological discourse in conjunction with their audience. As God-conscious rappers wrestle with the issue of human misery, they call black churches to task. For example, Michael Dyson notes "that Tupac aimed to enhance awareness of the divine, of spiritual reality, by means of challenging orthodox beliefs and traditional religious practices."[6] Rappers like Tupac are making meaning, while exploring the religious meaning of life. This is an intentional process framed by a unique, late-twentieth-century social context. Rappers of this genre claim they have been sent by God to speak to the masses in the 'hood. DMX (Dark Man X—X representing the unknown, a reach back to the Nation of Islam and Malcolm X) makes it clear in "Prayer" that God has selected him to serve as the voice of the divine for his generation.[7] DMX has included such a prayer on each of his projects. He has recently begun to include the words of his prayers on the inside covers of his compact discs.

DMX dominates the cover of the October 2001 *Vibe* magazine, and inside the issue he is the subject of an article titled "DMX: The Controversial Street Apostle Walks the Line between Heaven and Hell." In the article, DMX's relationship with the church is explored. He recounts a moment when he faced serious problems and was taken to a church by one of his friends:

> "Right before my first record came out, I was lost," he says. "I met a friend. I was on the streets, and we started walking. She looked in my eyes and said, 'Yo, what's wrong? Come with me. I want to show you something.' She brought me to a church. The pastor started talking to me, I broke down. It was then that I knew, there was something with this God thing for real. That same church, a nondenominational refuge at 407 Warburton Avenue in Yonkers, was purchased by X, who saved it from foreclosure and then gave it to the church's pastor. On every album, he includes a sermon, where he talks to God and prays for his people."[8]

DMX came to affirm that God is real, but he did not stay in or affiliate with the church.

Killah Priest's "B.I.B.L.E.," subtitled "Basic Instructions Before Leaving Earth" (on *Heavy Mental*), portrays the institutionalized church as irrelevant and duplicitous. Killah Priest claims that he went to church searching for truth but was sorely disappointed because the church took up offerings, but he never saw evidence of those funds coming back to help the community.[9] Killah Priest raps about his break from the church and contends that it is only after this break that he was able to discover Truth. God knows about the broken promises of America and the dried-up dreams of ghetto kids. His rhymes are clear, as he claims that those who struggle as they deal with crime are actually those who are blessed and loved by God. Those who are busted and locked up because they are trying to make ends meet are also blessed.[10] Killah Priest maintains that God has anointed those who go through the struggles of inner-city poverty as "Kings and Queens."[11]

A Pause for the Cause: A Word on the Process—Signs and Symbols

A key to understanding God-conscious rap and recognizing it as a new religious discourse is seeing it as a process of semiosis. "By semiosis we mean an action, an influence, which is, or involves, a cooperation of three subjects, such as a sign, its object and its interpretant."[12] The semiotic process involves religious-evolutionary construction through a constant interaction of the three: sign, symbol, and interpreter. In the case of God-conscious rap there is a circular (rather than linear) relationship in the semiotic process. In this semiotic convention there is (1) the rap music; (2) the appropriation of religious symbols and signs; and (3) the interpretants seeking meaning within the context of the social arrangements. As these three properties interact, the construction of a *socio-theo-rap-ology* and religion occurs.

The theoretical undergirding for this analysis of God-conscious rap is rooted in "sociotheological semiotics." Sociotheological semiotics contends that theological constructs are products of the social settings in which they are framed. These theological constructs have social constructive properties in the form of "sociotheo" signs and symbols. When rappers take familiar religious symbols and use them as platforms or vehicles for religious expression and then reinterpret them and re-present them with their own interpretation and meaning, they are engaging in sociotheological semiotics. They are using old religious signs and symbols as a vehicle to make new meanings by offering new interpretation of these symbols that are contextually relevant. It is in the social frame of the inner city in which these theological tenets are re-formed and re-framed.

This genre of music offers a sociotheological interpretation of the inner-city world, attempting to make sense of the seeming chaos by answering the questions that have historically been given privilege in the circles of organized and institutionalized religion. In essence, rap theology offers a religious "dogma." However, the expression of religious discourse in rap music is seen not only through the lyrics but also in its signs, symbols, and images. The lyrics as constructed in connection with the inner-city sociocultural context embody the nuances and precision of a religious frame that is situated in the specific sacred space called the 'hood.

The early years of this theological expression reflected a relative religious orthodoxy, in relation to Christianity and Islam. As the genre developed during the late 1980s and 1990s, however, the meanings and interpretations of the theological concepts changed. Rappers took familiar religious symbols like Jesus Christ, suffering, martyrdom, and the blood images of sacrifice and made them meaningful within a context where hip-hop sensibilities and aesthetics rule. When, for example, "homies" who were shot down in drive-bys were likened to Jesus Christ, saints, or martyrs of the 'hood, the imagery provided a religious orientation and focus with a hyped twist. While other modalities of religious discourse have condemned the violence of the streets, some rap music has glorified the violence. Rap music has justified retaliation and developed the defendable theological argument that those who have died at the hand of the streets were actually going to "ghetto heaven." While the notion of the gangsta's heaven as an alternate eschatology is vital, it must be noted that the first major theme in this mode of theological discourse is deity. In rap's religious discourse there appears to be an assent to a God, but this God is distinctly different from God as described in orthodox Christianity or Islam. The definition of God in rap's religious discourse has been complimented by a lexicon and template for forms of rituals, and prayer(s), methods for worship, an explanation and definition of what truth is, and how one is to know truth.

By the late 1990s, the transition from lyrics laced with religious overtones to lyrics completely dedicated to the definition of God and other religious themes had been made. Rap had effectively woven together a systematic Word about the ultimate. The rhymes represented truth, a truth that resonated with the lived experience of inner-city working-class African Americans. The genre effectively became an informed theology.

Alpha and Omega: Tracking the Beginning and Pointing toward the End

Tupac Shakur's 1991 *2Pacalypse Now*, with cuts such as "Young Black Male," "Rebel Underground," and "If My Homie Calls," deals with issues related to the idea of justified retribution with the hope of divine intervention. By 2000, rappers like Ja Rule had gone a step further, adding texture to the framework established by Tupac. Ja Rule asked a probing question: What if God were one of us? If God traded places with those who are struggling to make a life in the inner city, would God be involved in the same activities? The answer is yes. Ja Rule rejects the God presented by Christianity, while justifying the behavior of those in the 'hood by saying if God were one of us God's ethics would be 'hood ethics.

Moving beyond the theological formulations of the days of Tupac, Ja Rule "humanizes" God in a radical way. The incarnational principle as presented in Christianity is morphed into a God made fully human in the 'hood. God is not perfect, without sin. As Ja Rule puts it on his *Venni Vetti Vecci* compact disc, "He who believeth in Ja Shall not be condemned. But he that believeth not Is condemned already. Only because He has not believed."[13] Who is God? Is Ja Rule God? Has he become God? Yes, and more to the point, God is us. We are God. The incarnational principle has taken on new meaning and new dimensions. In fact, as rapper Common remarks, hip-hop might be considered one's God.[14]

Life after death, or eschatology, is a pressing question addressed within religious doctrine. In this regard, socio-theo-rap-ology attempts to make sense of both the moment and method of death as well as the afterlife. Tupac provides important information concerning this dimension of rap theology. In my talks and interviews about theology with hundreds of young African Americans in the inner city of Pittsburgh, the names of certain rappers continually surfaced. As we would talk about God, religion, and theology, someone was bound to say, "Well, you know Tupac says. . . ." An illustration of this phenomenon is neatly situated in the events, interpretations, and reaction to the death of Tupac Shakur by many of the "street theologians" I encountered in inner-city Pittsburgh, in 1996.

I preached the Sunday morning message—"A Tribute to a Soldier"—at Trinity African Methodist Episcopal Church in Pittsburgh on September 15, 1996, two days after the untimely death of Tupac Shakur. The young African Americans with whom I shared our grief before and after the message were clear on the purpose of Tupac's life, and they knew that he had gone to a place called "heaven." His life and work had an enormous impact on them, much like the impact civil rights leaders had on the lives of an earlier generation. As we discussed Tupac's music video, *I Ain't Mad at Cha*, some concluded that Tupac had prophesied his death. "Tupac," I was told, "understood us, he knew what it was like, he knew what was going down, he knew what was coming, he knew they was go' kill him." In the video, Tupac is shown being shot to death during a drive-by. The video tells the story of Tupac and his friend, to whom Tupac returns, as a type of angel, to help. Among other things, this video asserts that one does not have to be connected to a formal, institutionalized religion to get into heaven.

Is there a "heaven" for a "G"? Is there a paradise, a mansion, for a gangsta? Bone Thugs-n-Harmony, in their cut "At The Crossroads," contend that gangstas and others will meet at a place called the "crossroads," a place where life meets death. The followers of this worldview do not have to go to church or other organized, established religious institutions to negotiate their transition into the afterlife because they can access God and heaven from the streets. One can be a member of the community, live in the streets, die in the streets, embrace this new religious worldview, and secure an eternal reward.

Back to the Text: Exegeting the Lyrics

Certain principles of syncretism appear to be operative in God-conscious rap: it borrows and merges theological ideas and concepts from major religions that are then reinterpreted and reframed to form a core of beliefs. One example is a reference to a type of Jesus, but it is not the Jesus of Christianity. Tupac Shakur refers to the Jesuz of rap religion as "Black Jesuz." The first and most obvious reinterpretation of Jesus is the intentional spelling of the name with a "z" instead of an "s." In the cut "Searching for Black Jesuz," this Jesuz is a saint, but one who hurts like thugs hurt, who engages in illegal behavior as "thugs" must. Jesuz is not above them; he sins, and he does whatever it takes to survive.[15] Black Jesuz is not one to be worshiped in a building, but rather worshiped through everyday, 'hood experiences. The God of God-conscious rap has only hints of transcendence. God becomes one of us, in the words of Ja Rule. To push the humanization of God further, one cut on Common's compact disc entitled *G.O.D. ("Gaining One's Definition")* defines God as coming into a sense of self-awareness.[16] You do not need anyone to assist you in finding God, and there is no call for corporate worship or common rituals. The ritual and process of worship is as personal as the quest itself.

As those who ascribe to the principles of this religious discourse begin to structure rituals around the accompanying music, styles, rhythms, and behaviors, an ethos emerges. This discourse is meant to be repeated and lived—ritualized—in the streets, by the people. The ritual is tied to the streets (holy ground)—the birthplace of rap music. According to the rapper Witchdoctor, on "A.S.W.A.T., Healin Ritual," ritual is not something a person has to be led in by a clergy-person or shaman. Rather, one discovers and develops her or his own proscribed and repeated activities. For Witchdoctor, a ritual is something one does at home, on holy ground, and the music and lyrics of God-conscious rap are a part of the ritual.[17] Therefore, to repeat or engage in the words of socio-theo-rap is to create and engage in religious ritual. The streets of the 'hood, which have been demonized by the media, the police, and others, are transformed into a space of profound value and worth. Localizing ritual and worship in the 'hood is a primary characteristic that brings this discourse of God-conscious rap full circle: humanity—God—renewed humanity.

The religious discourse of God-conscious rap continues to evolve and address questions that have historically been reserved for more established religious institutions and doctrine. It appears that this trend will continue as rappers become even more explicit in their lyrics, unapologetically making reference to the divine and claiming connection to this source of "ghetto" life. Where will this lead? As DMX, Ja Rule, and others of this genre develop a stable of rappers underneath their tutelage, and as other major proponents of this genre work on new projects, it is reasonable to believe that God-conscious rap will become more refined and defined.

NOTES

1. Michael Eric Dyson, *Holler If You Hear Me: In Search of Tupac Shakur* (New York: Basic Civitas Books, 2001), 202.

2. Heidi Siegmund, "Gods and Monsters," *Vibe* magazine, October 2001, 96.

3. William J. Wilson, "The Ghetto Underclass," in William J. Wilson and Loic D. Wacquant, *The Cost of Racial Exclusion* (Newbury Park, CA: Sage, 1993), 41.

4. Tricia Rose, *Black Noise: Rap Music and Black Culture in Contemporary America* (Hanover, NH: Wesleyan University Press, 1994), 102.

5. Anthony B. Pinn, *Varieties of African American Religious Experiences* (Minneapolis: Fortress Press, 1998), 4.

6. Dyson, *Holler If You Hear Me*, 204.

7. Earl Simmons (aka DMX), *And Then There Was X*, Island Def Jam Music Group, 1999.

8. Siegmund, "Gods and Monsters," 96.

9. Killah Priest, *Heavy Mental*, Geffen Records, 1998.

10. Ibid.

11. Ibid.

12. Umberto Eco, *A Theory of Semiotics*, (Bloomington: Indiana University Press, 1979), 15.

13. Ja Rule, "Only Begotten Son," on *Venni Vetti Vecci*, Def Jam Music Group, 1999.

14. Common, *One Day It'll Make Sense*, Relativity Records, 1997.

15. Tupac Shakur, *2Pac + Outlawz*, Interscope Records, 1999.

16. Common, *One Day It'll Make Sense*.

17. Witchdoctor, *A.S.W.A.T. Healin' Ritual*, Interscope Records, 1998.

Selected Bibliography

Books and Articles

Albee, Edward, *The Death of Bessie Smith: A Play in Eight Scenes* (New York: Dramatist Play Service, 1959).

Albertson, Chris, *Bessie* (Stein & Day: New York, 1971).

Adler, B., and Janette Beckman, eds., *Rap: Portraits and Lyrics of a Generation of Black Rockers* (New York: St. Martin's Press, 1991).

Amnesty International, *United States of America: Rights for All* (London: Amnesty International USA, 1998).

Anderson, Victor, *Beyond Ontological Blackness: An Essay on African American Religious and Cultural Criticism* (New York: Continuum, 1995).

Appiah, Kwame Anthony, and Henry Louis Gates, eds., *Identities* (Chicago: University of Chicago Press, 1995).

Asante, Molefi K., and Mark T. Mattison, *Historical and Cultural Atlas of African-Americans* (New York: Macmillan, 1992).

Attali, Jacques, *Noise: The Political Economy of Music* (Minneapolis: University of Minnesota Press, 1985).

Austin, Allan D. *African Muslims in Antebellum America: A Sourcebook* (New York/London: Garland, 1984).

Baker, Houston A., Jr., *Black Studies, Rap, and the Academy* (Chicago: University of Chicago Press, 1993).

Baker, Houston, *Blues, Ideology and Afro-American Literature* (Chicago: University of Chicago Press, 1984).

Barboza, Steven, ed., *American Jihad: Islam after Malcolm X* (New York: Doubleday, 1993).

Barlow, William, *"Looking Up at Down": The Emergence of Blues Culture* (Philadelphia: Temple University Press, 1989).

Barrett, Leonard E., *The Rastafarians* (Boston: Beacon Press, 1997).

Barrett, Leonard E., *Soul-Force* (New York: Anchor Press, 1974).

Barth, Karl, *Theologian of Freedom,* edited by Clifford Green (Minneapolis: Fortress Press, 1991).

Bayles, Martha, *Hole in the Soul: The Loss of Beauty and Meaning in American Popular Music* (Chicago: University of Chicago Press, 1996).

Bebey, Francis, *African Music: A Peoples Art* (New York: Lawrence Hill Books, 1975).

Benitez-Rojo, Antonio, *The Repeating Island: The Caribbean and the Postmodern Perspective,* 2d ed. (Durham, NC: Duke University Press, 1996).

Berendt, Joachim-Ernst, *The Third Ear: On Listening to the World* (New York: An Owl Book, Henry Holt, 1992).

Blassingame, John W., *The Slave Community: Plantation Life in the Antebellum South* (New York: Oxford University Press, 1972).

Boyd, Todd, *Am I Black Enough for You? Popular Culture from the 'Hood and Beyond* (Bloomington and Indianapolis: Indiana University Press, 1997).

Bynum, Edward Bruce, *The African Unconscious: Roots of Ancient Mysticism and Modern Psychology* (New York: Teachers College Press, 1999).

Campbell, Helen, *Turnip Blues* (Duluth, MN: Spinsters Ink, 1998).

Camus, Albert, *The Rebel: An Essay on Man in Revolt* (New York: Vintage International, 1991).

Canizares, Raul, *The Life and Works of Marie Laveau: Gris-Gris, Cleansings, Charms, Hexes, Original Publications* (New York: Plainview, 2001).

Carby, Hazel, "Women, Migration and the Formation of a Blues Culture," in *Cultures in Babylon: Black Britain and African America* (London: Verso, 1999).

Chang, Nancy, *The Silencing of Political Dissent: How the USA Patriot Act Undermines the Constitution* (New York: Open Media, 2001).

Chernoff, John Miller, *African Rhythm and African Sensibility: Aesthetics and Social Action in African Musical Idioms* (Chicago: University of Chicago Press, 1979).

Collins, Allyson, *Shielded from Justice: Police Brutality and Accountability in the United States* (New York: Human Rights Watch, 1998).

Comblin, Jose, *Called to Freedom: The Changing Context of Liberation Theology* (Maryknoll, NY: Orbis Books, 1998).

Cones, James H., *The Spirituals and the Blues* (Maryknoll, NY: Orbis Books, 1972).

Cooper, Carolyn, *Noises in the Blood* (London: Macmillan Education, 1993).

Costello, Mark, and David Foster Wallace, *Signifying Rappers: Rap and race in the urban present* (New York: Ecco Press, 1990).

Cross, Brian, *It's Not about a Salary . . . Rap, Race and Resistance in Los Angeles* (New York: Verso, 1993).

Davaney, Sheila Greeve, and Dwight N. Hopkins, *Changing Conversations: Religious Reflection and Cultural Analysis* (New York and London: Routledge, 1997).

Davis, Angela, *Blues Legacies and Black Feminism,: Gertrude "Ma" Rainey, Bessie Smith and Billie Holiday* (New York: Pantheon Books, 1998).

Davis, Eisa, "Sexism and the Art of Feminist Hip Hop Maintenance," in Rebecca Walker, ed., *To Be Real: Telling the Truth and Changing the Face of Feminism* (New York: Anchor Books, 1995).

Dent, Gina, ed., *Black Popular Culture* (Seattle: Bay Press, 1992).

Donziger, Stephen, *The Real War on Crime: Report of the National Criminal Justice Commission* (New York: HarperCollins, 1996).

Du Bois, W. E. B., *The Souls of Black Folk* (New York: Library of America Edition, 1990 [1903]).

Dussel, Enrique, *The Invention of the Americas: Eclipse of "the Other" and the Myth of Modernity* (New York: Continuum, 1995).

Dyson, Michael Eric, *Holler If You Hear Me: In Search of Tupac Shakur* (New York: Basic Civitas Books, 2001).

Dyson, Michael Eric, *Between God and Gangsta Rap: Bearing Witness to Black Culture* (New York: Oxford University Press, 1996).

Dyson, Michael Eric, *Making Malcolm: The Myth and Meaning of Malcolm X* (New York: Free Press, 1995).

Dyson, Michael Eric, *Reflecting Black: African-American Cultural Criticism* (Minneapolis: University of Minnesota Press, 1993).

Early, Gerald, ed., *Lure and Loathing: Essays on Race, Identity, and the Ambivalence of Assimilation (*New York: Penguin Books, 1994).

Eco, Umberto, *A Theory of Semiotics* (Bloomington: Indiana University Press, 1979).

Emerson, Rana A., 'Where My Girls At?' Negotiating Black Womanhood in Music Videos," *Gender and Society* 16, no. 1 (February 2002): 115–135

Esteva, Gustavo, and Madhu Suri Prakash, *Grassroots Postmodernism: Remaking the Soil of Cultures* (New York: Zed Books, 1998).

Feagin, Joe R., *Racist America: Roots, Current Realities and Future Reparations* (New York: Routledge, 2000).

Floyd, Samuel A., *The Power of Black Music: Interpreting Its History from Africa to the United States* (New York: Oxford University Press, 1995).

Frankenberg, Ruth, *The Social Construction of Whiteness: White Women, Race Matters* (Minneapolis: University of Minnesota Press, 1993).

Fulop, Timothy E., and Albert Raboteau, eds., *African-American Religion: Interpretative Essays in History and Culture* (New York: Routledge, 1997).

Gates, Henry Louis, Jr., *The Signifying Monkey: A Theory of Afro-American Literary Criticism* (New York: Oxford University Press, 1988).

George, Nelson, *The Death of Rhythm & Blues* (New York: Pantheon Books, 1988).

George, Nelson et al., eds., *Fresh: Hip Hop Don't Stop* (New York: Random House, 1985).

Gilroy, Paul, *The Black Atlantic: Modernity and Double Consciousness* (Cambridge, MA: Harvard University Press, 1993).

Gilroy, Paul, *There Ain't No Black in the Union Jack: The Cultural Politics of Race and Nation* (Chicago: University of Chicago Press, 1991).

Girard, Rene, *Violence and the Sacred,* translated by Patrick Gregory (Baltimore: Johns Hopkins University Press, 1977).

Gold, Jonathan. "Dr. Dre and Snopp Doggy Dogg: One Nation under a G Thang." *Rolling Stone,* Issue 666, September 30, 1993

Gooding-Williams, R., ed., *Reading Rodney King, Reading Urban Uprising* (New York: Routledge, 1993).

Gordon, Lewis, ed., *Existence in Black: An Anthology of Black Existential Philosophy* (New York: Routledge, 1997).

Griffin, Farah Jasmine, *If You Can't Be Free, Be A Mystery: In Search of Billie Holiday* (New York: Free Press, 2001).

Grossberg, Lawrence, Cary Nelson, and Paula Treichler, eds., *Cultural Studies* (New York: Routledge, 1992).

Haddad, Yvonne Y., and Jane I. Smith, eds., *Muslim Communities in North America* (Albany: State University of New York Press, 1994).

Harrison, Daphne Duval, *Black Pearls: Blues Queens of the 1920s,* (New Brunswick, NJ: Rutgers University Press, 1988).

Haskins, Jim, *Queen of the Blues: A Biography of Dinah Washington* (New York: William Morrow, 1987).

Heywood, Ian, and Barry Sandywell, eds., *Interpreting Visual Culture: Explorations in the Hermeneutics of the Visual* (New York: Routledge, 1999).

Heywood, Leslie, and Jennifer Drake, eds., *Third Wave Agenda: Being Feminist, Doing Feminism* (Minneapolis: University of Minnesota Press, 1997).

Hill-Collins, Patricia, *Black Feminist Thought: Knowledge, Consciousness and the Politics of Empowerment* (New York: Routledge, 1994).

Hinkle, Gerald H., *Art as Event: An Aesthetic for the Performing Arts* (Washington, DC: University Press of America, 1979).

Hurston, Zora Neale, *Tell My Horse: Voodoo and Life in Haiti and Jamaica* (New York: Harper and Row, 1990).

James, Joy, ed., *States of Confinement: Policing, Detention and Prisons* (New York: St. Martin's Press, 2000).

Johnson, E. Patrick, "Feeling the Spirit in the Dark: Expanding Notions of the Sacred in the African- American Gay Community," *Callaloo* 21.2 (1998): 399–416.

Jones, Hettie, *Big Star, Fallen Mama: Five Women in Black Music* (New York: Viking Press, 1974).

Jones, LeRoi, *Blues People: The Negro Experience in White American and the Music That Developed from It* (New York: Morrow Quill Paperbacks, 1963).

Judy, Ronald A. T., *(Dis)Forming the American Canon: African-Arabic Slave Narratives and the Vernacular* (Minneapolis: University of Minnesota Press, 1993).

Keil, Charles, "Motion and Feeling in Music," *Journal of Aesthetics and Art Criticism* 24, no. 3 (1996): 337–349.

Kelley, Robin D. G., *Yo' Mama's Disfunktional! Fighting the Culture Wars in Urban America* (Boston: Beacon Press, 1997).

Kochman, Thomas, *Black and White Styles in Conflict* (Chicago: University of Chicago Press, 1981).

Kozol, Jonathan, *Amazing Grace: The Lives of Children and the Conscience of a Nation* (New York: Crown, 1995).

Krims, Adam, *Rap Music and the Poetics of Identity* (New York: Cambridge University Press, 2000).

Krims, Adam, ed., *Music/Ideology: Resisting the Aesthetic* (Amsterdam, Netherlands: G+B Arts International/Overseas Publishers Association, 1998).
Kroker, Arthur, *The Possessed Individual: Technology and the French Postmodern* (New York: St Martin's Press, 1992).
Kruger, Barbara, and Phil Mariani, eds., *Remaking History* (New York: New Press, 1999).
Lambek, Michael, *Reader in the Anthropology of Religion* (London: Basil Blackwell, 2002).
Latifah, Queen, with Karen Hunter, *Ladies First: Revelations of a Strong Woman* (New York: William Morrow, 1999).
Long, Charles, *Significations: Signs, Symbols, and Images in the Interpretation of Religion* (Philadelphia: Fortress Press, 1986).
Malcolm X, *The Autobiography of Malcolm X* (New York: Ballatine, 1973).
Mayo, Kierna, "Queen Latifah: The Last Good Witch," in *Hip Hop Divas* (New York: Vibe Books, 2001).
Miller, Jerome C., *Search and Destroy: African-American Males in the Criminal Justice System* (New York: Cambridge University Press, 1996).
Morgan, Joan, *When Chickenheads Come Home to Roost: My Life as a Hip Hop Feminist* (New York: Simon and Schuster, 1999).
Murphy, Joseph, *Working the Spirit: Ceremonies of the African Diaspora* (Boston: Beacon Press, 1994).
Murrell, Nathanial S., et al., eds., *Chanting Down Babylon* (Philadelphia: Temple University Press, 1998).
Nelson, Havelock, and Michael A. Gonzales, *Bring the Noise: A Guide to Rap Music and Hip Hop Culture* (New York: Harmony Books, 1991).
Nelson, Jill, ed., *Police Brutality: An Anthology* (New York: W. W. Norton, 2000).
Oliver, Paul, *The Blues Fell This Morning: The Meaning of the Blues* (New York: Cambridge University Press, 1979, 1990).
O'Meally, Robert G., ed., *Living with Music: Ralph Ellison's Jazz Writings* (New York: Modern Library Edition/Random House, 2001).
Omi, Michael, and Howard Winant, *Racial Formation in the United States from the 1960s to the 1990s,* 2d ed. (New York: Routledge, 1994).
Otto, Rudolph, *The Idea of the Holy,* translated by John W. Harvey (London: Oxford University Press, 1950).
Parenti, Christian, *Lockdown America: Police and Prisons in the Age of Crisis* (New York: Verso, 1999).
Perkins, William Eric, ed., *Droppin' Science: Critical Essays on Rap Music and Hip Hop Culture* (Philadelphia: Temple University Press, 1996).
Perkinson, James W., "The Body of White Space: Beyond Stiff Voices, Flaccid Feelings and Silent Cells," in N. Tuana et al., *Revealing Male Bodies,* 228–261. (Bloomington: Indiana University Press, 2002).

Perkinson, James W., "Theology and the City: Learning to Cry, Struggling to See," *Cross Currents* 51/1 (Spring 2001): 95–114

Perkinson, James W., "Rage with a Purpose, Weep without Regret: A White Theology of Solidarity," *Soundings* 82, nos. 3–4 (Fall–Winter 1999): 437–463

Placksin, Sally, *American Women in Jazz: 1900 to the Present: Their Worlds, Lives and Music* (New York: Wideview Books, 1982).

Phillips, Kevin, *Wealth and Democracy: A Political History of the American Rich* (New York: Broadway Books, 2002).

Phillips, Kevin, *The Politics of Rich and Poor: Wealth and the Reagan Electorate in the Reagan Aftermath* (New York: Harper Perennial, 1990).

Pinn, Anthony B., "How Ya Livin'? Notes on Rap Music and Social Transformation," *Western Journal of Black Studies* 23, no. 1 (1999): 10–21

Pinn, Anthony B., *Varieties of African American Religious Experiences* (Minneapolis: Fortress Press, 1998).

Pinn, Anthony B., "Gettin' Grown: Gangsta Rap Music and Notions of Manhood," *Journal of African- American Men* 2, no. 1 (Summer 1996): 61–73

Pinn, Anthony B., *Why, Lord? Suffering and Evil in Black Theology* (New York: Continuum, 1995).

Raboteau, Albert, *Slave Religion: The "Invisible Institution" in the Antebellum South* (New York: Oxford University Press, 1978).

Rose, Tricia, *Black Noise: Rap Music and Black Culture in Contemporary America* (Hanover, NH: Wesleyan University Press, published by University Press of New England, 1994).

Sackheim, Eric, compiler, *The Blues Lines: A Collection of Blues Lyrics from Leadbelly to Muddy Waters* (Hopewell, NJ: Ecco Press, 1969).

Sernett, Milton C., ed., *Afro-American Religious History: A Documentary Witness* (Durham, NC: Duke University Press, 1985).

Sherman, Arloc, *Extreme Child Poverty Rises Sharply in 1997* (Washington, DC: Children's Defense Fund, 1999).

Simmons, Russell, with Nelson George, *Life and Def: Sex, Drugs, Money, + God* (New York: Crown, 2001).

Smith, Theophilus, *Conjuring Culture: Biblical Formations of Black America* (New York: Oxford University Press, 1994).

Snoop Dogg, with Davin Seay, *The Doggfather: The Times, Trials, and Hardcore Truths of Snoop Dogg* (New York: William Morrow, 1999).

Spencer, Jon Michael, *The Rhythms of Black Folk: Race, Religion and Pan-Africanism* (Trenton, NJ: Africa World Press, 1995).

Spencer, Jon Michael, ed., *Sacred Music of the Secular City: From Blues to Rap.* A special issue of *Black Sacred Music: A Journal of Theomusicology* 6, no. 1 (Spring 1992).

Spencer, Jon Michael, ed., *The Theology of American Popular Music.* A special issue of *Black Sacred Music: A Journal of Theomusicology* 3, no. 2 (Fall 1989).

Stallybrass, Peter, and Allon White, *The Politics and Poetics of Transgression* (Ithaca, NY: Cornell University Press and Methuen Books, 1986).
Stockman, Steve, *Walk On: The Spiritual Journey of U2* (Lake Mary, FL: Relevant Books, 2001).
Taylor, Don, *Marley and Me* (Kingston, Jamaica: Kingston Publishers, 1994).
Taylor, Mark L., *The Executed God: The Way of the Cross in Lockdown America* (Minneapolis: Fortress Press, 2001).
Thompson, Robert Farris, *Flash of the Spirit: African and Afro-American Art and Philosophy* (New York: Vintage Books, 1983).
Brent Turner, Richard, *Islam in the African American Experience* (Bloomington and Indianapolis: Indiana University Press, 1997).
Turner, Victor, *Dramas, Fields and Metaphors: Symbolic Action in Human Society* (London and Ithaca, NY: Cornell University Press, 1974).
Ventura, Michael, *Shadow Dancing in the USA* (New York: St. Martin's Press, 1985).
Walker, Alice, *In Search of Our Mothers' Gardens: Womanist Prose* (New York: Harvest/Harcourt Brace Jovanovich, 1983).
Welch, Sharon, *A Feminist Ethic of Risk* (Minneapolis: Fortress Press, 1999).
West, Cornel, *Race Matters* (Boston: Beacon Press, 1993).
West, Cornel, "On Afro-American Popular Music: From Bebop to Rap," in *Prophetic Fragments,* 177–188. (Trenton, NJ: Eerdmans/Africa World Press, 1988).
West, Cornel, *Prophesy Deliverance: An African-American Revolutionary Christianity* (Philadelphia: Westminster Press, 1982).
White, Hayden, *Tropics of Discourse: Essays in Cultural Criticism* (Baltimore: Johns Hopkins University Press, 1978).
White, Timothy, *Catch a Fire: The Life of Bob Marley* (New York: Henry Holt, 1983).
Willis, Susan B., *Specifying: Black Women Writing the American Experience* (Madison: University of Wisconsin Press, 1987).
Wilmore, Gayraud S., ed., *African American Religious Studies: An Interdisciplinary Anthology* (Durham, NC: Duke University Press, 1989).
Wilson, William J., and Loic D. Wacquant, *The Cost of Racial Exclusion* (Newbury Park, CA: Sage, 1993).
Wood, Forrest G., *The Arrogance of Faith: Christianity and Race in America from the Colonial Era to the Twentieth Century* (New York: Alfred Knopf, 1990).
Woods, Joe, "Malcolm X and the New Blackness," in Joe Woods, ed., *Malcolm X: In Our Image* (New York: St. Martin's Press, 1992).
Zaretsky, Irving I., and Mark P. Leone, ed., *Religious Movements in Contemporary America* (Princeton, NJ: Princeton University Press, 1974).

Partial Discography

A Tribe Called Quest, *The Love Movement* (Jive Records, 1998).
A Tribe Called Quest, *Beats, Rhymes and Life* (Jive Records, 1996).

Arrested Development, *Zingalamaduni* (Chrysalis Records, 1994).
Arrested Development, *3 Years, 5 Months and 2 Days in the Life of . . .* (Chrysalis Records, 1992).
B. B. Jay, *Universal Concussion* (Jive Records, 2000).
Boogie Down Productions, *By All Means Necessary* (Jive Records, 1989).
Boogie Down Productions, *Criminal Minded* (Jive Records, 1987).
Common, *One Day It'll Make Sense* (Relativity Records, 1997).
DJ Maj, *Full Plates* (Gotee Records, 2001).
DMX, *And Then There Was X* (Island Def Jam Music Group, 1999).
Dooney, *Peculiar Records Compilation,* vol. 1 (Peculiar Records, 2000).
E-Roc, *Avalanche* (Grapetree Records, 1999).
Easop, *The Time Has Come* (Life or Death Records, 1999).
Elle R.O.C., *I Die Daily* (Bettie Rocket Record, 2001).
GT Compilation Volume II Muzik Ta Ride 2 (Grapetree Records, 1997).
Ice Cube, *Death Certificate* (Priority Records, 1991).
Ja Rule, *Venni Vetti Vecci* (Def Jam Music Group, 1999).
Killah Priest, *Heavy Mental* (Geffen Records, 1998).
King Cyz, *Life or Death* (Nu Wyne Records, 2001).
Knowdaverbs, *The Action Figure* (Gotee Records, 2000).
L. G. Wise, *Ghetto Fables: Da Ain't Told* (Grapetree Records, 2000).
Lil' Raskull, *Certified Southern Hits* (Grapetree Records, 1999).
Lil' Raskull, *Gory to Glory* (Grapetree Records, 1997).
Charles Manchild, *Christside: Holy Hip-Hop* (LoveOne Edu-Tainment, 2001).
Ms. Dynasty, *The Hostile Takeover* (Tommy Boy Records, 2001).
Public Enemy, *Muse-Sick-N-Hour-Message* (Def Jam, 1994).
Public Enemy, *It Takes a Nation of Millions* (Def Jam, 1988).
Priesthood, *Keepin It Real* (Metro One Music, 2001).
Queen Latifah, *Black Reign* (Motown/Pgd, 1994).
Queen Latifah, *All Hail the Queen* (Tommy Boy Records, 1989).
Sage Francis, *Personal Journals* (ASIN, 2002).
ScarFace, *Mr. ScarFace is Back* (Virgin Records, 1995).
ScarFace, *The Diary* (Noo Trybe Records, 1994).
The Roots, *Things Fall Apart* (Uni/Mac, 1999).
The Roots, *Illadelph Halflife* (Geffen Records, 1996).
Tupac Shakur, *2Pac + Outlawz* (Uni/Interscope Records, 1999).
Tupac Shakur, *The Don Killuminati: The Seven Day Theory* (Uni/Interscope, 1996).
Sister Souljah, *360 Degrees of Power* (Epic, 1991).
Unity Klan, *As It Is Written* (Eternal Funk Records, 2001).
Wyclef Jean, *The Ecleftic: 2 Sides II a Book* (Sony Music Entertainment, 2000).

About the Contributors

Garth Kasimu Baker-Fletcher is on the faculty of Hood Theological Seminary. His publications include *Somebodyness: Martin Luther King, Jr., and the Theory of Dignity* and *Xodus: An African American Male Journey.*

William C. Banfield is the Endowed Chair in Arts and Humanities and Associate Professor of Music at the University of St. Thomas. In addition to being an accomplished composer, he is the editor of *Musical Landscapes in Color: Conversations with Black American Composers.*

Noel Leo Erskine is an Associate Professor of Theology at the Candler School of Theology (Emory University). His publications include *Decolonizing Theology: A Caribbean Perspective* and *King among the Theologians.*

Juan M. Floyd-Thomas is an Assistant Professor in the History Department at Texas Christian University. His publications include "The Burning of Rebellious Thoughts: MOVE as Revolutionary Black Humanism" *The Black Scholar* 32, no. 1 (Spring 2002): 11–21. He is currently working on a book dealing with the intersections of black religion and social reform movements in Harlem.

Leola A. Johnson is an Assistant Professor in Communication Studies at Macalester College. Her interests in mass media as social and cultural institutions have resulted in a book project about Iceberg Slim, the pimp writer whose 1968 autobiography is being produced as a Hollywood film.

James W. Perkinson is Associate Professor of Ethics and Director of the Doctor of Ministry Program at the Ecumenical Theological Seminary. His publications include "The Body of White Space: Beyond Stiff Voices, Flaccid Feelings and Silent Cells," in N. Tuana et al., editors, *Revealing Male Bodies.*

Anthony B. Pinn is Professor of Religious Studies at Macalester College. His publications include *Varieties of African American Religious Experience,*

Terror and Triumph: The Nature of Black Religion, and, as editor, *By These Hands: A Documentary History of African American Humanism* (available from NYU Press).

Mark Lewis Taylor is Professor Theology at Princeton Theological Seminary. His publications include *Remembering Esperanza: A Cultural-Political Theology for North American Praxis* and *The Executed God: The Way of the Cross in Lockdown America*.

Ralph C. Watkins is an Assistant Professor of Sociology at Augusta State University. His interests in Urban Sociology and Theology have resulted in a book titled *A Black Theology of the "Hood,"* to be published by Scholars Press.

Index